The International Society for Science & Religion was established in 2002 to promote education through the support of inter-disciplinary learning and research in the fields of science and religion. Our current membership of 140 comes from all major faith traditions and includes non-religious scholars. Inducted by nomination only, they are drawn from leading research institutions and academies worldwide. The Society embraces all perspectives that are supported by excellent scholarship.

In 2007, the Society began the process of creating a unique resource, *The ISSR Library*, a comprehensive reference and teaching tool for scholars, students, and interested lay readers. This collection spans the essential ideas and arguments that frame studies in science, religion, and the human spirit.

The Library has been selected through a rigorous process of peer review. Each constituent volume makes a substantial contribution to the field or stands as an important referent. These books exhibit the highest quality of scholarship and present distinct, influential viewpoints, some of which are controversial. While the many perspectives in these volumes are not individually endorsed by the ISSR, each reflects a facet of the field that is worthy of attention.

Accompanying the Library is *The ISSR Companion to Science and Religion*, a volume containing brief introductory essays on each of the Library's constituents. Users are encouraged to refer to the *Companion* or our website for an overview of the Library.

Mind and Emergence

Mind and Emergence

From Quantum to Consciousness

PHILIP CLAYTON

OXFORD
UNIVERSITY PRESS

*This book has been printed digitally and produced in a standard specification
in order to ensure its continuing availability*

OXFORD
UNIVERSITY PRESS

Great Clarendon Street, Oxford OX2 6DP

Oxford University Press is a department of the University of Oxford.
It furthers the University's objective of excellence in research, scholarship,
and education by publishing worldwide in

Oxford New York

Auckland Cape Town Dar es Salaam Hong Kong Karachi
Kuala Lumpur Madrid Melbourne Mexico City Nairobi
New Delhi Shanghai Taipei Toronto
With offices in
Argentina Austria Brazil Chile Czech Republic France Greece
Guatemala Hungary Italy Japan South Korea Poland Portugal
Singapore Switzerland Thailand Turkey Ukraine Vietnam

Oxford is a registered trade mark of Oxford University Press
in the UK and in certain other countries

Published in the United States
by Oxford University Press Inc., New York

ISBN 978-0-19-929143-4

Preface

How humans construe the world and their place in it matters deeply, even ultimately, to humans. Some of us are *physicalists*, holding that all things that exist are physical entities, composed out of, and thus ultimately explainable in terms of, the laws, particles, and energies of microphysics. Others are *dualists* because they believe that at least humans, and perhaps other organisms as well, consist both of these physical components and of a soul, self, or spirit that is essentially non-physical. *Emergence*, I shall argue, represents a third option in the debate and one that is preferable to both of its two main competitors. Wherever on the continuum of options one falls, one is likely to hold that position with great passion. What we believe about ourselves and our place in the universe, about science and history and the contents of our own consciousness, will make a crucial difference to our understanding of ourselves and of the world we inhabit.

A book on mind and emergence has the potential to unleash suspicion from both sides. Physicalists may close the cover when they encounter the word 'mind', since they know that nothing like mind exists in the physical world. Dualists' reservations have exactly the opposite motivation: mind or spirit could never emerge out of matter because the two are intrinsically different. No notion of mind derived from matter could ever be adequate to what is meant by soul or spirit or God. Hence, they conclude, one knows in advance that emergence theories must fail.

I approach this project with the sense that each of these two views omits a crucial part of the story. On the one hand, the physicalist stance leaves out our experience as conscious agents in the world. Not only do humans have the experience of thinking and willing and deciding; we also continually experience the fact that these thoughts and volitions actually *do* something—they are causally efficacious in the world. When after some reflection I decided to rewrite the last sentence, I consciously initiated a sequence of causes that led to your experience of reading these words, of liking or disliking them, and of reflecting on whether or not they are true. Dualism, on the other hand, is undercut by the increasingly strong correlations that neuroscientists are demonstrating between states of the central nervous system and conscious states. The neural correlates of consciousness do not *prove* that dualism is false, any more than they prove that there will someday be a complete reduction of consciousness to physiology. But successes in the neurosciences do suggest that your consciousness is at least partially derived from a particular biological system, your brain and central nervous system, in interaction with a set of physical, historical, and presumably also linguistic and cultural factors.

Emergence is the view that new and unpredictable phenomena are naturally produced by interactions in nature; that these new structures, organisms, and ideas are not reducible to the subsystems on which they depend; and that the newly evolved realities in turn exercise a causal influence on the parts out of which they arose. The emergence thesis suggests that consciousness or what we call mind is derived from and is dependent upon complex biological systems. But consciousness is not the only emergent level; in one sense it is merely another in a very long series of steps that have characterized the evolutionary process. It may be a particularly interesting and complex level, including as it does the entire intellectual, cultural, artistic, and religious life of humanity. Certainly, for us as human agents, consciousness—both in its private, first-person manifestations and in the others who make up our social world—matters ultimately. But consciousness is not utterly unique; conscious phenomena also manifest important analogies to emergent realities at much earlier points in evolutionary history. In so far as it recognizes that consciousness is in one sense 'just another emergent level', emergence theory is not dualism in disguise.

Neither dualism nor reductive physicalism, then, tells the complete story. Drawing the arguments from both philosophy and contemporary science, I will defend the thesis that mind—causally efficacious mental properties—emerges from the natural world, as a further step in the evolutionary process. The naturalness of mind, but also its *differentia specifica*, becomes evident only when one looks closely at how biological evolution works and what it produces.

A book on the emergence of mind cannot shy away from the question of the nature of emergent mind. After establishing a position on the relation of human beings to the rest of evolutionary history, a philosopher must then ask: what, more generally, is the place of mind in the natural world? Can mind be fully understood within the context of a naturalistic and scientific study of the world? How might the emergence of mind be related to the question of transcendent mind? Can one who takes seriously the methods and results of the natural sciences make any sense of claims for the influence of transcendent mind on the world? If one is to follow the line of argument in the direction in which it naturally leads, one must not be shy about extending the discussion into the domain of religious beliefs. For those with interests in the philosophy of religion or theology, the light that emergence sheds on religion may represent its most crucial feature. Nonetheless, theologians and other believers who appeal to the emergence concept should not do so blithely, as the concluding chapter will show. The emergence argument has a logic of its own, and it may require certain modifications to traditional versions of theism and to traditional theologies. Even for those without religious beliefs, the application of emergence to religion offers an intriguing thought experiment, one which may increase or decrease one's sense of the viability of this notion for explaining more inner-worldly phenomena such as epigenetic forces or human mental experience.

The net result of this exploration of emergence, I trust, will be a fuller understanding of the strengths of a concept that is receiving much attention today, as well as of the criticisms to which it is vulnerable. In the end, I hope to show, emergence offers a new and more fruitful paradigm for interpreting a wide variety of phenomena running from physics to consciousness, and perhaps beyond.

Bits and pieces of the developing argument have appeared in a variety of publications over the half a dozen years that I have been engaged in this research; full references are contained in the Bibliography. In particular, some portions of an earlier version of Chapter 3 appeared in the volume, *Science and Ultimate Reality: Quantum Theory, Cosmology and Complexity*, co-edited by John Barrow, Paul Davies, and Charles Harper. Every segment of the argument has however been reworked in the effort to construct a single coherent argument concerning mind and emergence.

Any multi-year research project incurs an impressive variety of debts. There may be conviction, and sometimes even truth, without intersubjective testing and agreement. But without the community of inquirers (and those who make it possible) there would be no justified knowledge. I am grateful:

- to the John Templeton Foundation for a generous grant through their first Research Grant Competition, which made possible a much more intense examination of the science and philosophy of emergence than I would otherwise have been able to achieve. Parts of the text were completed during a Templeton-sponsored programme known as the Stanford Emergence Project; I have profited from the work with Stanford scientists and philosophers and from those who flew in to participate in the various conferences and consultations at Stanford.
- to the 123 scientists of the seven-year CTNS programme 'Science and the Spiritual Quest', whose courage to explore religious and spiritual questions without lowering the highest standards of scientific enquiry was a model for this book and whose intellectual efforts contributed to the conclusions reflected in these pages;
- to Steven Knapp, provost of Johns Hopkins University, my major intellectual collaborator on this project, as on many before it;
- to my research assistants during this period: Kevin Cody, Andrea Zimmerman, Jheri Cravens, Dan Roberts, and Zach Simpson.
- and, finally, to the members of my family, who during these particular years have paid a greater price than they should ever have had to pay.

Contents

List of Illustrations

From Reduction to Emergence

It is widely but falsely held that there are only two major ways to interpret the world: in a physicalist or in a dualist fashion. The mistaken belief in this dichotomy has its roots in the confrontation of Newtonian physics with the metaphysical systems that still dominated in the seventeenth century, which were built up out of Greek, Christian, and medieval elements—but we will not worry here about the historical backgrounds to the conflict. It is the thesis of this book that the days of this forced dilemma are past.

The case stands on three legs. Two of these—the revolution in metaphysics brought about by Kant, German Idealism, and process thought; and the revolution in the theory of knowledge brought about by non-objectivist epistemologies, contextualist philosophies of science, and inherent limits on knowledge discovered within the sciences themselves—I have explored in other publications and will not reargue here.[1] The present argument against the physicalism-dualism dichotomy is derived from a third source: the revolution brought about by the sciences of evolution. The evolutionary perspective has fatally undercut both sides of the once regnant either/or: physicalism, with its tendency to stress the sufficiency of physics, and dualism, with its tendency to pull mind out of the evolutionary account altogether.

The evolutionary perspective which is realigning the long-established philosophical frontiers is the core presupposition of the most successful scientific explanation we have of biological phenomena. More accurately, it is a component in all biological explanations and a label for a large number of specific empirical results. Now to say that biological evolution directly undercuts physicalism and dualism would be a category mistake. Scientific theories have to be turned into philosophical arguments before they can support or undercut philosophical positions (except, of course, when philosophers make direct errors about empirical facts or scientific theories, as not infrequently occurs). In the following pages I argue that *emergence* is the philosophical position—more accurately, the philosophical elabora-

tion of a series of scientific results—that best expresses the philosophical import of evolutionary theory.

Thus we should say, if the argument turns out to be successful,
that it is emergence which undercuts the hegemony of the physicalist-
dualism dichotomy. There are now not two but three serious
ontological options. And, of the three, emergence is the naturalist
position most strongly supported by a synthetic scientific perspective—that is, by the study of natural history across the various levels
that it has produced—as well as by philosophical reflection.

THE RISE AND FALL OF REDUCTIONISM

The discussion of emergence makes no sense unless one conducts
it against the backdrop of reductionism. Emergence theories presuppose that the project of explanatory reduction—explaining all
phenomena in the natural world in terms of the objects and laws
of physics—is finally impossible. For this reason, the overview of
emergence theories in the twentieth century needs to begin by
reviewing the difficulties that have come to burden the programme
of reductionism.

In its simple form, at least, the story of the rise and fall of reductionism is not difficult to tell (I return to the complexities in later
pages). Once upon a time there was a century dominated by the ideal
of reductionism. It was a century in which some of the deepest dreams
of science were fulfilled. Building on Newton's laws, Maxwell's equations and Einstein's insights, scientists developed a body of theory
capable of handling the very small (quantum physics), the very fast
(special relativity, for speeds approaching c), and the very heavy (general relativity, or what one might call gravitational dynamics). Chemistry was, for all intents and purposes, completed. Crick and Watson
discovered the structure of the biochemical information system that
codes for all biological reproduction and heritable mutations, and a
short while ago the mapping of the human genome was completed.
Breakthroughs in neuroscience promised the eventual explanation of
cognition in neurophysiological terms, and evolutionary psychology
brought evolutionary biology to bear on human behaviour. Each
success increased optimism that so-called bridge laws would eventually link together each of the sciences into a single system of law-
based explanation with physics as its foundation.

Yet, the story continues, these amazing successes were followed
by a series of blows to the reductionist program.[2] Scientists encoun-

tered a number of apparently permanent restrictions on what physics can explain, predict, or know: relativity theory introduced the speed of light as the absolute limit for velocity, and thus as the temporal limit for communication and causation in the universe (no knowledge outside our 'light cone'); Heisenberg's uncertainty principle placed mathematical limits on the knowability of both the location and momentum of a subatomic particle; the Copenhagen theorists came to the startling conclusion that quantum mechanical indeterminacy was not merely a temporary epistemic problem but reflected an *inherent* indeterminacy of the physical world itself; so-called chaos theory showed that future states of complex systems such as weather systems quickly become uncomputable because of their sensitive dependence on initial conditions (a dependence so sensitive that a finite knower could *never* predict the evolution of the system—a staggering limitation when one notes what percentage of natural systems exhibit chaotic behaviours); Kurt Gödel showed in a well-known proof that mathematics cannot be complete . . . and the list goes on.

In one sense, limitations to the program of reduction*ism*, understood as a philosophical position about science, do not affect everyday scientific practice. To do science still means to try to explain phenomena in terms of their constituent parts and underlying laws. Thus, endorsing an emergentist philosophy of science is in most cases consistent with business as usual in science. In another sense, however, the reduction-versus-emergence debate does have deep relevance for one's understanding of scientific method and results, as the following chapters will demonstrate. The 'unity of science' movement that dominated the middle of the twentieth century, perhaps the classic expression of reductionist philosophy of science, presupposed a radically different understanding of natural science—its goals, epistemic status, relation to other areas of study, and final fate—than is entailed by emergence theories of science. Whether the scientist ascribes to the one position or the other will inevitably have effects on how she pursues her science and how she views her results.

THE CONCEPT OF EMERGENCE

In a classic definition el-Hani and Pereira identify four features generally associated with the concept of emergence:

1. *Ontological physicalism*: All that exists in the space-time world are the basic particles recognized by physics and their aggregates.

2. *Property emergence*: When aggregates of material particles attain an appropriate level of organizational complexity, genuinely novel properties emerge in these complex systems.

3. *The irreducibility of the emergence*: Emergent properties are irreducible to, and unpredictable from, the lower-level phenomena from which they emerge.

4. *Downward causation*: Higher-level entities causally affect their lower-level constituents.[3]

Each of these four theses requires elaboration; some require modification. The defence of emergence in the following pages refers to a set of claims no weaker than the four theses, but modified as follows.

Concerning (1), ontological physicalism

The first condition is poorly formulated. It does correctly express the anti-dualistic thrust of emergence theories. But the emergence thesis, if correct, undercuts the claim that physics is the fundamental discipline from which all others are derived. Moreover, rather than treating all objects that are not 'recognized by physics' as mere aggregates, it suggests viewing them as emergent entities (in a sense to be defined). Thus I suggest it is more accurate to begin with the thesis of ontological monism:

> (1′) *Ontological monism*: Reality is ultimately composed of one basic kind of stuff. Yet the concepts of physics are not sufficient to explain all the forms that this stuff takes— all the ways it comes to be structured, individuated, and causally efficacious. The one 'stuff' apparently takes forms for which the explanations of physics, and thus the ontology of physics (or 'physicalism' for short) are not adequate. We should not assume that the entities postulated by physics complete the inventory of what exists. Hence emergentists should be monists but not physicalists.

Concerning (2), property emergence

The discovery of genuinely novel properties in nature is indeed a major motivation for emergence. Tim O'Connor has provided a sophisticated account of property emergence. For any emergent property P of some object O, four conditions hold:

(i)   *P* supervenes on properties of the parts of *O*;
(ii) *P* is not had by any of the object's parts;
(iii) *P* is distinct from any structural property of *O*;
(iv) *P* has direct ('downward') determinative influence on the pattern of behaviour involving *O*'s parts.[4]

Particular attention should be paid to O'Connor's condition (ii), which he calls the feature of *non-structurality*. It entails three features: 'The property's being potentially had only by objects of some complexity, not had by any of the object's parts, [and] distinct from any structural property of the object' (p. 97).

Concerning (3), the irreducibility of emergence

To say that emergent properties are irreducible to lower-level phenomena presupposes that reality is divided into a number of distinct levels or orders. Wimsatt classically expresses the notion: 'By level of organization, I will mean here compositional levels— hierarchical divisions of stuff (paradigmatically but not necessarily material stuff) organized by part-whole relations, in which wholes at one level function as parts at the next (and at all higher) levels . . . '[5] Wimsatt, who begins by contrasting an emergentist ontology with Quine's desert landscapes, insists that 'it is possible to be a reductionist and a holist too' (p. 225). The reason is that emergentist holism, in contrast to what we might call 'New Age holism', is a controlled holism. It consists of two theses: that there are forms of causality that are not reducible to physical causes (on which more in a moment), and that causality should be our primary guide to ontology. As Wimsatt writes, 'Ontologically, one could take the primary working matter of the world to be causal relationships, which are connected to one another in a variety of ways—and together make up patterns of causal networks' (p. 220).

It follows that one of the major issues for emergence theory will involve the question of when exactly one should speak of the emergence of a new level within the natural order. Traditionally, 'life' and 'mind' have been taken to be genuine emergent levels within the world—from which it follows that 'mind' cannot be understood dualistically, à la Descartes. But perhaps there are massively more levels, perhaps innumerably more. In a recent book the Yale biophysicist Harold Morowitz, for example, identifies no fewer than twenty-eight distinct levels of emergence in natural history from the big bang to the present.[6]

The comparison with mathematics helps to clarify what is meant by emergent levels and why decisions about them are often messy. Although mathematical *knowledge* increases, mathematics is clearly an area in which one doesn't encounter the emergence of something new. Work in mathematics involves discovering logical entailments: regularities and principles that are built into axiomatic systems from the outset. Thus it is always true that if you want to know the number of numerals in a set of concurrent integers, you subtract the value of the first from the value of the last and add one. It is not as if that rule only begins to pertain when the numbers get really big. By contrast, in the natural world the quantity of particles or degree of complexity in a system does often make a difference. In complex systems, the outcome is more than the sum of the parts. The difficult task, both empirically and conceptually, is ascertaining when and why the complexity is sufficient to produce the new effects.

Concerning (4), downward causation

Many argue that downward causation is the most distinctive feature of a fully emergentist position—and its greatest challenge. As O'Connor notes, 'an emergent's causal influence is irreducible to that of the micro-properties on which it supervenes: it bears its influence in a direct, "downward" fashion in contrast to the operation of a simple structural macro-property, whose causal influence occurs *via* the activity of the micro-properties that constitute it'.[7]

Such a causal influence of an emergent structure or object on its constituent parts would represent a type of causality that diverges from the standard philosophical treatments of causality in modern science. This concept of downward causation, which may be the crux of the emergence theory debate, will occupy us further in the coming chapters. Authors seeking to defend it often criticize the strictures of modern 'efficient' causality and seek to expand the understanding of causality, perhaps with reference to Aristotle's four distinct types of causal influence. The trouble is that material causality—the way in which the matter of a thing causes it to be and to act in a particular way—is no less 'physicalist' than efficient causality, and final causality—the way in which the goal towards which a thing strives influences its behaviour—is associated with vitalist, dualist, and supernaturalist accounts of the world, accounts that most emergentists would prefer to avoid. Formal causality—the influence of the form, structure, or function of an object on its activities—is thus probably the most fruitful of these Aristotelian options. Several authors have begun formulating a broader theory of causal influence,[8] although much work remains to be done.

THE PRE-HISTORY OF THE EMERGENCE CONCEPT

It is widely conceded that George Henry Lewes first introduced the term 'emergence'.[9] Precursors to the concept can nonetheless be traced back in the history of Western philosophy at least as far as Aristotle. Aristotle's biological research led him to posit a principle of growth within organisms that was responsible for the qualities or form that would later emerge. Aristotle called this principle the *entelechy*, the internal principle of growth and perfection that directs the organism to actualize the qualities that it contains in a merely potential state. According to his doctrine of 'potencies', the adult form of the human or animal emerges out of its youthful form. (Unlike contemporary emergence theories, however, he held that the complete form is already present in the organism from the beginning, like a seed; it just needs to be transformed from its potential state to its actual state.) As noted, Aristotle's explanation of emergence included 'formal' causes, which operate through the form internal to the organism, and 'final' causes, which pull the organism (so to speak) towards its final telos or 'perfection'.

The influence of Aristotle on the Hellenistic, medieval, and early modern periods cannot be overstated. His conception of change and growth was formative for the development of Islamic thought and, especially after being baptized at the hands of Thomas Aquinas, it became foundational for Christian theology as well. In many respects biology was still under the influence of something very much like the Aristotelian paradigm when Darwin began his work.

A second precursor to emergence theory might be found in the doctrine of *emanation* as first developed by Plotinus in the third century CE[10] and greatly extended by the Neoplatonic thinkers who followed him. Plotinus defended the emergence of the entire hierarchy of being out of the One through a process of emanation. This expansion was balanced by a movement of finite things back up the ladder of derivation to their ultimate source. The Neoplatonic model allowed both for a *downward* movement of differentiation and causality and an *upward* movement of increasing perfection, diminishing distance from the Source, and (in principle) mystical reunification with the One. Unlike static models of the world, emanation models allowed for a gradual process of becoming. Although the Neoplatonic philosophers generally focused on the downward emanation that gave rise to the intellectual, psychological and physical spheres respectively (*nous, psychê,* and *physika* or *kosmos* in Plotinus), their notion of emanation allowed for the emergence of new species as well. In those cases where the emanation was understood in a temporal sense, as with Plotinus, the emanation doctrine provides an important antecedent to doctrines of biological or universal evolution. Finally, process philosophies of the last 150 years are also important contributors to emergence theory[8]; they will be dealt with further below.

When science was still natural philosophy, emergence played a productive heuristic role. After about 1850, however, emergence theories were several times imposed unscientifically as a metaphysical framework in a way that blocked empirical work. Key examples include the neo-vitalists (e.g. H. Driesch's theory of entelechies) and neo-idealist theories of the interconnection of all living things (e.g. Bradley's theory of internal relations) around the turn of the century, as well as the speculations of the British Emergentists in the 1920s concerning the origin of mind (on whom more in a moment).

Arguably, the philosopher who should count as the great modern advocate of emergence theory is Hegel. In place of the notion of static being or substance, Hegel offered a temporalized ontology, a philosophy of universal becoming. The first triad in his system moves from Being as the first postulation to Nothing, its negation. If these two stand in blunt opposition, there can be no development in reality. But the opposition between the two is overcome by the category of Becoming. This triad is both the first step in the system and an expression of its fundamental principle. Always, in the universal flow of 'Spirit coming to itself', oppositions arise and are overcome by a new level of emergence.

As an idealist, Hegel did not begin with the natural or the physical world; he began with the world of ideas. At some point, ideas gave rise to the natural world, and in Spirit the two are reintegrated. The idealism of Hegel's approach to emergent processes had to be corrected if it was to be fruitful for science, though it would be some eighty years before science began to play a major role in understanding emergence. First it was necessary to find a more materialist starting point, even if it was not yet one driven by the natural sciences. Feuerbach's 'inversion' of Hegel represented a start in this direction. For Feuerbach the laws of development were still necessary and triadic (dialectical) in Hegel's sense. But for the author of *The Essence of Christianity*, the development of spiritual ideas began with the human species in its physical and social reality ('species-being'). Karl Marx made the inversion more complete by anchoring the dialectic in the means of production. Now economic history, the study of the development of economic structures, became the fundamental level and ideas were reduced to a 'super-structure', representing the ideological after-effects or *ex-post-facto* justifications of economic structures.

The birth of sociology (or, more generally, social science) in the nineteenth century is closely tied to this development. Auguste Comte, the so-called father of sociology, provided his own ladder of evolution. But now science crowned the hierarchy, being the rightful heir to the Age of Religion and the Age of Philosophy. The work of Comte and his followers (especially Durkheim), with their insistence that higher-order human ideas arise out of simpler antecedents, helped establish an emergentist understanding of human society. Henceforth studies of the human person would have to begin not with the realm of ideas or Platonic forms but with the elementary processes of the physical and social worlds.

WEAK AND STRONG EMERGENCE

Although the particular labels and formulations vary widely, commentators are widely agreed that twentieth-century emergence theories fall into two broad categories. These are best described as 'weak' and 'strong' emergence—with the emphatic insistence that these adjectives refer to the degree of emergence and do not prejudice the argumentative quality of the two positions.[11] Strong emergentists maintain that evolution in the cosmos produces new, ontologically distinct levels, which are characterized by their own distinct laws or regularities and causal forces. By contrast, weak emergentists insist that, as new patterns emerge, the fundamental causal processes remain those of physics. As emergentists, these thinkers believe that it may be essential to scientific success to explain causal processes using emergent categories such as protein synthesis, hunger, kin selection, or the desire to be loved. But, although such emergent structures may essentially constrain the behaviour of lower-level structures, they should not be viewed as active causal influences in their own right.

Weak emergentists grant that different sorts of causal interactions seem to dominate 'higher' levels of reality. They agree with strong emergentists, for example, that evolution forms structures which, as emergent wholes, constrain the motions of their parts. But our inability to recognize in these emerging patterns new manifestations of the same fundamental causal processes is due primarily to our ignorance. For this reason weak emergence is sometimes called 'epistemological emergence', in contrast to strong or 'ontological' emergence. Michael Silberstein and John McGreever nicely define the contrast between these two terms:

> A property of an object or system is epistemologically emergent if the property is reducible to or determined by the intrinsic properties of the ultimate constituents of the object or system, while at the same time it is very difficult for us to explain, predict or derive the property on the basis of the ultimate constituents. Epistemologically emergent properties are novel only at a level of description. . . . Ontologically emergent features are neither reducible to nor determined by more basic features. Ontologically emergent features are features of systems or wholes that possess causal capacities not reducible to any of the intrinsic causal capacities of the parts nor to any of the (reducible) relations between the parts.[12]

It is not difficult to provide a formal definition of emergence in the weak sense: 'F is an emergent property of S *if* (a) there is a law to the effect that all systems with this micro-structure have F; but (b) F cannot, even in theory, be deduced from the most complete knowledge of the basic properties of the components $C_1, \ldots, C_n$' of the system.[13]

Both weak and strong emergence represent a conceptual break with the reductive physicalist positions to which they are responding. The differences between them are significant and shall concern us more in due course. Weak emergence, because it places a stronger stress on the continuities between physics and subsequent levels, stands closer to the 'unity of science' perspective. It has won a number of important advocates in the sciences and in philosophy from the end of the heyday of British Emergentism in the early 1930s until the closing decades of the century. But a number of philosophers have recently disputed its claim to represent a genuine alternative to physicalism. If the charge proves true, as I think it does, weak emergence will leave us saddled with the same old dichotomy between physicalism and dualism, despite its best efforts to the contrary.

The contrasts between weak and strong theories of emergence— both the issues that motivate them and the arguments they employ—are important. Yet their common opposition to reductive physicalism is a sign of significant common ground between the two positions. Before we enter into a no-holds-barred contest between them, it is crucial to explore their shared history and the numerous lines of connection between them. By attempting a conceptual reconstruction of the history of emergentism in the twentieth century, we will win a clearer picture of the similarities and the oppositions between the two related schools of thought. First the combined resources of the two schools must be marshalled in order to make a decisive case against the metaphysics of physicalism; only then can we turn to the issues that continue to divide them.

STRONG EMERGENCE: C. D. BROAD

I begin with perhaps the best known work in the field, C. D. Broad's *The Mind and its Place in Nature*. Broad's position is clearly not dualist; he insists that emergence theory is compatible with a fundamental monism about the physical world. He contrasts this emergentist monism with what he calls 'Mechanism' and with weak emergence:

On the emergent theory we have to reconcile ourselves to much less unity in the external world and a much less intimate connexion between the various sciences. At best the external world and the various sciences that deal with it will form a kind of hierarchy. We might, if we liked, keep the view that there is only one fundamental kind of stuff. *But we should have to recognise aggregates of various orders.*[14]

Emergence, Broad argues, can be expressed in terms of laws ('trans-ordinal laws') that link the emergent characteristics with the lower-level parts and the structure or patterns that occur at the emergent level. But emergent laws do not meet the deducibility requirements of, for example, Hempel's 'covering law' model;[15] they are not metaphysically necessary. Moreover, they have another strange feature: 'the only peculiarity of [an emergent law] is that we must wait till we meet with an actual instance of an object of the higher order before we can discover such a law; and . . . we cannot possibly deduce it beforehand from any combination of laws which we have discovered by observing aggregates of a lower order' (p. 79).

These comments alone would not be sufficient to mark Broad as a strong rather than weak emergentist. Nor do his comments on biology do so. He accepts teleology in nature, but defines it in a weak enough sense that no automatic inference to a cosmic Designer is possible. Broad also attacks the theory of entelechies (p. 86) and what he calls 'Substantial Vitalism', by which he clearly means the work of Hans Driesch. Broad rejects biological mechanism because 'organisms are not machines but are systems whose characteristic behaviour is emergent and not mechanistically explicable' (p. 92). He thus accepts 'Emergent Vitalism', while insisting that this watered down version of Vitalism is an implication of emergence and not its motivation: 'What must be assumed is not a special tendency of matter to fall into the kind of arrangement which has vital characteristics, but a general tendency for complexes of one order to combine with each other under suitable conditions to form complexes of the next order' (p. 93). Emergentism is consistent with theism but does not entail it (p. 94).

It is in Broad's extended treatment of the mind–body problem that one sees most clearly why the stages of emergence leading to mind actually entail the strong interpretation. Mental events, he argues, represent another distinct emergent level. But they cannot be explained in terms of their interrelations alone. Some sort of 'Central Theory' is required, that is, a theory that postulates a mental 'Centre' that unifies the various mental events as 'mind' (pp. 584ff.). Indeed, just as Broad had earlier argued that the notion of a material event requires the notion of material substance, so now he argues that the idea of mental events requires the notion of mental substance (pp. 598ff.). Broad remains an emergentist in so far as the 'enduring whole', which he calls 'mind' or 'mental particle', 'is analogous, not to a body, but to a material particle' (p. 600). (Dualists, by contrast, would proceed from the postulation of mental substance to the definition of individual mental events.) The resulting strong emergentist position lies between dualism and weak emergence. Broad derives his concept of substance from *events* of a particular type (in this case, mental events), rather than presupposing it as ultimate. Yet he underscores the emergent reality of each unique level by speaking of actual objects or specific emergent substances (with their own specific causal powers) at that level.

Broad concludes his *magnum opus* by presenting seventeen metaphysical positions concerning the place of mind in nature and boiling them down ultimately to his preference for 'emergent materialism' over the other options. It is a materialism, however, far removed from most, if not all, of the materialist and physicalist positions of the second half of the twentieth century. For example, 'Idealism is not incompatible with materialism' as he defines it (p. 654)—something that one cannot say of most materialisms today. Broad's (redefined) materialism is also not incompatible, as we have already seen, with theism.

Conway Lloyd Morgan became perhaps the most influential of the British Emergentists of the 1920s. I reconstruct the four major tenets of his emergentist philosophy before turning to an initial evaluation of its success.

First, Morgan could not accept what we might call Darwin's *continuity principle*. A gradualist, Darwin was methodologically committed to removing any 'jumps' in nature. On Morgan's view, by contrast, emergence is all about the recognition that evolution is 'punctuated': even a full reconstruction of evolution would not remove the basic stages or levels that are revealed in the evolutionary process.

In this regard, Morgan stood closer to Alfred Russel Wallace than to Darwin. Wallace's work focused in particular on qualitative novelty in the evolutionary process. Famously, Wallace turned to divine intervention as the explanation for each new stage or level in evolution. Morgan recognized that such an appeal would lead sooner or later to the problems faced by any 'God of the gaps' strategy. In the conviction that it must be possible to recognize emergent levels without shutting down the process of scientific inquiry, Morgan sided against Wallace and with 'evolutionary naturalism' in the appendix to *Emergent Evolution*. He endorsed emergence not as a means for preserving some causal influence *ad extra*, but because he believed scientific research points to a series of discrete steps as basic in natural history.

Second, Morgan sought a philosophy of biology that would leave an adequate place for the emergence of radically new life forms and behaviours. Interestingly, after Samuel Alexander, Henri Bergson is one of the most cited authors in *Emergent Evolution*. Morgan resisted Bergson's conclusions ('widely as our conclusions differ from those to which M. Bergson has been led', p. 116), and for many of the same reasons that he resisted Wallace: Bergson introduced the *élan vital* or vital energy as a force from outside nature.[16] Thus Bergson's *Creative Evolution* combines a Cartesian view of non-material forces with the pervasively temporal perspective of late nineteenth-century evolutionary theory. By contrast, the underlying forces for Morgan are thoroughly immanent in the natural process. Still, Morgan stands closer to Bergson than this contrast might suggest. For him also, 'creative evolution' produces continually novel types of phenomena. As Rudolf Metz noted,

It was through Bergson's idea of creative evolution that the doctrine of novelty [became] widely known and made its way into England, where by a similar reaction against the mechanistic evolution theory, Alexander and Morgan became its most influential champions. Emergent evolution is a new, important and specifically British variation of Bergson's creative evolution.[17]

Third, Morgan argued powerfully for the notion of levels of reality. He continually advocated a study of the natural world that would look for novel properties at the level of a system taken as whole, properties that are not present in the parts of the system. Morgan summarizes his position by arguing that the theory of

levels or orders of reality . . . does, however, imply (1) that there is increasing complexity in integral systems as new kinds of relatedness are successively supervenient; (2) that reality is, in this sense, in process of development; (3) that there is an ascending scale of what we may speak of as richness in reality; and (4) that the richest reality that we know lies at the apex of the pyramid of emergent evolution up to date. (p. 203)

The notion of levels of reality harkens back to the Neoplatonic philosophy of Plotinus, who held that all things emanate outward from the One in a series of distinct levels of reality (*Nous, Psyché*, individual minds, persons, animals, etc.). In the present case, however, the motivation for the position is not in the first place metaphysical but scientific: the empirical study of the world itself suggests that reality manifests itself as a series of emerging levels rather than as permutations of matter understood as the fundamental building blocks for all things.

Finally, Morgan interpreted the emergent objects at these various levels in the sense of strong emergence. As his work makes clear, there are stronger and weaker ways of introducing the idea of levels of reality. His strong interpretation of the levels, according to Blitz, was influenced by a basic philosophy text by Walter Marvin. The text had argued that reality is analysable into a series of 'logical strata', with each new stratum consisting of a smaller number of more specialized types of entities:

To sum up: The picture of reality just outlined is logically built up of strata. The logical and mathematical are fundamental and universal. The physical comes next and though less extensive is still practically, if not quite, universal. Next comes the biological, extensive but vastly less extensive than the chemical. Finally, comes the mental and especially the human and the social, far less extensive.[18]

Emergence is interesting to scientifically minded thinkers only to the extent that it accepts the principle of parsimony, introducing no more metaphysical superstructure than is required by the data themselves. The data, Morgan argued, require the strong interpretation of emergence. They support the conclusions that there are major discontinuities in evolution; that these discontinuities result in the multiple levels at which phenomena are manifested in the natural world; that objects at these levels evidence a unity and integrity, which require us to treat them as wholes or objects or agents in their own right; and that, as such, they exercise their own causal powers on other agents (horizontal causality) and on the parts of which they are composed (downward causation). Contrasting his view to 'weaker' approaches to ontology, Morgan treats the levels of reality as *substantially* different:

There is increasing richness in stuff *and in substance* throughout the stages of evolutionary advance; there is redirection of the course of events at each level; this redirection is so marked at certain critical turning-points as to present 'the apparent paradox' that the emergently new is incompatible in 'substance' with the previous course of events before the turning-point was reached. All this seems to be given in the evidence. (p. 207; italics added)

Introducing emergent levels as producing new substances means attributing the strongest possible ontological status to wholes in relation to their parts. Blitz traces Morgan's understanding of the whole–part relation back to E. G. Spaulding. Spaulding had argued that 'in the physical world (and elsewhere) it is an established empirical fact that parts as non-additively organized form a whole which has characteristics that are qualitatively different from the characteristics of the parts'.[19] Significantly, Spaulding drew most of his examples from chemistry. If emergence theories can point to emergent wholes only at the level of mind, they quickly fall into a crypto-dualism (or perhaps a not-so-crypto one!); and if they locate emergent wholes only at the level of life, they run the risk of sliding into vitalism. Conversely, if significant whole–part influences can be established already within physical chemistry, they demonstrate that emergence is not identical with either vitalism or dualism.

How are we to evaluate Morgan's *Emergent Evolution*? The strategy of arguing for emergent substances clashes with the monism that I defended above, and a fortiori with all naturalist emergence theories. Morgan's strategy is even more regrettable in that it was unnecessary; his own theory of *relations* would actually have done the same work without recourse to the substance notion. He writes, 'There is perhaps no topic which is more cardinal to our interpretation . . . than that which centres round what I shall call relatedness' (p. 67). In fact, relation forms the core of his ontology: 'It is as an integral whole of relatedness that any individual entity, or any concrete situation, is a bit of reality' (p. 69; note the close connection to contemporary interpretations of quantum physics). Since the relations at each emergent level are unique, complexes of relations are adequately individuated:

> May one say that in each such family group there is not only an incremental resultant, but also a specific kind of integral relatedness of which the constitutive characters of each member of the group is an emergent expression? If so, we have here an illustration of what is meant by emergent evolution. (p. 7)

Or, more succinctly: 'If it be asked: What is it that you claim to be emergent?—the brief reply is: Some new kind of relation', for 'at each ascending step there is a new entity in virtue of some new kind of relation, or set of relations, within it' (p. 64). As long as each relational complex evidences unique features and causal powers, one does not need to lean on the questionable concept of substance in order to describe it.

Let's call those theories of emergence 'very strong' or 'hyper-strong' which not only (*a*) individuate relational complexes, (*b*) ascribe reality to them through an ontology of relations, and (*c*) ascribe causal powers and activity to them, but also (*d*) treat them as individual substances in their own right. The recent defence of 'emergent dualism' by William Hasker in *The Emergent Self* provides an analogous example: 'So it is not enough to say that there are emergent properties here; what is needed is an *emergent individual*, a new individual entity which comes into existence as a result of a certain functional configuration of the material constituents of the brain and nervous system.'[20] The connection with a theory of substantival entities becomes explicit when Hasker quotes with approval an adaptation of Thomas Aquinas by Brian Leftow: 'the human fetus becomes able to host the human soul . . . This happens in so lawlike a way as to count as a form of natural supervenience. So if we leave God out of the picture, the Thomist soul is an "emergent individual".'[21]

Clearly, emergence theories cover a wide spectrum of ontological commitments. According to some, the emergents are no more than patterns, with no causal powers of their own; for others they are substances in their own right, almost as distinct from their origins as Cartesian mind is from body. An emergence theory that is to be useful in the philosophy of science will have to accept some form of the law of parsimony: emergent entities and levels should not be multiplied without need. From a scientific perspective it is preferable to explain mental causation by appealing only to mental properties and the components of the central nervous system, rather than by introducing mental 'things' such as minds and spirits. I have argued that Morgan's robust theory of emergent relations would have done justice to emergent levels in natural history, and even to downward causation, without the addition of emerging substances. Morgan, in his attempt to avoid the outright dualism of Wallace and Bergson, would have been better advised to do without them.

STRONG EMERGENCE SINCE 1960

Emergence theory in general, and strong emergence in particular, began to disappear off the radar screens during the mid-1930s and did not reappear for some decades. Individual philosophers such as Michael Polanyi continued to advocate emergence positions. Generally, however, the criticisms of the British Emergentists—for instance, by Stephen Pepper in 1926 and by Arthur Papp in 1952[22]—were taken to be sufficient. Pepper argued, for example, that although evolution produces novelty, there is nothing philosophically significant to say about it; neither indeterminism nor emergence can make novelty philosophically productive.

In 1973, Pylyshyn noted that a new cognitive paradigm had 'recently exploded' into fashion.[23] Whatever one's own particular position on the developments, it is clear that by the 1990s emergence theories were again major topics of discussion in the sciences and philosophy (and the media). Now one must proceed with caution in interpreting contemporary philosophy, since histories of the present are inevitably part of what they seek to describe. Nonetheless, it is useful to consider the immediate pre-history of strong views in contemporary emergence theory. Two figures in particular played key roles in the re-emergence of interest in strong emergence: Michael Polanyi and Roger Sperry.

Michael Polanyi

Writing in the heyday of the reductionist period, midway between the British Emergentists of the 1920s and the rebirth of the emergence movement in the 1990s, Michael Polanyi was a sort of lone voice crying in the wilderness. He is perhaps best known for his theories of tacit knowledge and the irreducibility of the category of personhood, views that were in fact integrally linked to his defence of emergence. In his theory of tacit knowing, for instance, Polanyi recognized that thought was motivated by the anticipation of discovery: 'all the time we are guided by sensing the presence of a hidden reality toward which our clues are pointing'.[24] Tacit knowing thus presupposes at least two levels of reality: the particulars, and their 'comprehensive meaning' (*TD* 34). Gradually Polanyi extended this 'levels of reality' insight outward to a variety of fields, beginning with his own field, physical chemistry, and then moving on to the biological sciences and to the problem of consciousness.[25] In his view even physical randomness was understood as an emergent phenomenon (*PK* 390–1); all living things, or what he called 'living mechanisms', were classed with machines as systems controlled by their functions, which exercise a downward causation on the biological parts (e.g. *KB* 226–7; *PK* 359ff.). Processes such as the composition of a text serve as clear signs that human goals and intentions are downward causal forces that play a central role in explaining the behaviour of *homo sapiens*. Polanyi combined these various argumentative steps together into an overarching philosophy of emergence:

> The first emergence, by which life comes into existence, is the prototype of all subsequent stages of evolution, by which rising forms of life, with their higher principles, emerge into existence. . . . The spectacle of rising stages of emergence confirms this generalization by bringing forth at the highest level of evolutionary emergence those mental powers in which we had first recognized our faculty of tacit knowing. (*TD* 49)

Several aspects of Polanyi's position are reflected in contemporary emergence theories and served to influence the development of the field; I mention just three.[26]

(1) Active and passive boundary conditions

Polanyi recognized two types of boundaries: natural processes controlled by boundaries; and machines, which function actively to bring about effects. He characterized this distinction in two different ways: in terms of foreground and background interests, and in terms of active and passive constraints. Regarding the former distinction, he argued, a test tube constrains the chemical reaction taking place within it; but when we observe it, 'we are studying the reaction, not the test tube' (*KB* 226). In watching a chess game, by contrast, our interest 'lies in the boundaries': we are interested in the chess master's strategy, in *why* he makes the moves and what he hopes to achieve by them, rather than in the rule-governed nature of the moves themselves.

More important than the backgrounding and foregrounding of interest, Polanyi recognized that the 'causal role' of the test tube is a passive constraint, whereas intentions *actively* shape the outcome in a top–down manner: 'when a sculptor shapes a stone or a painter composes a painting, our interest lies in the boundaries imposed on a material and not in the material itself' (*KB* 226). Messages from the central nervous system cause neurotransmitter release in a much more active top–down fashion than does the physical structure of microtubules in the brain. Microtubule structure is still a constraining boundary condition, but it is one of a different type, namely a passive one.[27]

(2) The 'from–at' transition and 'focal' attention

Already in the Terry Lectures, Polanyi noticed that the comprehension of meaning involved a movement from 'the proximal'—that is, the particulars that are presented—to the 'distal', which is their comprehensive meaning (*TD* 34). By 1968 he had developed this notion into the notion of 'from–at' conceptions. Understanding meaning involves turning our attention from the words to their meaning; 'we are looking *from* them *at* their meaning'.[28] Polanyi built from these reflections to a more general theory of the 'from–to' structure of consciousness. Mind is a 'from–to experience'; the bodily mechanisms of neurobiology are merely 'the subsidiaries' of this experience (*KB* 238). Or, more forcibly, 'mind is the meaning of certain bodily mechanisms; it is lost from view when we look *at* them focally'.[29]

Note, by the way, that there are parallels to Polanyi's notion of mind as focal intention in the theory of consciousness advanced by the quantum physicist Henry Stapp, especially in his *Mind, Matter, and Quantum Mechanics*. These parallels help to explain why Stapp is often classified as a strong emergentist.[30] Both thinkers believe that we can comprehend mind as the function of 'exercising discrimination' (*PK* 403 n 1). If Polanyi and Stapp are right, their view represents good news for the downward causation of ideas, since it means that no energy needs to be added to a system by mental activity, thereby preserving the law of the conservation of energy, which is basic to all physical calculations.

(3) The theory of structure and information

Like many emergence theorists, Polanyi recognized that structure is an emergent phenomenon. But he also preserved a place for downward causation in the theory of structure, arguing that 'the structure and functioning of an organism is determined, like that of a machine, by constructional and operational principles that control boundary conditions left open by physics and chemistry' (*KB* 219). Structure is not simply a matter of complexity. The structure of a crystal represents a complex order without great informational content (*KB* 228); crystals have a maximum of stability that corresponds to a minimum of potential energy. Contrast crystals with DNA. The structure of a DNA molecule represents a high level of chemical improbability, since the nucleotide sequence is not determined by the underlying chemical structure. While the crystal does not function as a code, the DNA molecule can do so because it is very high in informational content relative to the background probabilities of its formation.

Polanyi's treatment of structure represents an interesting anticipation of contemporary work in information biology.[31] Terrence Deacon, for example, argues that 'it is essential to recognize that biology is not merely a physical science, it is a semiotic science; a science where significance and representation are essential elements. . . . [Evolutionary biology] stands at the border between physical and semiotic science.'[32] Perhaps other elements in Polanyi's work could contribute to the development of information biology, which is still in the fledgling phases.

At the same time that emergence theory has profited from Polanyi, it has also moved beyond his work in some respects. I briefly indicate two such areas:

(1) Polanyi was wrong on morphogenesis

He was very attracted by the work of Hans Driesch, which seemed to support the existence of organismic forces and causes (*TD* 42–3, *PK* 390, *KB* 232). Following Driesch, Polanyi held that the morphogenetic field pulls the evolving cell or organism towards itself. He was also ready to argue that the coordination of muscles, as well as the recuperation of the central nervous system after injury, was 'unformalizable . . . in terms of any fixed anatomical machinery' (*PK* 398). While admitting that the science of morphogenetic fields had not yet been established, he hitched his horse to its future success: 'once . . . emergence was fully established, it would be clear that it represented the achievement of a new way of life, induced in the germ plasm by a field based on the gradient of phylogenetic achievement' (*PK* 402). He even cites an anticipation of the stem cell research that has been receiving so much attention of late: the early work by Paul Weiss, which showed that embryonic cells will grow 'when lumped together into a fragment of the organ from which they were isolated' (*KB* 232). But we now know that it is not necessary to postulate that the growth of the embryo 'is controlled by the gradient of potential shapes', and we don't need to postulate a 'field' to guide this development (ibid.). Stem cell research shows that the cell nucleus contains the core information necessary for the cell's development.

(2) Polanyi's sympathy for Aristotle and vitalism clashes with core assumptions of contemporary biology

Aristotle is famous for the doctrine of *entelechy*, whereby the future state of an organism (say, in the case of an acorn, the full-grown oak) pulls the developing organism towards itself. In a section on the functions of living beings, Polanyi spoke of the causal role of 'intimations of the potential coherence of hitherto unrelated things', arguing that 'their solution establishes a new comprehensive entity, be it a new poem, a new kind of machine, or a new knowledge of nature' (*TD* 44). The causal powers of non-existent (or at least not-yet-existent) objects make for suspicious enough philosophy; they make for even worse science. Worse from the standpoint of biology was Polanyi's advocacy of Bergson's *élan vital* (*TD* 46), which led him to declare the affinity of his position with that of Teilhard de Chardin.

The doctrine of vitalism that Polanyi took over from Driesch meant, in fact, a whole-scale break with the neo-Darwinian synthesis, on which all actual empirical work in biology today is based. Beyond structural features and mechanical forces, Polanyi wanted to add a broader 'field of forces' that would be 'the gradient of a potentiality: a gradient arising from the proximity of a possible achievement'

(*PK* 398). He wanted something analogous to 'the agency of a centre seeking satisfaction in the light of its own standards' (ibid.). What we do find in biology is the real-world striving that is caused by the appetites and behavioural dispositions of sufficiently complex organisms. The operation of appetites cannot be fully explained by a Dawkinsian reduction to the 'selfish gene', since their development and expression are often the result of finally tuned interactions with the environment. Nevertheless, combinations of genes can code for appetites, and the environment can select for or against them, without one's needing to introduce mysterious forces into biology.

In the end, Polanyi went too far, opting for 'finalistic' causes in biology (*PK* 399). It is one thing to say that the evolutionary process 'manifested itself in the novel organism', but quite another to argue that 'the maturation of the germ plasm is *guided* by the potentialities that are open to it through its possible germination into new individuals' (*PK* 400). It is one thing to say that the evolutionary process has given rise to individuals who can exercise rational and responsible choices; but it breaks with all empirical biology to argue that 'we should take this active component into account likewise down to the lowest levels' (*PK* 402–3). This move would make all of biology a manifestation of an inner vitalistic drive; and that claim is inconsistent with the practice of empirical biology.

Donald MacKay

I should briefly mention the important early work on emergence by Donald MacKay. MacKay was one of the pioneers in Artificial Intelligence (AI) research; he was also a theist whose arguments for the complementarity of science and faith were influential in Great Britain in the middle of the century.[33] MacKay recognized that an integrated account of human behaviour required the use of multiple levels of explanation: 'we need a whole hierarchy of levels and categories of explanation if we are to do justice to the richness of the nature of man'.[34] The goal is not to translate mental terms into (say) electrochemical terms but rather to trace the correspondences between the two levels of description. 'They are neither *identical* nor *independent*, but rather *complementary*' (30).

MacKay was certainly not a dualist: he predicted that there would not be gaps in neurophysiological explanations and insisted that one 'not try what the French philosopher Descartes suggested, looking in the brain for signs of non-physical forces exerted by the soul; but it would make sense to look in the brain (if we could) for physical happenings whose pattern was correlated with that of conscious activities such as examining-one's-motives, or making-up-one's-mind' (32–3). Yet he did tend to draw a sharp distinction between 'the outside view' and 'the inside view' of the human person.[35] In the end MacKay's work is best classified as a version of strong emergence because he combined the theory of a hierarchy of explanatory levels with an insistence on the causal influence of consciousness. Convinced of the disanalogy between humans and computing machines, MacKay defended 'the intimate two-way relationship that exists between the physical activity of the brain and the conscious experience of the individual'.[36]

Roger Sperry

In the 1960s, at a time when such views were not only unpopular but even anathema, Roger Sperry began defending an emergentist view of mental properties. As a neuroscientist, Sperry would not be satisfied with any explanation that ignored or underplayed the role of neural processes. At the same time, he realized that consciousness is not a mere epiphenomenon of the brain; instead, conscious thoughts and decisions *do something* in brain functioning. Sperry was willing to countenance neither a dualist, separationist account of mind, nor any account that would dispense with mind altogether. As early as 1964, by his own account, he had formulated the core principles of his view.[37] By 1969 emergence had come to serve as the central orienting concept of his position:

The subjective mental phenomena are conceived to influence and govern the flow of nerve impulse traffic by virtue of their encompassing emergent properties. Individual nerve impulses and other excitatory components of a cerebral activity pattern are simply carried along or shunted this way and that by the prevailing overall dynamics of the whole active process (in principle—just as drops of water are carried along by a local eddy in a stream or the way the molecules and atoms of a wheel are carried along when it rolls downhill, regardless of whether the individual molecules and atoms happen to like it or not). Obviously, it also works the other way around, that is, the conscious properties of cerebral patterns are directly dependent on the action of the component neural elements. Thus, a mutual interdependence is recognized between the sustaining physico-chemical processes and the enveloping conscious qualities. The neurophysiology, in other words, controls the mental effects, and the mental properties in turn control the neurophysiology.[38]

Sperry is sometimes interpreted as holding only that mental language is a redescription of brain activity as a whole. But this interpretation is mistaken; he clearly does assert that mental properties have causal force: 'The conscious subjective properties in our present view are interpreted to have causal potency in regulating the course of brain events; that is, the mental forces or properties exert a regulative control influence in brain physiology.'[39]

The initial choice of the term 'interactionism' came as a result of Sperry's work with split-brain patients. Because these patients' *corpus callosum* had been severed, no neurophysiological account could be given of the unified consciousness that they still manifested. Thus, he reasoned, there must be interactions at the emergent level of consciousness, whereby conscious states exercise a direct causal influence on subsequent brain states, perhaps alongside other causal factors. Sperry referred to this position as 'emergent interactionism'. He also conceded that the term 'interaction' is not exactly the appropriate term:

Mental phenomena are described as primarily supervening rather than intervening, in the physiological process. . . . Mind is conceived to move matter in the brain and to govern, rule, and direct neural and chemical events without interacting with the components at the component level, just as an organism may move and govern the time–space course of its atoms and tissues without interacting with them.[40]

Sperry is right to avoid the term 'interaction' if it is understood to imply a causal story in which higher-level influences are interpreted as specific (efficient) causal activities that push and pull the lower-level components of the system. As Jaegwon Kim has shown, if one conceives downward causation in that manner, it would be simpler to tell the whole story in terms of the efficient causal history of the component parts themselves.

Sperry was not philosophically sophisticated, and he never developed his view in a systematic fashion. But he did effectively chronicle the neuroscientific evidence that supports some form of downward or conscious causation, and he dropped hints of the sort of philosophical account that must be given: a theory of downward causation understood as whole–part influence. Thus Emmeche, Køppe, and Stjernfelt develop Sperry's position using the concepts of part and whole. On their interpretation, the higher level (say, consciousness) constrains the outcome of lower-level processes. Yet it does so in a manner that qualifies as causal influence:

The entities at various levels may enter part–whole relations (e.g., mental phenomena control their component neural and biophysical sub-elements), in which the control of the part by the whole can be seen as a kind of functional (teleological) causation, which is based on efficient material as well as formal causation in a multinested system of constraints.[41]

I suggest that a combination of Sperry's approach to the neuroscientific data and to the phenomenology of consciousness or *qualia*—combined with an ontology of part–whole relations and a theory of downward causation that builds upon it—represents the most hopeful strategy for developing an adequate theory of strong emergence today.

WEAK EMERGENCE: SAMUEL ALEXANDER

We turn now to the opposing school, weak emergence, which has probably been the more widespread position among twentieth-century philosophers. Recall that weak emergence grants that evolution produces new structures and organizational patterns. We may happen to speak of these structures as things in their own right; they may serve as irreducible components of our best explanations; and they might even *seem* to function as causal agents. But the real or ultimate causal work is done at a lower level, presumably that of physics. Our inability to recognize in these emerging patterns new manifestations of the same fundamental processes is due primarily to our ignorance and should not be taken as a guide to ontology. The first major advocate of this view, and its classic representative, is Samuel Alexander.

Samuel Alexander's *Space, Time and Deity* presents a weak emergentist answer to the mind–body problem and then extends his theory outward into a systematic metaphysical position. Alexander's goal was to develop a philosophical conception in which evolution and history had a real place. He presupposed both as givens: there really are bodies in the universe, and there really exist mental properties or mental experience. The problem is to relate them. Alexander resolutely rejected classical dualism and any idealist view that would make the mental pole primary (e.g. Leibniz, and British Idealists such as F. H. Bradley); yet, like the other emergentists already discussed, he refused to countenance physicalist views that seek to reduce the phenomenon of mind to its physical roots. Mind, he concluded, must emerge in some sense from the physical.

Spinoza's work provided a major inspiration for Alexander. At any given level of reality, Spinoza held, there is only one (type of) activity. Thus in the mind–body case there cannot be both mental causes and physical causes; there can be only one causal system with one type of activity. Alexander argued in a similar manner: 'It seems at first blush paradoxical to hold that our minds enjoy their own causality in following an external causal sequence, and still more that in it [sc. the mind] influencing the course of our thinking we contemplate causal sequence in the objects'.[42] As a result, although minds may 'contemplate' and 'enjoy', they cannot be said to *cause*.

Recall that the continuum between strong and weak emergence turns on how strong is the role of the active subject or mental pole. As one of the major defenders of the weak view of mental emergents, Alexander's view pushes strongly towards the physical pole. The real causality in nature seems to come from events in the external world. Some causal strings are actual; others are only imagined: 'Plato in my dreams tells me his message as he would in reality' (ii. 154). For example, suppose you think of the city Dresden and of a painting by Raphael located there. 'When thinking of Dresden makes me think of Raphael, so that I feel my own causality, Dresden is not indeed contemplated as the cause of Raphael, but Dresden and Raphael are contemplated as connected by some causal relation *in the situation which is then* [that is, then becomes] *my perspective of things*' (ii. 154).

Alexander extends this core causal account from sensations to a universal theory of mind. Our motor sensors sense movement of objects in the world; we are aware of our limbs moving. Our eyes detect movement external to us in the world. Thus, 'My object in the sensation of hunger or thirst is the living process or movement of depletion, such as I observe outside me in purely physiological form in the parched and thirsting condition of the leaves of a plant.' It's a mistake to think that 'the unpleasantness of hunger is . . . psychical' or to treat hunger 'as a state of mind' (ii. 171). Here Alexander's position stands closest to the 'non-reductive physicalist' view in contemporary philosophy of mind: 'It is no wonder then that we should suppose such a condition to be something mental which is as it were presented to a mind which looks on at it; and that we should go on to apply the same notion to colours and tastes and sounds and regard these as mental in character' (ibid.).

In order to generalize this position into a global metaphysical position, Alexander uses 'mind' in a much broader sense than as consciousness alone. In fact, at times 'mind' and 'body' threaten to become purely formal concepts: the 'body' aspect of anything stands for the constituent factors into which it can be analysed, and the 'mind' aspect always represents the new quality manifested by a group of bodies when they function as a whole.[43] This generalization allows him to extend his answer to the mind–body problem to all of nature, producing a hierarchical metaphysics of emergence. As he defines the hierarchy,

Within the all-embracing stuff of Space-Time, the universe exhibits an emergence in Time of successive levels of finite existence, each with its characteristic empirical quality. The highest of these empirical qualities known to us is mind or consciousness. Deity is the next higher empirical quality to the highest we know. (ii. 345)

The result is a ladder of emergence of universal proportions. I take the time to reconstruct the steps of this ladder in some detail, since they give the first clear sense of what a theory of natural history looks like when developed in terms of a hierarchy of emergent levels:[44]

1. At the base of the ladder lies Space-Time. Time is 'mind' and space is 'body'; hence time is 'the mind of space'. Space-Time is composed of 'point-instants'. The early commentators on Alexander found this theory hard to stomach. It has not improved with age.

2. There must be a principle of development, something that drives the whole process, if there is to be an ongoing process of emergence. Thus Alexander posited that 'there is a nisus in Space-Time which, as it has borne its creatures forward through matter and life to mind, will bear them forward to some higher level of existence' (ii. 346). This 'nisus' or creative metaphysical principle bears important similarities to the principle of Creativity in Whitehead's thought.

3. Thanks to the nisus, Space-Time becomes differentiated by 'motions'. Certain organized patterns of motions (today we would call them energies) are the bearers of the set of qualities we refer to as matter. So, contra Aristotle, matter itself is emergent. (Quantum field theory has since offered some support for this conception: e.g. in *Veiled Reality* Bernard d'Espagnat describes subatomic particles as products of the quantum field, hence as derivatives of it.[45])

4. Organizations of matter are bearers of macrophysical qualities and chemical properties. This constitutes emergence at the molecular level.

5. When matter reaches a certain level of complexity, molecules become the bearers of life. (This response is consistent with contemporary work on the origins of life, which postulates a gradual transition from complex molecules to living cells.)

6. Alexander didn't adequately cover the evolution of sentience

but should have. Thus he could have covered the evolution of simple volition (e.g. the choice of where to move), symbiosis (reciprocal systems of organisms), sociality, and primitive brain processing as extensions of the same framework of bodies and their emergent holistic properties, which he called 'mind'. Certainly Alexander's hierarchy would have to give careful attention to the stages of actual evolutionary development if it is to pass as a conceptual reconstruction of natural history.

7. Some living structures then come to be the bearers of the quality of mind or consciousness proper, 'the highest empirical quality known to us'. This is the notion of the emergence of mind that I have already touched on above.

8. But Alexander did not stop with mind. At a certain level in the development of mind, he held, mind may be productive of a new emergent quality, which he called 'Deity'. Here he evidenced a rather substantial (verging on complete) agnosticism. We know of Deity only that it is the next emergent property, that it is a holistic property composed of parts or 'bodies', and that it results from an increased degree of complexity. To be consistent with the productive principle of the hierarchy, Alexander had to postulate that Deity is to the totality of minds as our mind is to (the parts of) our bodies. It follows that Deity's 'body' must consist of the sum total of minds in the universe:

One part of the god's mind will be of such complexity and refinement as mind, as to be fitted to carry the new quality of deity. . . . As our mind represents and gathers up into itself its whole body, so does the finite god represent or gather up into its divine part its whole body [namely, minds] . . . For such a being its specially differentiated mind takes the place of the brain or central nervous system with us. (ii. 355)

Alexander also ascribed certain moral properties to Deity. Beyond these minimal descriptions, however, one can say nothing more of its nature:

That the universe is pregnant with such a quality we are speculatively assured. What that quality is we cannot know; for we can neither enjoy nor still less contemplate it. Our human altars still are raised to the unknown God. If we could know what deity is, how it feels to be divine, we should first have to have become as gods. What we know of it is but its relation to the other empirical qualities which precede it in time. Its nature we cannot penetrate. (ii. 247)

I present Alexander's theory of Deity in some detail for several reasons. First, it shows that the position one takes on the physicalism–emergence–dualism debate will have significant implications for what views one can or cannot consistently hold regarding the nature of a divine agent (if one exists). Moreover, one might well have supposed that only a strong emergentist could introduce language of deity. Yet here we have a case of theological language being introduced as an intrinsic part of a hierarchy of weak emergence. Nor is Alexander the only theorist to seek to include the predicate of deity, though perhaps not a separately existing God, into a primarily physicalist metaphysic; recent proposals by Michael Arbib and Carl Gillett move in similar directions.[46] Nonetheless Alexander, if he is to remain a weak emergentist, must consistently refuse to talk of the actual existence of a spiritual being, God; whatever spiritual qualities he introduces must be predicated of the one natural universe:

As actual, God does not possess the quality of deity but *is the universe as tending to that quality.* . . . Thus there is no actual infinite being with the quality of deity; but there is an actual infinite, the whole universe, with a nisus toward deity; and this is the God of the religious consciousness, though that consciousness habitually forecasts the divinity of its object as actually realized in an individual form. . . . The actual reality which has deity is the world of empiricals filling up all Space-Time and tending towards a higher quality. Deity is a nisus and not an accomplishment. (ii. 361–2, 364)

Alexander's view remains a classic expression of the weak emergentist position. No new entities are postulated, and yet the emergent nature of reality requires one to supply explanations appropriate to each new level: 'The emergence of a new quality from any level of existence means that at that level there comes into being a certain constellation or collocation of the motions belonging to that level, and possessing the quality appropriate to it, and this collocation possesses a new quality distinctive of the higher complex'.[47] The *properties* of things become more mental or spiritual as one moves up the ladder of emergence, but the constituents and the causes do not. Like Spinoza's famous view (in *Ethics*, book 2: bodies form wholes, and the wholes themselves can be treated as bodies or parts within yet larger wholes), Alexander nowhere introduces separate mental or spiritual entities. There are no emergent causes, even though the higher levels, if they are complex enough, may manifest properties that *seem* to be the result of higher-order causes. In its highly complex forms the universe may become fairly mysterious, even divine; but the appearance of mystery is only what one would expect from a universe that is 'infinite in all directions'.[48]

Although it is a bold and fascinating attempt, one that became perhaps the most influential philosophy of emergence in the twentieth century, Alexander's position fails to answer many of the questions to which it gives rise. If time is the 'mind of space', time itself must be directional or purposive. But such teleology is rather foreign to the spirit of modern physics and biology. Nor does Alexander's notion of *nisus* relieve the obscurity. Nisus stands for the creative tendency in Space-Time: 'There is a nisus in Space-Time which, as it has borne its creatures forward through matter and life to mind, will bear them forward to some higher level of existence' (ii. 346). Yet creative advance does not belong to the furniture of physics. If time is 'the advance into novelty', then there is an 'arrow' to time. But what is the source of this arrow in a purely physical conception? Wouldn't it be more consistent with the physicalism toward which Alexander leans if he held that time consists of a (potentially) infinite whole divided into point-instants, without purpose or directionality?

Concerning the mind–body debate, one wants to know what consciousness is and what causal powers, if any, pertain to it and it alone. Alexander is not helpful here. Of course, neuroscience scarcely existed in the 1910s. What he did say about minds and brains is hardly helpful today: 'consciousness is situated at the synapsis of juncture between neurones' (ii. 129). But if Alexander offers nothing substantive on the mind–brain relation, how are contemporary philosophers to build on his work? At first blush it looks as if the only thing left of his position after the indefensible elements are removed is a purely formal specification: for any given level *L*, 'mind' is whatever whole is formed out of the parts or 'bodies' that constitute *L*. But a purely formal theory of this sort will not shed much light on the knotty, domain-specific problems that we will encounter in the philosophy of biology and the philosophy of mind (Chapters 3 and 4).

Strong emergentists will add a further reservation, one that, I suggest, foretells the eventual unravelling of the weak emergentist approach: Alexander does not adequately conceptualize the newness of emergent levels, even though his rhetoric repeatedly stresses the importance of novelty. If life and mind are genuinely emergent, then living things and mental phenomena must play some sort of causal role; they must exercise causal powers of their own. Indeed,

Alexander himself wants to maintain that a mental response is not separable into parts but is a whole (ii. 129). In the end, however, he turns his back on the conceptual resources that are available for specifying *in what sense* the entities and causes that evolution produces can finally be understood as wholes on their own, and not merely as aggregates of their constituent parts.

THE CHALLENGE OF WEAK EMERGENCE

In the coming pages I will argue that strong emergence represents the better overall interpretation of natural history. Still, at the outset of the discussion it is important to note that many scientists and philosophers in the twentieth century have in fact advocated positions more similar to Alexander's than to Broad's or Morgan's. The preponderance of the weak emergence position is reflected, for example, in the great popularity of the supervenience debate, which flourished in the 1980s and 1990s (see Chapter 4 below). The concept of supervenience, which seeks to preserve both the dependence of mental phenomena on brain states and the non-reducibility of the mental, could in principle be neutral between strong and weak emergence. But most of the standard accounts of supervenience also accept the causal closure of the world and a lawlike, even necessary entailment relationship between supervenient and subvenient levels. When interpreted in this way, supervenience theories stand much closer to the goals of weak emergentists such as Samuel Alexander.[49] Similarly, the language that scientists are trained to employ inclines them towards weak emergentist positions (though I will later argue that nothing inherent in the scientific method requires this conclusion). Neuroscientists, for example, may often speak of conscious states in common-sense terms, as if they viewed them as playing a causal role in a patient's condition. But, they usually add, to give a neuroscientific account of consciousness *just is* to explain conscious phenomena solely in terms of neurophysiological causes and constraints.

It is widely supposed that those answers to the mind–body problem are to be preferred which preserve the causal closure of the world and hold open the possibility that mental phenomena are related in a lawlike way to states of the central nervous system. Only if these two assumptions are made, we are told, will it be possible to develop a natural science of consciousness. And isn't one better advised to wager on the *possibility* of scientific advances in some field than arbitrarily to rule out that possibility in advance? Not surprisingly, if one is a physicalist, as the majority of Anglo-American philosophers today seem by their own testimony to be, then one will be inclined to wager on the side of bottom–up causation alone—after all, that's what the term 'physicalism' means. But, as we will see, the bottom–up, unity-of-science wager of physicalism has been allowed to spread well beyond its borders, so that it has come to be identified with any study that might pass as scientific or naturalistic. In countering this illicit move, I shall show that the deeper commitment to a study of natural phenomena as they manifest themselves may actually require one to question, and perhaps set aside, this pre-commitment to the metaphysics of physicalism.

Nonetheless I think it is important to acknowledge in advance that weak emergence is the position to beat. Many start with intuitions that are in conflict with weak emergence; after all, the man or woman on the street would find the denial of mental causation highly counter-intuitive. But when one engages the dialogue from the standpoint of the neurosciences or contemporary Anglo-American philosophy, one enters a playing field on which a physicalist approach has the upper hand. To the extent that it stands closer to the physicalist metaphysic, weak emergence will seem initially to be the form of emergentism easiest on the palate. A major part of my narrative involves the attempt to show why this initial impression does not stand up to closer examination.

CONCLUSION

The stakes of the battle have been clear from the opening page. Over the last hundred years or so thinkers have been forced to wrestle with the astounding facts of evolution and to search for the most adequate interpretation of the world, and of humankind, that accords with these facts. The ensuing battle over the philosophical interpretation of evolution has been dominated by two major contenders: physicalism and emergence. (Dualists have not been as involved in this debate since, at least with regard to the question of mind, their major role has been to criticize the neo-Darwinian synthesis rather than to interpret it.) Both of these two views are theories about the ultimate causes, and hence the ultimate explanations, of phenomena in the natural world. Physicalists claim that the causes are ultimately microphysical causes operating on physical particles and physical energies. Biological phenomena will not be fully explained until the physical (read: physics-based) principles that underlie the biology have been brought to light. Emergentists, by contrast, claim that biological evolution represents a paradigm of explanation that is significantly different from physics, though one that must of course remain consistent with physical law. Exactly what this new evolutionary paradigm is, and how it is different from that of physics, will concern us in detail in the coming chapters.

NOTES

1. On the metaphysics see Clayton, *The Problem of God in Modern Thought* (Grand Rapids, Mich.: Eerdmans, 2000) and the sequel, *From Hegel to Whitehead: Systematic Responses to the Modern Problem of God* (in preparation). On the epistemology, see my *Explanation from Physics to Theology* (New Haven: Yale University Press, 1989).

2. See, among many others, Austen Clark, *Psychological Models and Neural Mechanisms: An Examination of Reductionism in Psychology* (Oxford: Clarendon Press, 1980); Hans Primas, *Chemistry, Quantum Mechanics and Reductionism: Perspectives in Theoretical Chemistry*, 2nd corr. edn. (Berlin: Springer-Verlag, 1983); Evandro Agazzi (ed.), *The Problem of Reductionism in Science* (Episteme, vol. 18; Dordrecht: Kluwer Academic Publishers, 1991); Terrance Brown and Leslie Smith (eds.), *Reductionism and the Development of Knowledge* (Mahwah, NJ: L. Erlbaum, 2003). Also helpful are Sven Walter and Heinz-Dieter Heckmann (eds.), *Physicalism and Mental Causation: The Metaphysics of Mind and Action* (Exeter: Imprint Academic, 2003) and Carl Gillett and Barry Loewer (eds.), *Physicalism and its Discontents* (New York: Cambridge University Press, 2001), e.g. Jaegwon Kim's article, 'Mental Causation and Consciousness: The Two Mind–Body Problems for the Physicalist'.

3. Charbel Nino el-Hani and Antonio Marcos Pereira, 'Higher-Level Descriptions: Why Should We Preserve Them?' in Peter Bøgh Andersen, Claus Emmeche, Niels Ole Finnemann, and Peder Voetmann Christiansen (eds.), *Downward Causation: Minds, Bodies and Matter* (Aarhus: Aarhus University Press, 2000), 118–42, p. 133.

4. See Timothy O'Connor, 'Emergent Properties', *American Philosophical Quarterly*, 31 (1994), 97–8.

5. See William C. Wimsatt, 'The Ontology of Complex Systems: Levels of Organization, Perspectives, and Causal Thickets', *Canadian Journal of Philosophy*, suppl. 20 (1994), 207–74, p. 222.

6. Harold Morowitz, *The Emergence of Everything: How the World Became Complex* (New York: Oxford University Press, 2002).

7. O'Connor, 'Emergent Properties', 97–8. Fundamental for this debate are the works of Donald Campbell, e.g. '"Downward Causation" in Hierarchically Organised Biological Systems', in F. J. Ayala and T. H. Dobzhansky (eds.), *Studies in the Philosophy of Biology* (Berkeley: University of California Press,

1974), 179–86, and 'Levels of Organisation, Downward Causation, and the Selection-Theory Approach to Evolutionary Epistemology', in G. Greenberg and E. Tobach (eds.), *Theories of the Evolution of Knowing* (Hillsdale, NJ: Lawrence Erlbaum, 1990), 1–17.

8. See, *inter alia*, Rom Harré and E. H. Madden, *Causal Powers: A Theory of Natural Necessity* (Oxford: Blackwell, 1975); John Dupré, *The Disorder of Things: Metaphysical Foundations of the Disunity of Science* (Cambridge, Mass.: Harvard University Press, 1993); and Robert N. Brandon, 'Reductionism versus Wholism versus Mechanism', in R. N. Brandon (ed.), *Concepts and Methods in Evolutionary Biology* (Cambridge: Cambridge University Press, 1996), 179–204.

9. G. H. Lewes, *Problems of Life and Mind*, 2 vols. (London: Kegan Paul, Trench, Turbner, & Co., 1875).

10. More detail is available in Clayton, *Problem of God*, ch 3.

11. See Mark Bedau, 'Weak Emergence', *Philosophical Perspectives*, xi: *Mind, Causation, and World* (Atascadero, Calif.: Ridgeview, 1997), 375–99. E. J. Lowe ('The Causal Autonomy of the Mental', *Mind*, 102 (1993), 629–44, p. 634) claims to be the first to use the terms weak and strong, adapting his usage from John Searle's 'emergent$_1$' and 'emergent$_2$' in Searle, *The Rediscovery of the Mind* (Cambridge, Mass.: MIT Press, 1992), ch 5, 'Reductionism and the Irreducibility of Consciousness'. Note that 'weak' is not used in the literature as a term of derision. Donald Davidson ('Thinking Causes', in John Heil and Alfred Mele (eds.), *Mental Causation* (Oxford: Oxford University Press, 1995), 4 no. 4) cites Jaegwon Kim's use of the notion of 'weak' supervenience, agreeing with Kim that the term well expresses his (Davidson's) own understanding of mental events. Since my position on mental events is close to Davidson's anomalous monism, I happily follow his terminological suggestion. Weak supervenience, as we will see, corresponds to strong emergence; strong supervenience corresponds to (at most) weak emergence (see Ch. 4 below).

12. See Michael Silberstein and John McGreever, 'The Search for Ontological Emergence', *Philosophical Quarterly*, 49 (1999), 182–200, p. 186. The same distinction between epistemological and ontological, or weak and strong, emergence lies at the centre of Jaegwon Kim's important 'Making Sense of Emergence', the feature article in a *Philosophical Studies* special issue on emergence; see Kim, 'Making Sense of Emergence', *Philosophical Studies*, 95 (1999), 3–36.

13. Ansgar Beckermann, Hans Flohr, and Jaegwon Kim (eds.), *Emergence or Reduction? Essays on the Prospects of Nonreductive Physicalism* (New York: W. de Gruyter, 1992), 104.

14. C. D. Broad, *The Mind and its Place in Nature* (London: Routledge & Kegan Paul, 1925), 77.

15. On the covering law model, see classically Carl Hempel and Paul Oppenheim, 'Studies in the Logic of Explanation', *Philosophy of Science*, 15 (1948), 135–75, repr. in Hempel, *Aspects of Scientific Explanation* (New York: Free Press, 1965); see also Ernst Nagel, *The Structure of Science* (London: Routledge & Kegan Paul, 1961).

16. I thus agree with David Blitz that Morgan's work is more than an English translation of Bergson.

17. Rudolf Metz, *A Hundred Years of British Philosophy*, ed. J. H. Muirhead (London: G. Allen & Unwin, 1938), 656, quoted in David Blitz, *Emergent Evolution: Qualitative Novelty and the Levels of Reality*, Episteme, 19 (Dordrecht: Kluwer, 1992), 86. Blitz's work is an invaluable resource on the early influences on Morgan's thought.

18. Walter Marvin, *A First Book in Metaphysics* (New York: Macmillan, 1912), 143–4, quoted in Blitz, *Emergent Evolution*, 90.

19. E. G. Spaulding, *The New Rationalism* (New York: Henry Holt & Co., 1918), 447, quoted in Blitz, *Emergent Evolution*, 88.

20. William Hasker, *The Emergent Self* (Ithaca, NY: Cornell University Press, 1999), 190.

21. Brian Leftow, comment delivered at the University of Notre Dame, 5 Mar 1998, quoted ibid., 195–6.

22. Stephen Pepper, 'Emergence', *Journal of Philosophy*, 23 (1926), 241–5; Arthur Pap, 'The Concept of Absolute Emergence', *British Journal for the Philosophy of Science*, 2 (1952), 302–11.

23. See Z. W. Pylyshyn, 'What the Mind's Eye Tells the Mind's Brain: A Critique of Mental Imagery', *Psychological Bulletin*, 80 (1973), 1–24, p. 1, cited frequently by Roger Sperry.

24. *The Tacit Dimension*, henceforth *TD* (Garden City, NY: Doubleday Anchor Books, 1967), 24.

25. On the latter see esp. *Knowing and Being: Essays by Michael Polanyi*, henceforth *KB*, ed. Marjorie Grene (London: Routledge & Kegan Paul, 1969), esp. part 4, 'Life and Mind'.

26. I am grateful to Walter Gulick for his clarifications of Polanyi's position and criticisms of an earlier draft of the following argument. See Gulick, 'Response to Clayton: Taxonomy of the Types and Orders of Emergence', in *Tradition and Discovery*, 29/3 (2002–3), 32–47.

27. Gulick argues (see n. 26) that Polanyi is not actually this clear in his usage of the terms; if so, these comments should be taken as a rational reconstruction of his view.

28. *KB* 235–6, my emphasis.

29. Ibid.; cf. 214. Polanyi writes later, 'We lose the meaning of the subsidiaries in their role of pointing to the focal' (*KB* 219). For more on Polanyi's theory of meaning, see Polanyi and Harry Prosch, *Meaning* (Chicago: University of Chicago Press, 1975).

30. Henry P. Stapp, *Mind, Matter, and Quantum Mechanics* (Berlin and New York: Springer-Verlag, 1993). A feature article by Stapp on this topic is forthcoming in *Behavioral and Brain Sciences* (2004). Stapp's use of von Newmann's interpretation of the role of the observer in quantum mechanics represents a very intriguing form of dualism, since it introduces consciousness not for metaphysical reasons but for physical ones. For this very reason, however, it

stands rather far from classical emergence theory, in which natural history as a narrative of (and source for) the biological sciences plays the central role.

31. Hubert Yockey, *Information Theory and Molecular Biology* (Cambridge: Cambridge University Press, 1992). See Ch. 3 for a fuller treatment of this topic.

32. Terrence Deacon, 'Evolution and the Emergence of Spirit', SSQ workshops, Berkeley CA, 2001–2, unpublished paper, 6.

33. See e.g. Donald MacKay, *Science and the Quest for Meaning* (Grand Rapids, Mich.: Eerdmans, 1982). His 1986 Gifford Lectures were edited by his wife Valery MacKay and published posthumously as *Behind the Eye* (Oxford: Basil Blackwell, 1991). MacKay defended the complementarity thesis in *Science, Chance and Providence* (Oxford: Oxford University Press, 1978) and in *The Clockwork Image* (London: InterVarsity Press, 1974). An equally influential proponent of the complementarity of science and faith in this period was C. A. Coulson, a predecessor of Roger Penrose as Rouse-Ball Professor of mathematics at Oxford; see e.g. *Christianity in an Age of Science* (London: Oxford University Press, 1953); *Science and the Idea of God* (Cambridge: Cambridge University Press, 1958); and *Science, Technology, and the Christian* (New York: Abingdon Press, 1960). But as we will see, MacKay went beyond Coulson's insistence on complementarity, anticipating some of the central features of an emergentist theory of mind.

34. Donald MacKay, *Human Science and Human Dignity* (Downers Grove, Ill.: InterVarsity Press, 1979), 28.

35. MacKay, *Behind the Eye*, 1–10.

36. MacKay, *Human Science*, 32.

37. Roger Sperry, 'Mind–Brain Interaction: Mentalism, Yes; Dualism, No', *Neuroscience*, 5 (1980), 195–206, cf. 196.

38. Roger Sperry, 'A Modified Concept of Consciousness', *Psychological Review*, 76 (1969), 532–6.

39. Sperry, 'Mental Phenomena as Causal Determinants in Brain Function', in G. G. Globus, G. Maxwell, and I. Savodnik (eds.), *Consciousness and the Brain* (New York: Plenum, 1976), 165. See also Sperry, 'Consciousness and Causality', in R. L. Gregory (ed.), *The Oxford Companion to the Mind* (Oxford: Oxford University Press, 1987), 164–6.

40. See Sperry, 'Consciousness and Causality'.

41. Claus Emmeche, Simo Køppe, and Frederik Stjernfelt, 'Levels, Emergence, and Three Versions of Downward Causation', in Peter Bøgh Andersen *et al.*, *Downward Causation*, 13–34, p. 25.

42. Samuel Alexander, *Space, Time, and Deity*, the Gifford Lectures for 1916–18, 2 vols. (London: Macmillan, 1920), ii. 152. Subsequent references to this work appear in the text, preceded by volume number.

43. See Dorothy Emmet's introduction to *Space, Time, and Deity*, xv. The concept is reminiscent of Whitehead's well-known claim that mind is 'the spearhead of novelty'.

44. Again, see Dorothy Emmet's excellent introduction to *Space, Time, and Deity*, on which I have drawn in this reconstruction.

45. See Bernard d'Espagnat, *Veiled Reality: An Analysis of Present-Day Quantum Mechanical Concepts* (Reading, Mass.: Addison-Wesley, 1995).

46. The Gifford lectures by the neuroscientist Michael Arbib, almost 70 years after Alexander's Gifford lectures, make a similar move. According to Arbib, schemas can be extended upward to include God-language, yet no commitment needs to be made to the metaphysical existence of a god. See Arbib and Mary B. Hesse, *The Construction of Reality* (Cambridge: Cambridge University Press, 1986). For an explicitly emergentist position that combines a variant of physicalism with theological language, see Carl Gillett, 'Physicalism and Panentheism: Good News and Bad News', *Faith and Philosophy*, 20/1 (Jan. 2003), 1–21.

47. Alexander, *Space, Time, and Deity*, ii. 45. He also writes, 'The [emergent] quality and the constellation to which it belongs are at once new and [yet] expressible without residue in terms of the processes proper to the level from which they emerge' (ibid., emphasis added). Cf. Timothy O'Connor and Hong Yu Wong, 'Emergent Properties', *The Stanford Encyclopedia of Philosophy* (Winter 2002 edition), ed. Edward N. Zalta, at <http://plato.stanford.edu/archives/win2002/entries/properties-emergent/>, verified Oct. 2002.

48. See Freeman Dyson, *Infinite in All Directions*, Gifford lectures 1985 (New York: Harper & Row, 1988).

49. For standard criticisms of supervenience in the guise of non-reductive physicalism see Jaegwon Kim, *Supervenience and Mind: Selected Philosophical Essays* (Cambridge: Cambridge University Press, 1993); Kim, *Mind in a Physical World: An Essay on the Mind-Body Problem and Mental Causation* (Cambridge, Mass.: MIT Press, 1998); Kim (ed.), *Supervenience* (Aldershot: Ashgate, 2002).

2

Defining Emergence

The battle lines are now drawn. In addressing the ontological question about science—the question of what view of the world it supports—one must select among at least three major options: physicalism, emergence, and dualism. Our goal is to see what it means to advocate the emergentist option and why one might choose it over the alternatives.

It is already clear, however, that emergence is no monolithic term. Within the genus of interpretations of the natural world that it constitutes we have been able to identify two major competing species, commonly referred to as strong and weak emergence. The cumulative argument, I will suggest, favours strong emergence. That is, when the whole spectrum of emergent phenomena has been canvassed—from emergent phenomena in physics, through the study of organisms in their struggle to survive and thrive, and on to the phenomena of brain and mind—it is the perspective that best does justice to the entire range of phenomena. But the battle is hotly contested and, as we will see, some considerations also pull one towards the weak interpretation. The conflict between the two approaches, though often unrecognized, underlies much of the contemporary discussion; inevitably it will set the parameters for the debate as it unfolds in these pages.

THE PROBLEM OF DEFINITIONS

People often ask for a simple definition of emergence. The task proves not to be quite so simple, since in ordinary language the term is not used as a technical term. The *Oxford Universal Dictionary* lists thirteen definitions for 'emerge/emergence/emergent', of which the one closest to the term's technical meaning within emergence theory is 'that which is produced by a combination of causes, but cannot be regarded as the sum of their individual effects'. *Webster's*

Third New International Dictionary stresses the factor of newness in the last of its fifteen definitions: 'appearing as or involving the appearance of something novel in a process of evolution'. If forced to give a one-sentence definition, I would say that emergence is *the theory that cosmic evolution repeatedly includes unpredictable, irreducible, and novel appearances.*

But simple definitions fail to satisfy: either they combine features of multiple theories at the cost of superficiality, or they present one particular viewpoint without argument while passing silently over all others. One cannot move on to an examination of the relevant sciences without first pausing to clarify the concept of emergence. But let the reader beware: there are no neutral definitions; every conceptual clarification is actually a plea for the reader to look at the subject in a particular way. The following exposition is no exception—though I will make that case that it is more useful and more accurate than are the opposing approaches to the field.

The authors of one important recent analysis identify six key aspects of emergence: synergism (combined or cooperative effects between objects or systems), novelty, irreducibility, unpredictability, coherence, and historicity.[1] Most generally, emergent properties are those that arise out of some subsystem but are not reducible to that system. Emergence is about *more than but not altogether other than.*

Often one understands the most about a position by understanding what it is opposed to. Generally emergentist positions define themselves against two competitors: *physicalist* positions, which claim that explanations must be given in terms of the constituent parts of some physical system, and *dualist* positions, which claim a causal role for other sorts of things, such as souls or spirits, whose essence could never be derived from the basal physical properties. Tim Crane thus describes the basic two requirements for an emergentist position as 'dependence' and 'distinctness': 'mental properties are properties of physical objects', but 'mental properties are distinct from physical properties'.[2] That some kind of dependence relationship exists seems hard to deny: destroy enough molecules within a cell and you no longer have a cell; kill enough cells in an organ and the organ ceases to function; watch your discussion partner ingest enough alcohol and his sentences will cease to be coherent.

Emergence means that the world exhibits a recurrent pattern of novelty and irreducibility. In advocating this dual manifesto, emergence theorists tread a narrow path between two precipices. Should higher-order properties in fact be reducible to the underlying micro-physics, then (non-emergent) physicalism is true. But if the properties of life or mind are too novel, too different from the physical world, then emergence theorists are really closet dualists; in that case they might as well come out of the closet and display their true colours. Even if emergence theorists avoid both Scylla and Charybdis, critics argue, they may still fail. For merely to say 'not this, not that' doesn't convey very much; the concept of emergence must express a positive thesis. But, the critic continues, *novelty and irreducibility without dualism* may just be a negative specification. At worst the phrase says nothing more than that evolution produces phenomena that are not like what came before and not reducible to it, yet not different enough that they belong to another order of reality altogether.

FIVE DIFFERENT MEANINGS OF EMERGENCE

Before proceeding further with the definition question it might be helpful to consider what is the *topic* that emergence addresses. In the broader discussion one finds the term being used in multiple fields, some deeply concerned with scientific topics and others apparently incompatible with science. In fact, one can locate at least five distinct levels on which the term is applied. Care is required to avoid rampant equivocation. As one moves along the continuum between the levels, one observes a transition from very specific scientific domains to increasingly integrative, and hence increasingly philosophical, concepts.

E_1: theories of emergence within specific scientific fields

This category refers to occurrences of the term within the context of a specific scientific theory. E_1 thus describes features of a specified physical or biological system of which we have some scientific understanding. The scientists who construct these theories claim that the term, used in a theory-specific sense, is of value to contemporary science as a description of features or patterns of the natural world. Because of this specificity, however, there is no way to establish whether the term is being used analogously across theories, or whether it really means something utterly distinct in each theory in which it appears.

E_2: levels of emergence within the natural world

Used in this sense the term draws attention to broader features of the world that may eventually become part of a unified scientific theory. Emergence in this sense expresses postulated connections or laws that may in the future become the basis for one or more branches of science. One thinks, for example, of the role claimed for emergence in Stuart Kauffman's notion of a new 'general biology' or in certain proposed theories of complexity or self-organization.

E_3: patterns across scientific theories

Since it postulates features that are shared by multiple theories within science, E_3 is actually a meta-scientific term. Used in this sense, as it often is in the philosophy of science, the term is not drawn from a particular scientific theory; it is an observation about a significant pattern that allegedly connects a *range* of scientific theories. For example, consider the features that might be common to autocatalysis, complexity, and self-organization. We have some idea of what role each of these three terms plays in at least one branch of science; but it is also possible that they share certain significant features in common. E_3 draws attention to these features, whether or not any individual theory within science actually makes scientific use of the term 'emergence'. It thus serves a heuristic function, helping to highlight common features between theories. Recognizing such broader patterns can help to extend existing theories, to formulate insightful new hypotheses, or to launch new interdisciplinary research programmes.

E_4: a theory about the patterns in the transitions between sciences

Emergence in this sense is a broader theory about the evolutionary process. Like E_3 it claims that new systems or structures are formed at particular points and that these systems share certain common features. But emergence theories sometimes go beyond the task of describing common features across scientific fields; they sometimes attempt to explain why these patterns should exist. Such theories argue that the similarities and differences across emergent systems are part of a broader pattern in nature—an overall 'ladder of emergence', for example. Current work is being done, for example, to understand how chemical structures emerge out of the underlying physics, to reconstruct the biochemical dynamics that underlie the origins of life, and to conceive how complicated neural processes produce cognitive phenomena such as memory, language, rationality, and creativity. E_4-type theories attempt to discern the broader pattern that runs across each of these (and other) transition points in nature. As such, they are not themselves scientific theories. A scientific theory that explains how chemical structures are formed is unlikely to explain the origins of life, and neither theory will explain how self-organizing neural nets encode memories. Instead, E_4 theories explain why the transition between scientific theories should be as we find them to be in nature.

E_5: the metaphysics of emergence

Emergence in this sense is a metaphysical theory, in the sense that physicalism and dualism are also metaphysical theories. It claims that the nature of the world is such that it produces, and perhaps must produce, continually more complex realities in a process of ongoing creativity, and it is a thesis about the nature of what is produced. Each of the preceding four types of emergence may serve as evidence for E_5, but they alone will not prove it. Metaphysical theories are not limited to inferences from the available evidence; they are hypotheses about the nature of reality as a whole. In the final chapter of this work I examine the case for a metaphysics of emergence and the implications that follow from it.

AN EXAMPLE: EMERGENCE AT THE FOURTH LEVEL

We have seen that emergence can be elaborated as a scientific, a philosophical, a metaphysical, or even a religious thesis. I presuppose that a metaphysical theory of emergence, be it religious or anti-religious, theological or anti-theological, should be guided by the philosophy of science and, ultimately, by a scientific study of the place of emergence in the natural world.

But given that at least three of the types of emergence just summarized (E_3–E_5) are not directly scientific theories, one wonders what kind of traction the broader theories of emergence really have with the sciences. Can broader theories of emergence be undercut by science? Is the concept of emergence actually helpful for understanding certain trends in recent science? If it is, *which* of the emergentist positions currently on the market best reflects the relevant sciences? One cannot answer these questions, I suggest, without doing some work within the field of the philosophy of science. This field is useful, for example, for locating the *kind* of claim that emergence makes, for specifying how emergence claims might be assessed, and for guiding the process of evaluating them. Philosophers of science have also developed sophisticated theories of emergence, debating questions such as, 'Can emergent physical entities exercise causal powers of their own, or does physics cover all the types of causes one needs to introduce?' (I return to this question in a moment.)

As an example let's consider the case of E_4—the type of emergence involving patterns in the transitions between theories. In effect, it represents the suggestion that a specific series of questions be posed to scientists, and that they be considered in a specific order:

1. Is the term 'emergence', understood however one wishes to understand it, useful for summarizing current results in one's specific discipline?

2. Which results is it useful for summarizing?

3. When one summarizes these phenomena as emergent, which opposing view is one implicitly rejecting?

4. How strong is the case for emergence in this sense? How important, how useful, is the emergence framework in contrast to the other available frameworks?

Suppose one mentally lines up the collected responses to these questions. The data then lead to an interesting comparative project, for one must now ask:

5. Can one discover any significant similarities in the usages of the term 'emergence' as it appears in answer to the first four questions?

An informed answer to this final question allows one to create and test a theory of emergence as a meta-theory about the relationships between scientific disciples and fields. For emergence will be a significant phenomenon in the natural world if we can discover analogies between the *relationships between* various scientific disciplines. This is a second-order enquiry. Let the letters A, B, C . . . stand for the various disciplines: quantum physics, macrophysics, physical chemistry, biochemistry, cell biology, etc. Now focus on the relationships between the particular disciplines: A–B, B–C, C–D, D–E, etc. For convenience, we might label each of these relationships with a number: relation A–B is 1, relation B–C is 2, relation C–D is 3, and so forth. This allows us to pose the question concerning the similarities and differences between the relationships: how are 1, 2, 3, 4, etc. themselves related?

In my view this may be, in the entire emergence debate, the

most important point at which philosophy and science overlap. The question concerns the connection between scientific domains, and raising it may allow one to see something highly significant about the natural world that one would not otherwise have recognized. For example, the results may help scholars to recognize a hierarchy among the fields of science and to reconstruct the principles that give rise to it, whether they involve increasing complexity, or more complex feedback loops, or some other conceptual framework. In the end, talk of hierarchies in nature is theoretically serious only if the principle by which the hierarchy is constructed can be clearly formulated and tested—that is, if it is possible to show that it can be undercut by empirical results, present or future. This method allows in principle for such testing.

Only when this work has been done can one begin to assess the broader philosophical theories about emergence. In formulating the project and beginning to carry it out, the present book attempts to establish a theoretical framework adequate for testing the various claims about emergence being put forward by an increasing number of scientists, philosophers, and theologians. Philosophers ask, for example, how values might supervene on physical states, whether emergence presupposes or undercuts belief in the causal closure of the physical world, whether consciousness exercises its own causal powers or is merely a shorthand way of expressing a certain organization of the physical forces that physics studies, and whether the physical universe is the type of place that supports or undercuts the religious belief that the universe is spiritually significant. But even for those who have no interest in philosophical questions, the methodology proposed here holds promise for assessing the significance of the emergence concept within, and between, the sciences themselves.

DOUBTS ABOUT EMERGENCE

Of course, the positive programme just outlined gives rise to a number of questions, doubts, and reservations. Above all, one worries about the gap between scientific and philosophical methods, theories, and assumptions. Philosophy requires theories that are unified, consistent, and as conceptually exact as possible, theories that can be applied without ambiguity across a wide variety of fields. But any attempt to apply such a global philosophical theory to a range of different scientific disciplines immediately raises walls of scepticism. The theoretical contexts are so radically different for any two cases of emergent phenomena in the natural world—say, the emergence of the classical physical world from quantum mechanical states, and the emergence of cell-wide behaviours out of the DNA code—that attempts to apply a unitary philosophical theory may appear as the worst sort of philosophical hegemony. Nor does science fare much better. Almost by definition, scientists cannot convince philosophers that they have a more adequate solution to the problem, since there is no such thing as 'a science of emergence'. What science offers instead are the particular theories that we already know as the core theories of this or that scientific discipline. Of course, what the scientific theories describe are, at least in some cases, emergent phenomena. But this observation is meta-scientific or philosophical rather than directly scientific.

It is not difficult to describe in general terms how emergence might link science and philosophy. Take the particular level we have been considering (E_4). One would work to understand the theories and data that describe emergence in the natural world; one would then formulate a philosophical theory stating common features among the various instances of emergence; and one would then test this theory against the scientific examples to determine its adequacy. So far the theory. In actual practice this sort of cooperative venture is rather more difficult. First of all, one has to have some idea of what should count as examples of emergence *before* one begins to examine the various sciences, which means that the philosophy does not just follow the scientific work but also precedes it. Next, philosophers writing on emergence would have to commit themselves to formulating theories that could in fact be supported or undercut by results in the various scientific disciplines; where the results of the tests are ambiguous, philosophers and theologians would have to content themselves with higher doses of agnosticism than is usual in their fields. Agreement to these conditions will not come easily. Further, because the disciplines involved stretch over a wide range from physics to population biology, it is probable that the resulting theory of emergence will provide, at best, a listing of family resemblances across the various disciplines. But family resemblance theories are usually not very attractive to analytic philosophers and traditional philosophers of science, who want more analytically rigorous theories.

To some it will seem strange that one needs to compromise on philosophical rigour in order to achieve genuine traction with science.

Are there not a number of cases in the philosophy of physics and philosophy of biology where close partnerships exist between scientific detail and philosophical reconstruction? For example, philosophers have played a major role in the interpretation of quantum mechanics, combining very detailed analytic work with a sophisticated understanding of the quantum physical theories involved.[3] Similar things can be said of the contributions of philosophers such as David Hull and Michael Ruse to discussions of evolutionary biology or of the role of game theorists in formulating models of kin selection and reciprocal altruism. But emergence is disanalogous, since a theory in this field will not be successful unless it is derived from more than one scientific discipline. By the nature of the case, emergence is an overarching concept that must pertain to theoretical structures and results in multiple fields. As a consequence it cannot draw too heavily on the details of theories in any particular discipline.

This argument explains my resistance to some of the emergence proposals made recently by Terrence Deacon.[4] Deacon's very clear presentation of three steps of emergent complexity offers a preciseness that one rarely finds elsewhere in the literature; his is perhaps the most sophisticated scientific theory of emergence currently available. Upon closer inspection, however, one realizes that its preciseness comes from a certain predominance of physics in his theory (more particularly, the level of thermodynamic complexity that allows natural selection to operate on the resulting system). This basic physical pattern can manifest itself in more complex forms, say, in cell biology or primate evolution. But on Deacon's view in the cited article, the process itself is not reiterated; stage-three emergence does not become a new starting point for a further process of emergent complexity leading to new emergent wholes. Instead, when the system reaches the point at which there is a self-contained feedback loop upon which the principles of natural selection can operate, the system has achieved all the ontological complexity there is to achieve; beyond this, nature just reiterates the same three-step process in a cycle of increasing physical complexity.

In contrast to this view, I will argue for an iterative model of emergence. As Deacon correctly describes, increasing complexity within a system under certain conditions gives rise to emergent entities or units. These units then become involved in more and more complex relationships until they produce further units which are basic causal agents in their own right, and the process begins again. If this iterative model is correct, it means that no single scientific discipline can express the precise nature of emergence; *emergence is a pattern that runs on a variety of different platforms.* As a consequence, no single scientific theory can provide the precise account of emergence that Deacon seeks.

DIVERGING APPROACHES TO THE SCIENCE AND PHILOSOPHY OF EMERGENCE

The foregoing discussion makes it possible now to specify several different approaches currently being taken by scholars as they explore emergence claims in the sciences and draw out their philosophical implications. In contrasting competing approaches it is impossible to remain neutral.

First, much of the suspicion about emergence within the scientific community stems from the sense that emergence is sometimes used as a 'magic pill'. That is, scientists complain that in certain treatments emergence seems to represent a strange mystical power within evolution that constantly works to lift the universe to new levels of reality. Could it be that emergentists have gained knowledge about a mysterious natural process, an elusive vital power that has eluded the grasp of scientists across the disciplines? Scientists responding to such claims are surely right to affirm that no one knows more about the universe *within the particular domains of the specialized sciences* than what the specific theories in those domains have established. Claims to possess a universal scientific theory that is supposed to explain everything at once should indeed be viewed with scepticism. (Of course, there may be speculative metaphysical positions that add insights not found in any particular science; at least nothing within science can rule these out. I return to this topic in a moment.)

Second, a number of thinkers, perhaps reacting against the excesses of the first group, treat emergence as a purely negative thesis. Viewed in this way, emergence becomes a theory about the limits of what science can ever accomplish. For example, science cannot reduce higher-level phenomena to lower-level explanations; it cannot explain wholes in terms of the parts alone; it cannot use physical explanations to exhaustively explain biological or psychological phenomena. Specific sciences may make their modest contributions, but no overarching, interconnected story can be told about the natural world—at least not one that may pass as knowledge.

We should evaluate this approach more positively than the previous one. Admittedly, claims about 'what cannot be known' are also knowledge claims and must be defended as well. Still, it is increasingly clear that the 'unity of science' programme has encountered some rather serious limitations, and emergence theories provide an effective means for explaining why the limitations exist. By itself, however, the negative thesis will not be sufficient. In the end emergence theorists will be unable to explain the limits on scientific knowledge unless they can provide some positive account of the broader structures—the feedback loops or whole-part constraints—that are responsible for the limits on bottom–up explanation.

Third, in response to the difficulties with the first two options, some treat emergence as the vanguard for the next round of progress within one or more particular sciences. Terry Deacon's emergence theory, for example, represents a reconstruction of the steps of increasing complexity in physics and chemistry that would eventually produce a fuller understanding of the operation of natural selection upon living systems. The rest of Deacon's theory then consists of a series of examples of natural selection at work: on proto-cells and cellular organisms, on animals competing within an environment, and even on brain structures and subsystems within the brain. Fundamentally new types of emergence do not occur at higher levels of complexity; rather, all are manifestations of the same basic structure.

The role of emergence in the work of Stuart Kauffman (considered in Chapter 3 below) is similar. Kauffman describes a living thing as a self-reproducing agent which carries out at least one thermodynamic work cycle. If his theory in *Investigations* is right, the biology of the future could be pursued with the same sort of rigour and conceptual clarity that one finds in thermodynamics. In fact, this is exactly what Kauffman has in mind when he proposes that we stand on the brink of 'a new general theory of biology'. Emergence serves two functions for Kauffman: to draw a line between physics and biology, showing why biology needs its own core principles; and to suggest that a new theoretical framework, that of autonomous agents defined in terms of work cycles, will arise once one concedes that biology is emergent *vis-à-vis* physics. But, as with Deacon's view, this approach does not suggest a broader iterating structure that one would expect to find repeated, say, in the emergence of mental phenomena.

The fourth school of emergence theory advocates the reiterating pattern approach defended in the present volume. Emergence is a repeating pattern that connects the various levels of evolution in the cosmos, and thus the various ways in which we come to know the world scientifically. With the second approach this view shares the sense that there are limits to what a single discipline (say, micro-physics) can explain about the world. Like the third, advocates of the pattern view are committed to developing detailed accounts of emergent phenomena in particular sciences. But unlike that view, we do not maintain that an account of emergence at any particular level can convey all of what one learns when one looks across the whole range of evolution for repeated instances of new emergents. In fact, *emergence just is that pattern that recurs across a wide range of scientific (and non-scientific) fields*. The full pattern only becomes visible when one steps back far enough to compare a large number of emergents in the natural world, including not only part–whole relations within particular fields but also the analogies that hold across the collection of such instances. Only when one perceives the recurrent emergentist structure of the natural world as a whole will one be in a position to offer a credible theory of how mind is related to the levels out of which it arises. Unless one keeps an eye on the whole range of similarities and differences, one will inevitably reduce mind downwards to its physical substrate or over-emphasize its separateness from the physical world, as dualists do.

DOWNWARD CAUSATION

It is fair to ask what is the most important defining characteristic of emergence. In the case of strong emergence theories the answer is: the concept of downward causation. I define downward causation as *the process whereby some whole has an active non-additive causal influence on its parts*. Cases of downward causation are clearest when the 'whole' in question is something we standardly pick out as a separate object in the world, such as cells, organs, organisms, and objects built by humans. Undoubtedly, claims for downward causa-tion are most controversial when they involve mental causes, as in Robert Audi's assertion that 'mental properties have causal power, i.e., can play a causally explanatory role in broadly causal general-izations'.[5] But not all, or even the majority, of putative cases of downward causation involve mental causes. In fact, if mental causes were the only instances of downward causation, the resulting position would support dualism rather than emergence. That is, the downward-operative causes would be signs that another order of reality altogether was at work in the world rather than signs that the one world produces wholes that in turn have a causal influence on their parts.

Strong emergence is a controversial thesis because the idea of downward causation is controversial. The quickest way to win an overview of the debate is to consider the four major contenders in the recent discussion, each of which has its ardent followers. One can deny the existence of any top–down causation in the world; one can maintain a dualist view of downward causation; or one can affirm a non-dualist, emergentist theory of top–down influences. The third possibility in turn subdivides into two major competitors: theories of *whole–part constraint* (weak emergence) and theories of active downward causation (strong emergence).

The strongest denial, of course, is the view that all causation is 'upward': causal influences proceed exclusively from constituting parts to constituted wholes. Thus the human agent may *believe* that the content of her thought has a causal influence on the action of her body. But in fact the operative causal forces are microphysical events, which in the brain take the form of electrochemically mediated interactions between neurons. It is these nerve cells that are operative in causing her muscles to contract and relax, resulting in the movements that other humans interpret as her actions in the world.

At the other end of the spectrum lies the dualist view of downward causation. Dualists hold that entities or forces which are ontologically of a qualitatively different kind from physical causes can nevertheless exercise determinative, top–down causal influence on human bodies and perhaps also on other physical systems. For example, if God places a soul into each human egg at the moment of fertilization, and if that soul later causes the individual to do things that the body would not have done without it, one has a case of downward causation in the strongest sense. The ambiguities arise when one tries to specify exactly what it means to be 'ontologically of a qualitatively different kind'. For example, an eel or elephant seems qualitatively different from an electron, yet one does not have to be a dualist to say that an elephant's movements can affect the motion of the electrons that are a part of it. Nor is it enough to say that for dualists the whole is more than the sum of its parts, since even weak emergentists affirm the same thing. It helps somewhat to note that dualists do not think that souls are constituted out of physical parts.

The clearest demarcation probably concerns the relations between the types of energy involved. When Descartes affirms that the soul affects the body through the pineal gland, he would presumably have to grant that the total energy of the physical system (if we could measure it) would be higher after the input of mind than before, or that brain changes could be made without any loss of energy. Particles in the brain, Descartes might have said, are now in different places than they were before the mental cause, even though no physical energy has been expended. Likewise, the nineteenth-century vitalists, who were dualists about the principle of life, would have to say that the 'vital principle' can bring about changes in the state of the organism without any decrease in the total amount of its physical energy. Something similar would have to hold for miracle claims, which are theologically dualist: the miraculously healed body would not have to expend calories for the healing, and perhaps it would be found to have a higher overall energy level after the healing than before. By contrast, downward causation for emergentists might involve transduction, the transformation of energy into forms of energy (say, mental energy) not well understood by contemporary science. But it would not involve any strange new addition of energy into the natural world.

The middle two senses of downward causation—whole–part constraint and top–down causation—are particularly important because they help to clarify the distinction between weak and strong emergence, which has already played a major role in the opening chapter. Whole–part constraint, which correlates with weak emergence, tends to treat emergent wholes as constraining factors rather than as active originators of causal activity. Complex structures like the cell or brain are wholes that emerge in evolutionary history; each whole, understood as a particular configuration of parts, can exercise a sort of constraining role on its parts. Likewise, when many electrons flow through a copper wire one observes the phenomenon of conduction (or, we say, the copper evidences the emergent property of conductivity), and when a number of water molecules are combined there is an increase in surface tension, which allows for the phenomenon of viscosity to emerge. The large number of integrated neural circuits in the brain constitutes an extremely complicated whole, which thus constrains the behaviour of its component parts and subsystems in very remarkable ways.

When we say that a person's thoughts or intentions 'cause' her to do something, we wrongly ascribe causal agency to a new causal entity, when in fact we should just say that the complexity of her central nervous system constrains her body's behaviours in a particular way.

For advocates of top–down causation, by contrast, something more is at work than the constraining influence of a large number of components operating as a system. In what follows I make the case for actual top–down causation, which is by definition to make a case for strong emergence.[6] The crux of the argument lies in the notion of distinct 'levels' within the natural world, with each level being defined by the existence of distinct laws and by distinct types of causal activity at that level.

The classic definition of downward causation appears in a 1974 essay by Donald Campbell.[7] In a later formulation of the position, Campbell makes downward causation dependent upon the existence of different laws that pertain to different levels within the natural world:

> Where natural selection operates through life and death at a higher level of organization, the laws of the higher level selective system determine in part the distribution of lower level events and substances. Description of an intermediate-level phenomenon is not completed by describing its possibility and implementation in lower level terms. Its presence, prevalence, or distribution . . . will often require reference to laws at a higher level of organization as well. . . . [F]or biology, all processes at the lower levels of a hierarchy are restrained by, and act in conformity to, the laws of the higher levels.[8]

Campbell's points are well taken: different disciplines are in fact defined by the different sets of laws that they use in predicting and explaining phenomena. Nor (in most cases) can one substitute the laws from some lower level for the laws used in a particular discipline. For reasons of complexity, predicting the behaviours of molecules, cells, or organisms is generally impossible if one relies only on natural laws at a lower level of the hierarchy. For example, it is impossible to describe Mary's decision to stop by the shop on the way home using well-formed equations in physics. The brain is such a complicated physical system that no interesting predictions of Mary's future brain states can be made using physics alone. In order to make any useful predictions at all, one has to take neurons, synapses, and action potentials as given, together with their causal powers, which means that physics is *not* adequate for one's task.

In addition, physical laws simply do not pick out the relevant aspects of the world for making sense of Mary's actions. For that one needs not only biological structures and the laws governing their behaviour, but also the theories and correlations of the social sciences, which are the special sciences relevant to predicting and comprehending human behaviour.[9] The significance of this argument is not always fully acknowledged. For example, physics cannot even pick out Mary as a well-formed object; Mary the person is not definable within physics.

Defining levels in terms of distinct laws and causes, as Donald Campbell has done, is much more fruitful than trying to define them in terms of the degree to which phenomena in the world strike us as novel or unexpected. Subjective perceptions regarding the novelty of particular causal systems are a highly unreliable means for drawing philosophical distinctions. Some highly dramatic events in the world turn out to have rather mundane scientific explanations (think of thunder and lightning), whereas others that seem rather commonsensical to human observers turn out to mark highly significant transitions in the empirical world (e.g. the difference between light from a star or from a galaxy, or the degree of red shift in the light coming to us from distant, quickly receding stars and galaxies). Note that this observation cuts two ways: one cannot dismiss a claimed case of emergence either because it is too mundane or because it is too startling to have an emergentist explanation.

Campbell and others avoid the subjectivist danger by defining emergent levels according to the particular laws and causes picked out by a particular scientific discipline. *Emergence is more about the existence of these (more or less) discrete levels than it is about a single theory of transition between levels.* As it happens, transitions between levels vary widely: chemistry is dependent on physics in a different way than organisms are dependent on cell behaviour, and both are different than the way that consciousness is tied to the states of the brain. Yet all three involve transitions between levels of reality at which different laws are operative.

This vast diversity in how nature makes the transitions between levels reminds us of the danger of basing the case for emergence primarily on the emergence of mind. If mind were indeed the only example of downward causation in nature, then basing an argument for strong emergence on mental causation would in fact demonstrate the truth of dualism rather than emergence. After all, emergence theory is a form of monism (see p. 60) which holds that the one 'stuff' of the world actually plays a greater diversity of causal roles in the world than old-time materialists thought (and, sadly, still think). It could also be labelled *ontological pluralism* because of the stress on multiple levels of laws and causes, but 'monism' better expresses the commitment of science to understand the interrelationship of levels as fully as possible. Still, only if family resemblances tie together the multiple instances of emergence across the natural world will the core thesis of emergence be supported. I thus turn in the next chapter to the case for downward causation in the biological sciences before returning to the question of emergent mental causation.

EMERGENCE AND PHYSICALISM

By this point the reader has already encountered a rather broad spectrum of distinctions, positions, and approaches to the emergence debate. Is the range of options so great that no clear concept of emergence can ever be obtained? When one compares the particular responses made by emergence theorists to the question of physicalism—still one of the most burning issues to be raised by contemporary science—one actually discovers only a rather limited number of core conceptual options. Since I have already covered the broader options (namely, the assertion of strong dualism and the denial of emergence altogether) I can now focus in on the three fundamental responses to the emergence question found in the philosophical literature. I present them in order of increasing distance from physicalism.

First, one often hears statements such as the following, 'I am not a physical reductionist because I do not think that the particles and laws of physics are sufficient to account for everything we find in the universe. Other explanatory principles are necessary as well.' Advocates of this rejoinder grant that states of affairs emerge in the course of evolution which it is useful for us to label with non-physics-based terms. Indeed, the concepts and predicates that we find ourselves using in explanations may even order themselves into layers, as strong emergentists think. Thus the neuroscientist Michael Arbib applies his notion of 'conceptual schemas' in a layered fashion: the schema of 'person' combines the schemas for 'the brain as a whole' and 'mental predicates'. One can invent broader conceptual schemas to link together various persons ('society' or 'history' or 'religion'), or one can divide the schema 'person' into further subcomponents. For example, 'the central nervous system' encompasses an immense array of neural subsystems, cell groups, cells, and ultimately the molecules and physical particles of which they are all composed.[10] Nonetheless, Arbib and others maintain, the principle of the causal closure of the physical world requires that all the actual causal work is done at the level of fundamental physical forces and particles. We may fruitfully construct schemas all the way up and down the conceptual hierarchy, from quarks to gods, but no ontological break with physicalism need be entailed by using language in this way.

That we use such an immense variety of conceptual levels is on this view *une façon de parler*, a manner of speaking. Biologists speak of the purposiveness of evolution or even of 'design'[11] without implying that a Creator actually exists who has purposes. Even hardcore neuroscientists will continue to speak of wants, wishes, and desires, just as folk psychologists do, even though they do not in the end believe in the actual existence of such causes. For this reason I suggest that we label the adherents of this first major position *façon de parler* emergentists. Thus, for example, when Jaegwon Kim insists that all actual causal interactions are to be traced back to microphysical particles and forces and to the laws that determine their behaviour, he clearly intends to espouse a strong version of metaphysical physicalism. That he continues to use folk-psychological terms in his publications and daily life merely reflects a manner of speaking; it does not contradict or negate his philosophical position. If Kim says that 'things emerge', as he sometimes does, he cannot mean more than that it is useful to construct conceptual schemas at a wide variety of levels.

The attempt to gain clarity on the question of emergence will be greatly enhanced if scholars do not advance this first position as a species of philosophical emergence. Of course physicalists will refer to the world around them using shorthand terms like intentions and thoughts. But what characterizes their position philosophically is the denial that intentions and thoughts actually exercise any downward causation, any causal efficacy of their own. *Façon de parler* emergentists are physicalists in precisely this sense. Conversely, only confusion will result if emergentists try to appropriate a position that lies at the heart of anti-emergentist physicalism.

Second, in contrast to the *façon de parler* emergentists there are a number of scientists and philosophers who want to remain as close as possible to physicalism yet who find themselves forced to acknowledge that emergent structures and their properties have some influence on the development of the physical world. These philosophers stand close to classical physicalism because they continue to centre their ontology on micro-physics. Carl Gillett speaks for this major school within emergence theory when he espouses physicalism in the sense that 'all individuals are constituted by, or identical to, micro-physical individuals, and all properties are realized by, or identical to, micro-physical properties'.[12] These philosophers rightly reject the false dichotomy propounded by Kim. Kim warns that if one gives up the 'causal closure of physics',

> there can in principle be no complete physical theory of physical phenomena, that theoretical physics, insofar as it aspires to be a complete theory, must cease to be pure physics and invoke irreducibly non-physical causal powers—vital principles, entelechies, psychic energies, elan vital, or whatnot. If that is what you are willing to embrace, why call yourself a 'physicalist'?[13]

Kim is right that emergentists—in any meaningful sense of the term—must give up the principle of the causal closure of physics. Emergentists such as Gillett respond that they can do so and still remain physicalists (in the sense of ascribing ontological priority to micro-physics) as long as they can specify a kind of 'determination' that is *non*-causal, that is, one that 'does not involve wholly distinct entities, and apparently involves no transfer of energy and/or mediation of force'.[14] Gillett follows Nancy Cartwright in calling this view 'patchwork physicalism'. Like the British Emergentists, Gillett accepts that there is a 'patchwork' of fundamental laws, 'including higher laws that refer ineliminably to . . . emergent properties . . . a mosaic of fundamentally determinative, and thus causally efficacious, entities' (43–4). Once again we find the appeal to laws and causes at multiple levels.

Crucial for this popular view is the observation that such emergent phenomena occur in systems involving the interaction of parts within some whole that they constitute. Were it a *separate* thing that co-determined an outcome, the ontology of physicalism would be broken, but these emergentist thinkers merely want to weaken physicalism slightly in comparison with classical formulations. Thus, they insist, as long as physical entities constitute systems that then constrain their motions in some specifiable way, nothing non-physical is at work. One thinks of Roger Sperry's frequently cited example: molecules contained in a wheel move in a way that one could not predict from an understanding of molecular interactions alone. Yet there is nothing 'spooky' about the motion of the wheel, and the motion of its molecules breaks no physical laws. Clearly the motion of the wheel 'determines' the motion of its parts; it is just a different kind of determination than bottom–up causal influences from micro-physics. Such is the other 'and very different kind of determination in cases of parts–wholes, realization or conditional powers' (42).

The literature already has a widely used term for this kind of non-causal determination of microphysical objects: *whole–part constraint*. It does seem true that Kim and other hard-core physicalists underappreciate the role of such constraints. Giving them their due produces a philosophically distinct physicalist position that diverges in interesting ways from *façon de parler* physicalism. For example, Gillett is a functionalist about the philosophy of mind and is willing to endorse a form of belief in God he calls 'panentheism', something that no hard-core physicalist would be willing to entertain.[15] The only unfortunate fact is that, rather than labelling his position 'weak emergence' or 'whole–part constraint emergence', Gillett insists on calling his position 'strong emergence'.[16] Since Gillett's definition of emergence clearly breaks with the strong emergence theories put forward by the British Emergentists and broadly used in the literature, while exactly summarizing what defenders of weak emergence and whole–part constraint advocate, his misnomer adds an unnecessary equivocation to the ongoing debate, threatening to produce the sort of confusion that causes newcomers to the debate to throw up their hands and give up on the notion of emergence altogether.

Third, given the clear distinctions between the previous positions, it is not difficult to define the standpoint of strong emergence. It includes all the features of weak emergence as Gillett and others have defended it, with the exception of their privileging of micro-physics. Although quantum physics offers the *first* constraining condition in evolution, there are clearly constraining and determining factors at other levels in the natural world besides micro-physics. Since these other factors influence the outcomes of processes in the world in a counterfactual fashion (had they not existed, the outcomes would have been different), there is no reason not to speak of them as actual causes. But as long as they are defined by laws and causal networks at a variety of different levels, one is not justified in privileging a physical interpretation over all others.[17] For this reason strong emergentists prefer the term 'monism' over the term 'physicalism'. (I follow Donald Davidson in this choice of terms.)

At this point in the argument one's opponents often run up the red flag of 'an anti-scientific attitude' or—what in their eyes amounts to the same thing—dualism. The charge, though dramatic (and rhetorically effective), is not accurate. The advocate of strong emergence need be no less committed to the scientific study of the natural world than those who hold the previous two views. Indeed, in one sense he is *more* committed. The position as defined here differs from weak emergence only in rejecting one metaphysical presupposition that the latter insists upon: the primacy of micro-physical causes and explanations. The strong emergentist notes that the reduction of biology—not to mention folk psychology—to micro-physics is a mere promissory note. (For that matter, the reduction of macro-physics to quantum physics is also a promissory note, and a highly contested one at that.) Until such causal reductions are accomplished, the strong emergentist holds that the more scientific course of action is to study the various levels of the natural world according to the laws that we currently possess that describe their behaviour. The addition of the micro-physics clause is, ironically, a meta-physical, and hence metaphysical, stipulation for which evidence is at present lacking. The unity of science—in the strong sense imagined by those who prioritize micro-physics— is a regulative ideal for scientific inquiry (Kant), an imagined end point at which expert opinion might converge (Peirce). But it is metaphysical wishful thinking to confuse regulative principles with currently established results of science.

Several of the core features of the strong emergence programme follow directly from these conclusions. First, they explain the partic- ular interest in the emergentist proposals being made by scientists such as Stuart Kauffman and Terrence Deacon. Both of these authors advance scientific causal accounts that reject the adequacy of microphysical accounts (except in the sense just defined), searching instead for fundamentally biological causes, processes, and laws. Likewise, these features support a more open-ended treatment of the brain–mind connection. Asking on what levels fundamental causal forces are at work and to what extent they can be reduced to other levels is an empirical question.[18] As philosophers we are sometimes tempted to lead with sharp conceptual distinctions and then to fit in the empirical and phenomenological data where we can. But the levels of brain studies and phenomenal awareness are connected in messy and ambiguous ways. The extent to which the causal connections and explanations will turn out to be micro-physical in nature is something to be discovered rather than laid down in advance. Thus the strong emergence programme does not espouse physicalism in the philosophy of mind, even though it would be easier and neater to do so. Were the reduction of mental properties to states of the central nervous system established, one would happily avoid the messiness of social scientific theories, concepts, and studies of human persons, since the resulting position would be more parsimonious and would yield a more unified science. Given the actual situation, though, one is mandated to treat the various human sciences and the sciences of culture in their own right as separate sets of empirical data, irreducible components in an overall understanding of human persons in all their biological and social complexity.

Do the phenomena of religion present themselves with the same autonomy as conscious experience does? Do religious experiences demand to be treated as a new emergent level as well? As attractive as this conclusion would be from a religious perspective, I do not think that it is true. From an emergentist standpoint alone, the existence of religious or spiritual experiences in humans need not represent anything more than a highly complex part of human social-biological existence. As the field of *Religionswissenschaft*, the social scientific study of religion, has shown, there is nothing about the range of religious phenomena that *requires* causal powers higher than those we know humans to possess. In some ways, it is human, all too human, to form religious beliefs, engage in religious practices, and have religious experiences. (Whether one views the pervasiveness of religiosity in human history and culture as positive or negative is another matter.)

Of course, the actual existence of a God who acts, a suprapersonal intentional agent without a natural evolutionary history, *would* introduce a causal level distinct from that of human being. Could this God be the result of yet another level of emergence? Yes and no. No, because a being that is able to pre-exist the entire physical cosmos cannot supervene, even weakly, on that cosmos. Hence the same sort of emergence that explains the evolution of human thought and culture could not be used to explain the origin and causal activity of such a being (unless deity were itself an emergent entity or set of properties[19]). But yes: there could be a conceptual progression from the sum total of naturally emergent phenomena to some sort of ground or source of all such phenomena. Nevertheless, it is crucial to acknowledge that this progression would represent at best a sort of argument from analogy, not a further rung on the ontological ladder of emergence. In the case of arguments from the world as a whole to its metaphysical source, the term 'dualism' is therefore justified. Combining theism and emergence yields a position that is theologically dualist but not (if my argument is successful) dualist with regard to human mind or consciousness.

CONCLUSION: EIGHT CHARACTERISTICS OF EMERGENCE

It is useful to conclude this analysis of the emergence concept with a summary of the core features of strong emergence as I will be using the term in the remaining chapters. Eight central theses characterize the position:

(1) Monism

There is one natural world made, if you will, out of stuff. Some have suggested that everyone who accepts this premise is a materialist. Although the Greek concept of matter (*hylê*) was sufficiently broad to be unobjectional, 'materialism' has taken on more limited connotations since the Enlightenment, largely because Descartes and the Cartesians set its cognate, *matter*, in opposition to *mind* in a way the Greeks would never have done. For this reason, I suggest using *monism* as the most neutral word available.

(2) Hierarchical complexity

This world appears to be hierarchically structured: more complex units are formed out of more simple parts, and they in turn become the 'parts' out of which yet more complex entities are formed. The rapid expansion of solid empirical work in complexity theory now allows us to quantify the increase in complexity, at least in some cases.

(3) Temporal or emergentist monism

This process of hierarchical structuring takes place over time: Darwinian evolution (and some forms of cosmological evolution) move from the simple to the more complex. Because new entities emerge in the process, I join with Arthur Peacocke[20] in advocating the label *emergentist monism*.

(4) No monolithic law of emergence

Many of the details of the process of emergence—the manner of the emergence of one level from another, the qualities of the emergent level, the degree to which the 'lower' controls the 'higher', etc.—vary greatly depending on which instance of emergence one is considering. Harold Morowitz,[21] for example, has identified more than two dozen levels, showing how radically different one instance of emergence can be from another. Emergence should thus be viewed as a term of family resemblance.

(5) Patterns across levels of emergence

It is possible to recognize and defend certain broad similarities shared in common by most of the various instances of emergence in natural history. I propose five in particular. For any two levels, L_1 and L_2, where L_2 emerges from L_1,

- (a) L_1 is prior in natural history
- (b) L_2 depends on L_1, such that if the states in L_1 did not exist, the qualities in L_2 would not exist.
- (c) L_2 is the result of a sufficient degree of complexity in L_1. In many cases one can even identify a particular level of criticality which, when reached, will cause the system to begin manifesting new emergent properties.
- (d) One can sometimes predict the emergence of some new or emergent qualities on the basis of what one knows about L_1. But using L_1 alone, one will not be able to predict (i) the precise nature of these qualities, (ii) the rules that govern their interaction (or their phenomenological patterns), or (iii) the sorts of emergent levels to which they in turn may give rise in due course.
- (e) L_2 is not reducible to L_1 in any of the standard senses of 'reduction' in the philosophy of science literature: causal, explanatory, metaphysical, or ontological reduction.

(6) Downward causation

I have also defended the more controversial thesis of downward causation: in some cases, phenomena at L_2 exercise a causal effect on L_1 which is not reducible to an L_1 causal history. This causal non-reducibility is not just epistemic, in the sense that we can't tell the L_1 causal story but (say) God could. It is ontological: the world is such that it produces systems whose emergent properties exercise their own distinct causal influences on each other and on (at least) the next lower level in the hierarchy. If we accept the intuitive principle that ontology should follow agency, then cases of emergent causal agency justify us in speaking of emergent objects (organisms, agents) in natural history. *Emergent properties* are new features of existing objects (e.g. conductivity is a property of electrons assembled under certain conditions); *emergent objects* become centres of agency on their own behalf (cells and organisms may be composed of smaller particles, but they are also the objects of scientific explanation in their own right).

(7) *Emergentist pluralism*

Some argue that (6) entails dualism. I disagree. Downward causation does mean that the position is 'pluralist', in so far as it asserts that really distinct levels occur within the one natural world and that objects on various levels can be ontologically primitive (can be entities in their own right) rather than being understood merely as aggregates of lower-level, foundational particles (ontological atomism). But to call this position 'dualist' is to privilege one particular emergent level—the emergence of thought out of sufficiently complex neural systems—among what are (if Morowitz is right) at least twenty-eight distinct emergent levels.

(8) *'Mind' as emergent*

The philosophical view I propose is not equivalent to 'dual aspect monism', a view that traditionally implied that there is no causal interaction between mental and physical properties, since they are two different aspects of the one 'stuff'. By contrast, the present view presupposes that both upward and downward influences are operative.

NOTES

1. Vladimir Archinov and Christian Fuchs (eds.), *Causality, Emergence, Self-Organisation*, a publication of the international working group on 'Human Strategies in Complexity: Philosophical Foundations for a Theory of Evolutionary Systems' (Moscow: NIA-Priroda 2003), 5–6.

2. See Tim Crane, 'The Significance of Emergence', in Carl Gillett and Barry Loewer (eds.), *Physicalism and its Discontents* (Cambridge: Cambridge University Press, 2001), 208.

3. The work of Jeremy Butterfield represents an excellent example of this genre. See Tomasz Placek and Jeremy Butterfield (eds.), *Non-Locality and*

Modality (Dordrecht: Kluwer Academic, 2002); Jeremy Butterfield and Constantine Pagonis (eds.), *From Physics to Philosophy* (Cambridge: Cambridge University Press, 1999); Jeremy Butterfield, Mark Hogarth, and Gordon Belot (eds.), *Spacetime* (Aldershot and Brookfield, Vt.: Dartmouth Publishing Co., 1996).

4. Terrence Deacon, 'The Hierarchic Logic of Emergence: Untangling the Interdependence of Evolution and Self-Organization', in Bruce H. Weber and David J. Depew (eds.), *Evolution and Learning: The Baldwin Effect Reconsidered* (Cambridge, Mass.: MIT Press, 2003).

5. Robert Audi, 'Mental Causation: Sustaining and Dynamic', in John Heil and Alfred Mele (eds.), *Mental Causation* (Oxford: Oxford University Press, 1993), 73.

6. For this reason it is especially interesting to watch the use or avoidance of one or the other term in the literature. Perhaps the most interesting case study is the work of Arthur Peacocke. In earlier years he used the more cautious 'whole–part constraints', gradually became emboldened to use the stronger 'top–down causation', became worried about dualism and ceased to use the stronger phrase, and now uses both phrases side by side without fully granting the philosophical difference between them.

7. See Donald Campbell, '"Downward Causation" in Hierarchically Organised Biological Systems', in F. J. Ayala and T. H. Dobzhansky (eds.), *Studies in the Philosophy of Biology* (Berkeley, Calif.: University of California Press, 1974), 179–86.

8. See Donald Campbell, 'Levels of Organisation, Downward Causation, and the Selection-Theory Approach to Evolutionary Epistemology', in G. Greenberg and E. Tobach (eds.), *Theories of the Evolution of Knowing* (Hillsdale, NJ: Lawrence Erlbaum, 1990), 1–17, p. 4.

9. In defence of special sciences, even at the cost of relaxing the hold of the 'unity of science' ideal, see Jerry Fodor, 'Special Sciences, or the Disunity of Science as a Working Hypothesis', in Ned Block (ed.), *Readings in Philosophy of Psychology*, 2 vols. (Cambridge, Mass.: Harvard University Press, 1980), i. 120–33.

10. See e.g. Michael Arbib, 'Schema Theory', in S. Shapiro (ed.), *The Encyclopedia of Artificial Intelligence* (New York: Wiley, 1992), 1427–43; Arbib, E. Jeffrey Conklin, and Jane C. Hill, *From Schema Theory to Language* (New York: Oxford University Press, 1987).

11. David J. Buller (ed.), *Function, Selection, and Design* (Albany, NY: SUNY Press, 1999).

12. See Carl Gillett, 'Non-Reductive Realization and Non-Reductive Identity: What Physicalism does Not Entail', in Sven Walter and Heinz-Deiter Heckmann (eds.), *Physicalism and Mental Causation* (Charlottesville, Va.: Imprint Academic, 2003), 23–49, p. 28.

13. See Jaegwon Kim, 'The Non-Reductivist's Troubles with Mental Causation', in Heil and Mele (eds.), *Mental Causation*, 189–210, p. 209. Cf. Carl Gillett,

'Strong Emergence as a Defense of Non-Reductive Physicalism: A Physicalist Metaphysics for "Downward" Determination', *Principia*, 6 (2003), 83–114.

14. Gillett, 'Non-Reductive Realization', 42.

15. See Carl Gillett, 'Physicalism and Panentheism: Good News and Bad News', *Faith and Philosophy*, 20/1 (Jan. 2003), 1–21.

16. 'A property instance X is strongly emergent, in an individual S, *if and only if* (i) X is realized by other properties/relations; and (ii) X partially non-causally determines the causal powers contributed by at least one of the fundamental properties/relations realizing X' (Gillett, 'Non-Reductive Realization', 37–8).

17. In one sense, of course, physics is privileged: it constrains explanations at all levels above it, but is not constrained by them. But one can accept this principle without accepting that all causes are physical causes.

18. At the end of both of the more recent articles, Gillett admits that the question about emergence will have to be decided by empirical enquiry. I am arguing that, were he to be consistent, he would have to say the same thing about the pre-commitment to micro-physicalism.

19. This limitation does not apply to those (such as Samuel Alexander and Weiland) who understand 'deity' as an emergent property of the physical world itself. See Chapter 5.

20. See Arthur Peacocke, 'The Sound of Sheer Silence', in Robert J. Russell *et al.* (eds.), *Neuroscience and the Person* (Vatican City: Vatican Observatory Publications, 1999).

21. See Harold Morowitz, *The Emergence of Everything: How the World Became Complex* (New York: Oxford University Press, 2002).

3

Emergence in the Natural Sciences

INTRODUCTION

The task now is to look at the role that emergence plays within, and in the relations between, the natural sciences. No pretence is made to completeness; each of the sciences covered here, and each of the relations between them, merits a book-length treatment of its own. In this early stage of the discussion, however, when scientists and philosophers are so unclear about what emergence might mean and where it occurs in the natural world, the most urgent task is to blaze a first path, however rough, through the underbrush.

In the previous chapter we saw that emergence is primarily about transitions between areas of scientific study. Once an entity or function has emerged—a cell, an organism, the collection of properties we call a person—it becomes the object of its own set of scientific studies. Now that the concept of emergence has been made clearer, one wants to know: what in the natural world actually counts as emergent? The examples, I will suggest, undercut the philosophy known as reductive physicalism. They do this by supporting a broad thesis about natural history that I am calling emergence—the thesis that evolution produces a variety of distinct levels of phenomena, each of which plays its own causal role in conjunction with its own set of laws or patterns. Between the two major interpretations of natural emergence, strong and weak, the data support the existence of the strong interpretation in at least some cases. Especially in the biological cases, what emerge are entities that become causal agents in their own right, not merely as aggregates of underlying particles and forces.

One recognizes a certain clash of cultures, reminiscent of C. P. Snow, in moving between the various parts of this inquiry.[1] Scientists tend to put much more weight on the concrete examples and treat the conceptual clarifications as a sort of throat-clearing, as if it were merely preparatory work for what really counts. Philosophers, by contrast, complain that the scientific examples are too detailed and would just as soon jump straight from the previous chapter to the next. Making a compelling case, however, requires both parts, and in no less detail than is given here. One also finds a cultural difference in responses to the theoretical choices. Philosophers generally perceive sharp conceptual differences between physicalism, weak, and strong emergence; one finds scores, if not hundreds, of works defending some particular version of one of these views against all comers. Scientists, by contrast, are more inclined to complain that there is no real difference between the three positions—or at least that the three should be treated as a matter of degree. Biologists, for example, are told in the process of their training that they are physicalists, which is a philosophical position that, I have argued, is inconsistent with standard theories and research practice in biology: technically, biologists should say that they are naturalists or students of natural history, not physicalists. Experience suggests that it will be difficult to convince scientific readers that, conceptually speaking, there are some real decisions to be made between the three alternatives.

PHYSICS TO CHEMISTRY

The present chapter focuses primarily on examples drawn from biochemistry and biology, with some assistance from neural networks and artificial systems theory. Before turning to those disciplines in some more detail, however, it is important to touch on recent uses of emergence within physics, if only to show that the term may also play a crucial role in interpreting relations between various physical theories. Although I will not attempt to analyse the peculiarities of physical emergence in much detail, even this passing look will show that physics has a role to play in a complete theory of scientific emergence.[2]

Phenomena emerge in the development of complex physical systems which, though verifiable through observation, cannot be derived from fundamental physical principles. Even given a complete knowledge of the antecedent states, we would not be able to predict their emergence with the particular qualities they have. One would not, for example, know about conductivity from a study of individual electrons alone; conductivity is a property that emerges only in complex solid state systems with huge numbers of electrons. Likewise, the fluid dynamics of chaotic hydrodynamic flows with vortices (say, the formation of eddies at the bottom of a waterfall) cannot be predicted from knowledge of the motions of individual particles. The quantum Hall effect and the phenomena of superconductivity are cited by Robert Laughlin and others as further examples of emergence.[3]

Such examples are convincing: physicists are familiar with a myriad of cases in which physical wholes cannot be predicted based on knowledge of their parts. Intuitions differ, though, on the significance of this unpredictability. Let's call the two options strong and weak unpredictability (linking this discussion with the heated debate on strong and weak emergence covered in the previous two chapters). Cases will be unpredictable in a weaker sense when it turns out that one could in principle predict aggregate states given suitably comprehensive information about the parts—even if predictions of system dynamics lie beyond present, or even future, limits on computability. But they will be unpredictable in a much stronger sense—that is, unpredictable even in principle—if the system-as-a-whole exercises some sort of causal influence that is more than the sum of its parts. Where an energy vector is understood as the sum of some collection of forces, even if completing the actual computation be beyond human abilities, we have weak unpredictability; where an energy transduction is not computable in advance but can only be ascertained based on subsequent observation, we have strong unpredictability.

Examples of physical emergence such as conductivity and fluid dynamics are already familiar to most readers; they could be multiplied at will. Recently, however, more radical claims have been raised about physical emergence. On the standard picture, for example, all that exists emerges from quantum mechanical potentialities, beginning with space-time itself. For example, Juan Maldacena argued recently that 'Space-time appears dynamically, due to the interactions in the quantum field theory at the boundary. It is an "emergent" property, appearing due to the interactions'. General relativity requires that space-time be treated like a four-dimensional fluid and not as a non-physical structuring separate from what exists within it (such as mass). Whether space-time emerges from quantum interactions, as Maldacena claims, is of course a more speculative matter.

In either case, the newer theories certainly require that the classical world be understood to emerge from the quantum world. A. Albrecht has written on the emergence of classicality in thermodynamics, and Wojciech Zurek argues that 'the path from the microscopic to macroscopic is emergent'. Zurek's work has demonstrated 'the status of decoherence as . . . a key ingredient of the explanation of the emergent classicality'.[4] It's thus appropriate, for example, to speak of 'the emergence of preferred pointer states' (Zurek, 'Decoherence' (2002), 17): even that paradigmatic touchstone of classical physics, the measure of a macrophysical state by the position of a pointer on a dial, must now be understood as an emergent phenomenon resulting from the decoherence of a quantum superposition.

It is easy to find simpler examples of the emergence of order through the evolution of physical systems. The formation of snow flakes, snow crystals, and other ice phenomena is frequently cited,[5] as are the patterns associated with large changes of scale, such as fractals.[6] The phenomena of fluid dynamics also offer some compelling examples,[7] such as the pattern of fluid convection known as the Bénard instability. The Bénard instability occurs in a fluid system far from thermodynamic equilibrium, when a stationary state becomes unstable and then manifests spontaneous organization.[8] In the Bénard case, the lower surface of a horizontal layer of liquid is heated. This produces a heat flux from the bottom to the top of the liquid. When the temperature gradient reaches a certain threshold value, conduction no longer suffices to convey the heat upward. At that point convection cells form at right angles to the vertical heat flow. The liquid spontaneously organizes itself into these hexagonal structures or cells.

Differential equations describing the heat flow exhibit a bifurcation of the solutions. This bifurcation expresses the spontaneous self-organization of large numbers of molecules, formerly in random motion, into convection cells. This represents a particularly clear case of the spontaneous appearance of order in a system. As we will see, many of the cases of emergent order in biochemistry and biology offer analogous cases of the spontaneous formation of ordered structures.

Consider, finally, the Pauli Exclusion Principle. The Pauli Principle is a physical law which stipulates that no two electrons of an atom can have the same set of four quantum numbers. Thus a maximum of two electrons can occupy an atomic orbital. The requirement of this simple principle on the way electrons fill up orbitals turns out to be basic for understanding modern chemistry. For example, one finds that each of the types of sublevel (s, p, d, f) must have its own particular electron capacity. As the orbitals are filled according to this simple rule, beginning with the lowest energy orbitals, the chemical characteristics that we know from the periodic table begin to emerge. A rather simple principle thus has as its outcome the complex chemical distribution of the elements. These emergent qualities are both diverse and unpredictable. (This example again raises the critical question of strong versus weak unpredictability discussed above.)

ARTIFICIAL SYSTEMS

As one moves towards chemical and, eventually, biological systems, the emerging structures, which are extremely large from a physics point of view, play a larger and larger causal and explanatory role. In order to trace the phenomena that result from increasing complexity, and the principles of their emergence, it is helpful to consider the insights offered by recent work on artificial systems. Three examples drawn from this field are especially illustrative: the emergence of 'gliders' in simulated evolutionary systems, the emergence of neural networks, and the emergence of system-level attributes in ant colonies.

I. Computer simulations study the processes whereby very simple rules give rise to complex emergent properties. John Conway's program 'Life', which simulates cellular automata, is already widely known. The program's algorithm contains simple rules that determine whether a particular square on a grid 'lights up' based on the state of neighbouring squares. When applied, the rules produce complex structures that evidence interesting and unpredictable behaviours. One of these, the 'glider,' is a five-square structure that moves diagonally across the grid, one step for every four cycles of the program.[9]

As in natural systems, further emergent complexity is added by the fact that the program 'tiles'. This term denotes the phenomenon in which composite structures are formed out of groups of simpler structures and evidence coherent behaviour over iterations of the program. What is true of a single square, for example, can also be true of a 3-by-3 array of squares. In this case one is dealing with a much more complex system: the resulting tile has 512 states and each of its eight inputs can take any of 512 values.[10]

Occurrences of the tiling phenomenon in the natural world, which George Ellis calls 'encapsulation',[11] reveal why emergent structures in the natural world play such a crucial role in scientific explanations. Composite structures are made up of simpler structures, and the rules governing the behaviour of the simple parts continue to hold throughout the evolution of the system. Yet in even as simple a system as Conway's 'Life', predicting the movement of larger structures in terms of the simple parts alone turns out to be extremely complex. Not surprisingly, in the messy real world of biology, behaviours of complex systems quickly become non-computable in practice. (Whether they are unpredictable in principle, i.e. strongly unpredictable, and if so why, remains a central question for emergence theory.) As a result—and, it now appears, necessarily—scientists must rely on explanations given in terms of the emerging structures and their causal powers. Actualizing the dream of a final reduction 'downwards', it now appears, has proven fundamentally impossible. Extending lower-level descriptions cannot do justice to the actual emergent complexity of the natural world as it has evolved.

Stephen Wolfram has recently attempted to formulate the core principles of rule-based emergence:

[E]ven programs with some of the very simplest possible rules yield highly complex behavior, while programs with fairly complicated rules often yield only rather simple behavior. . . . If one just looks at a rule in its raw form, it is usually almost impossible to tell much about the overall behavior it will produce.[12]

As an example of very similar rules producing widely discrepant outputs, Figure 3.1 shows Wolfram offering a sequence of elementary cellular automata 'whose rules differ from one to the next only at one position' in a Gray code sequence (ibid.).

2. Neural networks research comes to similar results from a very different starting point. Consider John Holland's work on developing visual processing systems. He begins with a simple representation of a mammalian visual system.[13] In neural networks research, rather than establishing laws in advance, one constructs a set of random interconnections between a large number of 'nodes' to form a network. The researcher then imposes relatively simple processing rules that emulate mammal perception. Crucially, the rules pertain to the synaptic junctions rather than to the overall architecture of the neural network. Thus they might include rules to govern the circulation of pulses based on variable threshold firing, 'fatigue' rules to simulate the inhibition of firing after a period of activity, and so forth. Researchers also program a 'shift to contrast' reflex, so that the 'eye' shifts successively to new points of contrast in

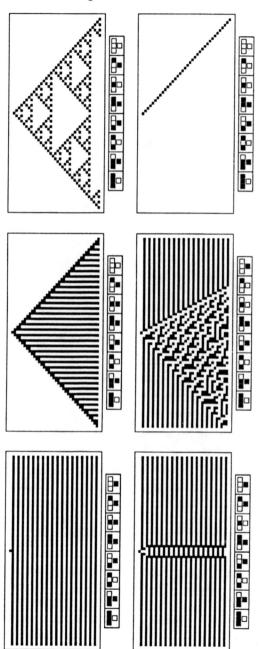

FIGURE 3.1 Wolfram's cellular automata.
From Stephen Wolfram, *A New Kind of Science*, copyright 2002
Reproduced with permission from Stephen Wolfram, LLC.

the presented image, such as to another vertex in a figure. One then runs multiple trials and measures learning via the system's output.

The idea is to see whether these simple systems can model visual memory in mammals. It seems that they can. Holland's systems, for example, exhibit the features of synchrony, or reverberation, as well as anticipation: groups of 'neurons' 'prepare' to respond to an expected future stimulus (p. 104). That is, groups of neurons light up in response to each of the vertices of the triangle, while 'fatigued' neurons don't. Particularly fascinating is the phenomenon of hierarchy: new groups of neurons form in response to groups that have already formed (p. 108). Thus a lighting of any of the three original groupings, which represent the vertices, causes a fourth area to light up, which represents the memory for 'triangle'.

3. Neural network models of emergent phenomena can model not only visual memory but also phenomena as complex as the emergence of ant colony behaviour from the simple behavioural 'rules' that are genetically programmed into individual ants. As John Holland's work has again shown, one can program the individual nodes in the simulation with the simple approach/avoidance principles that seem to determine ant behaviour (p. 228):

Flee when you detect a moving object; but

If the object is moving and small and exudes the 'friend' pheromone, then approach it and touch antennae.

The work of ant researchers such as Deborah Gordon confirms that the resulting programme simulates actual ant behaviours to a significant degree. Her work with ant colonies in turn adds to the general understanding of complex systems:

The dynamics of ant colony life has some features in common with many other complex systems: Fairly simple units generate complicated global behavior. If we knew how an ant colony works, we might understand more about how all such systems work, from brains to ecosystems.[14]

Even if the behaviour of an ant colony were nothing more than an aggregate of the behaviours of the individual ants, whose behaviour follows very simple rules,[15] the result would be remarkable, for the behaviour of the ant colony as a whole is extremely complex and highly adaptive to complex changes in its ecosystem. For example, Gordon finds, a given ant colony will have a particular set of characteristics (one might almost say, a particular personality) in comparison to others: one may be more aggressive and quick to respond, another more passive and patient. Moreover, the characteristics of colonies change year by year as they age, with youthful colonies growing and expending more energy and ageing colonies tending more towards stasis. What is remarkable about these higher-order patterns is that they emerge over a decade or so despite the fact that individual inhabitants live only about a year. (Of course the queen lives as long as the colony, but—the depiction in the film *Antz* notwithstanding—she exercises no ruling function or control over the colony.) Clearly, the complex adaptive potentials of the ant colony as a whole are emergent features of the aggregated system. The scientific task is to correctly describe and comprehend such emergent phenomena where the whole is more than the sum of the parts.

BIOCHEMISTRY

So far we have considered theoretical models of how it might be that nature builds highly complex and adaptive behaviours from relatively simple processing rules. Now we must consider actual cases in which significant order emerges out of (relative) chaos. The big question is how nature obtains order 'out of nothing', that is, how order is produced in the course of a system's evolution when it is not present in the initial conditions. (Generally this question seems to strike physicists as ill-formed, whereas biologists tend to recognize in it one of the core features in the evolution of living systems.) What are some of the mechanisms that make this emergence possible? We consider just three examples:

(1) Autocatalysis in biochemical metabolism.
Autocatalytic processes play a role in some of the most fundamental examples of emergence in the biosphere. These are relatively simple chemical processes with catalytic steps. Because they are easy to grasp, they form a good entré into the thermodynamics of the far-from-equilibrium chemical processes that lie at the base of the immensely more complicated biological systems.

Much of biochemistry is characterized by a type of catalysis in which 'the presence of a product is required for its own synthesis'.[16] Take a basic reaction chain where A→X, and X→E, but where X is involved in an autocatalytic process (ibid. 135): see Figure 3.2.

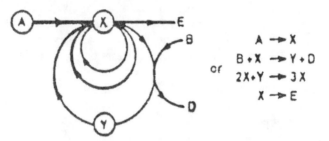

FIGURE 3.2.   A sample autocatalytic process.
From Ilya Prigogine, *Order out of Chaos*. Reprinted by permission of
Mrs Marina Prigogine.

For example, molecule X might activate an enzyme, which 'stabilizes' the configuration that allows the reaction. Similarly frequent are cases of *crosscatalysis*, namely cases where X is produced from Y and Y from X. In Figure 3.2 crosscatalysis is represented by the equation B + X→Y + D, that is, X in the presence of B produces Y and a by-product. The presence of Y in turn produces a higher quantity of X (here, 2X + Y→3X). The entire reaction loop is autocatalytic in producing E. Loops of this sort play a crucial role in metabolic functions.

(2) Belousov-Zhabotinsky reactions

The role of emergence becomes clearer as one considers more complex examples. Consider the famous Belousov-Zhabotinsky reaction[17] (see Figure 3.3). This reaction consists of the oxidation of an organic acid (malonic acid) by potassium bromate in the presence of a catalyst such as cerium, manganese, or ferroin. From the four inputs into the chemical reactor more than thirty products and intermediates are produced. The Belousov-Zhabotinsky reaction provides a fascinating example of a biochemical process where a high level of disorder settles into a patterned state. By interlocking a specific set of highly local autocatalytic reactions in a confined space, one can produce remarkable large-scale spatial patterns that undergo regular transformations in time.[18]

In more complex chemical systems, multiple states can be achieved far from equilibrium. That is, a given set of boundary conditions can produce one of a variety of stationary outcome states. The chemical composition of these outcome states serves as a 'control mechanism'

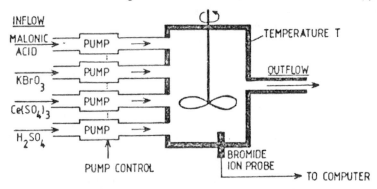

in biological systems. It would be fruitful to explore the similarities
between these multiple stationary outcomes and the 'attractors' or
'strange attractors' that mathematicians have explored, for example,
in the study of complex systems in physics.

One then wants to ask: what is the general feature of these
dissipative structures far from thermodynamic equilibrium? There
is much to recommend Prigogine's conclusion (p. 171):

One of the most interesting aspects of dissipative structures is their
coherence. The system behaves as a whole, as if it were the site of long-
range forces. . . . In spite of the fact that interactions among molecules do
not exceed a range of some 10^{-8} cm, the system is structured as though each
molecule were 'informed' about the overall state of the system.

Put in philosophical terms, the data suggest that emergence is not
merely epistemological but can also be ontological in nature. That
is, it is not just that *we* cannot predict emergent behaviours in these
systems from a complete knowledge of the structures and energies
of the parts. Instead, studying the systems suggests that structural
features of the system—which are emergent features of the system
as such and *not* properties pertaining to any of the parts—determine
the overall state of the system, and hence as a result the behaviour
of individual particles within the system. We find examples of
this phenomenon, which in discussions of emergence theory is
frequently referred to as 'downward causation', repeated across the
natural world. There is nothing 'spooky' or 'dualistic' about them:
the world naturally forms these more complex structures, which in

turn become causal agents that affect the dynamics of the micro-systems on which they depend.

The role of emergent features of systems is increasingly evident as one moves from the very simple systems so far considered to the sorts of systems one actually encounters in the biosphere. Figure 3.4 is a sketch by Stuart Kauffman of a simple autocatalytic set of the sort that occurs in nature.[19] This complicated sketch shows the reactions and the actions of catalysts in a set that involves only four food sets and seventeen other chemicals.

(3) Self-organization

We move finally to processes where random fluctuations give rise to organized patterns of behaviour between cells based on self-

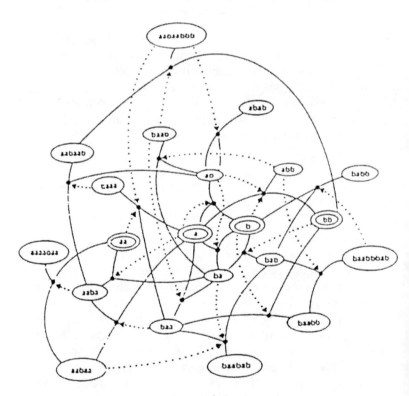

FIGURE 3.4.   Autocatalytic systems in nature.

From George Cowan, David Pines, and David Meltzer, *Complexity: Metaphors, Models, and Reality*. Copyright by Westview Press, a member of Perseus Books.

organization mechanisms. Consider the process of cell aggregation and differentiation in cellular slime moulds (specifically, in *Dictyostelium discoideum*). The slime mould cycle begins when the environment becomes poor in nutrients and a population of isolated cells joins into a single mass on the order of 10^4 cells (see Figure 3.5).[20] The aggregate migrates until it finds a higher nutrient source. Differentiation then occurs: a stalk or 'foot' forms out of about one-third of the cells and is soon covered with spores. The spores detach and spread, growing when they encounter suitable nutrients and eventually forming a new colony of amoebas.

Note that this aggregation process is randomly initiated. Autocatalysis begins in a random cell within the colony, which then becomes the centre of attraction (the attractor) for the cells around it. It begins to produce cyclic AMP. As cAMP is released in greater quantities into the extracellular medium, it catalyses the same reaction in the other cells, amplifying the fluctuation and total output. Cells then move up the gradient to the source cell, and other cells in turn follow their cAMP trail towards the attractor centre.[21]

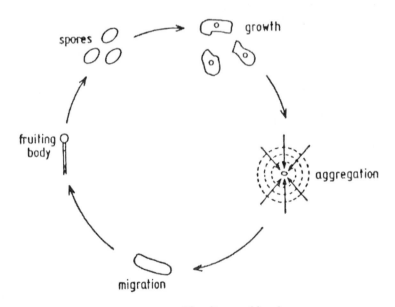

FIGURE 3.5.   The slime mold cycle.

From Ilya Prigogine, *Order out of Chaos*. Reprinted by permission of Mrs Marina Prigogine.

A similar randomly initiated process that produces highly adaptive behaviour is found in *coleoptera* (termite) larvae (see Figure 3.6). Here the aggregation process is induced through the release of a pheromone by the coleoptera. The higher their nutrition state, the higher the rate of release. Other larvae then move up the concentration gradient. The process is autocatalytic: the more larvae that move into a region, the more the attractiveness of that region is enhanced, until the nutrient source is finally depleted. It is also dependent on random moves of the larvae, since they will not cluster if they are too dispersed.

THE TRANSITION TO BIOLOGY

Ilya Prigogine did not follow the notion of 'order out of chaos' up through the entire ladder of biological evolution. But thinkers such as Kauffman, Goodman, de Duve, Gell-Mann, and Conway Morris have recently traced the role of the same principles in living systems.[22] Biological processes in general are the result of systems that create and maintain order (stasis) through massive energy input from their environment. In principle these types of processes could be the object of what Kauffman envisions as 'a new general biology', based on sets of still-to-be-determined laws of emergent ordering or self-complexification. Like the biosphere itself, these laws (if they indeed exist) are emergent: they depend on the underlying physical and chemical regularities but are not reducible to them. Kauffman writes,

I wish to say that life is an expected, emergent property of complex chemical reaction networks. Under rather general conditions, as the diversity of molecular species in a reaction system increases, a phase transition is crossed beyond which the formation of collectively autocatalytic sets of molecules suddenly becomes almost inevitable.[23]

Until a science has been developed that formulates and tests physics-like laws at the level of biology, the 'new general biology' remains an as-yet-unverified, though intriguing, hypothesis. Nevertheless recent biology, driven by the genetic revolution on the one side and by the growth of the environmental sciences on the other, has made explosive advances in understanding the role of self-organizing complexity in the biosphere. Four factors in particular play a central role in biological emergence:

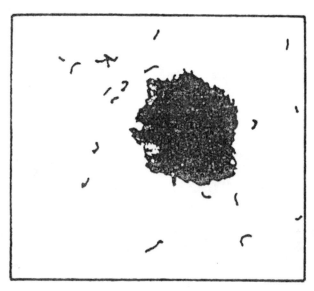

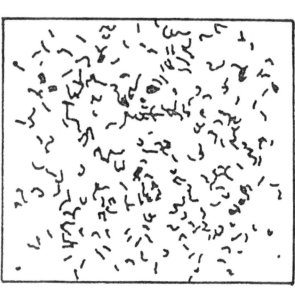

FIGURE 3.6.   Emergent behaviors in *coleoptera* larvae.
From Ilya Prigogine, *Order out of Chaos*. Reprinted by permission of Mrs Marina Prigogine.

(1) The role of scaling

As one moves up the ladder of complexity, macrostructures and macromechanisms emerge. In the formation of new structures, one might say, scale matters—or, better put, changes in scale matter. Nature continually evolves new structures and mechanisms as life forms move up the scale from molecules (c. 1 Ångstrom) to neurons (c. 100 micrometres) to the human central nervous system (c. 1 metre). As new structures are developed, new whole-part relations emerge.

John Holland argues that different sciences in the hierarchy of emergent complexity occur at jumps of roughly three orders of magnitude in scale. By that point systems have become too complex for predictions to be calculated, and one is forced to 'move the description "up a level"'.[24] The 'microlaws' still constrain outcomes, of course, but additional basic descriptive units must also be added. This pattern of introducing new explanatory levels iterates in a periodic fashion as one moves up the ladder of increasing complexity. To recognize the patterns is to make emergence an explicit feature of biological research. As of yet, however, science possesses only a preliminary understanding of the principles underlying this periodicity.

(2) The role of feedback loops

Feedback loops, examined above for biochemical processes, play an increasing role from the cellular level upwards. In plant–environment interactions, for example, one can trace the interaction of mechanisms, each of which is the complex result of its own internal autocatalytic processes. Plants receive nutrients, process them, and provide new materials to the environment (e.g. oxygen, pollen). The environment in turn takes up these materials and processes them, so that new resources become available to the plant (see Figure 3.7).

This sort of feedback dynamic is the basis for ecosystems theory: the particular behaviours of organisms bring about changes in their environment, which affect the organisms with which they interact; in turn, these organisms' complex responses, products of their own internal changes, further alter the shared environment, and hence its impact on each individual organism.

(3) The role of local–global interactions

In complex dynamical systems the interlocked feedback loops

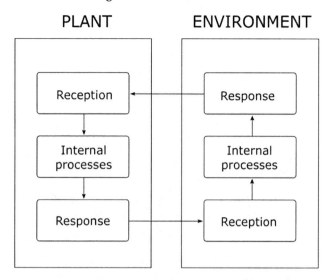

FIGURE 3.7.　Schematic summary of the plant-environment cycle.
Copyright Philip Clayton. Redrawn by Ben Klocek.

can produce an emergent global structure. Lewin[25] offers a schematic representation derived from the work of Chris Langton (see Figure 3.8).

In these cases, 'the global property—[the] emergent behaviour—feeds back to influence the behaviour of the individuals . . . that produced it' (ibid.). The global structure may have properties the local particles do not have. An ecosystem, for example, will usually evidence a kind of emergent stability that the organisms of which it is constituted lack. Nevertheless, it is impossible to predict the global effects 'from below', based on a knowledge of the parts of the system, because of the sensitive dependence on initial conditions (among other factors): minute fluctuations near the bifurcation point are amplified by subsequent states of the system. This form of 'downward' feedback process represents another instance of downward causation.

Figure 3.8 schematizes the idea of a global structure. In contrast to Chris Langton, Kauffman insists that an ecosystem is in one sense 'merely' a complex web of interactions. Yet consider a typical ecosystem of organisms of the sort that Kauffman analyses (see Figure 3.9).[26]

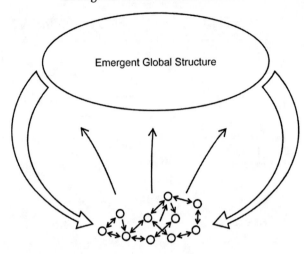

FIGURE 3.8.   Local-global interactions.
Permission granted by Chris Langton who frequently uses this drawing.
Redrawn by Ben Klocek.

Typically, in the study of complex environmental systems of this type one needs to move from directly quantitative methods to more qualitative modelling. For example, in assessing the impact of contaminants on particular populations, individual species, or habitats, toxicologists combine qualitative or 'top–down' methods with univariate and multivariate methods, since 'in a regional, multiple stressor assessment, the number of possible interactions increases combinatorially. Stressors are derived from diverse sources, receptors [i.e., organisms] are often associated with a variety of habitats, and one impact can lead to additional impacts. These interactions are painted upon a complex background of natural stressors, effects, and historical events'.[27] In short, particular research interests may compel one to focus attention on holistic features of the system as a necessary step towards reconstructing the interactions of the components within them. Langton's emphasis on 'global' features draws attention to the system-level features and properties, whereas Kauffman's 'merely' emphasizes that no mysterious outside forces need to be introduced in the process (such as e.g. Sheldrake's 'morphic resonance'[28]). Since the two dimensions are complementary, neither alone is scientifically adequate; the explosive complexity manifested in the evolutionary process involves the interplay of *both* systemic features and component interactions.

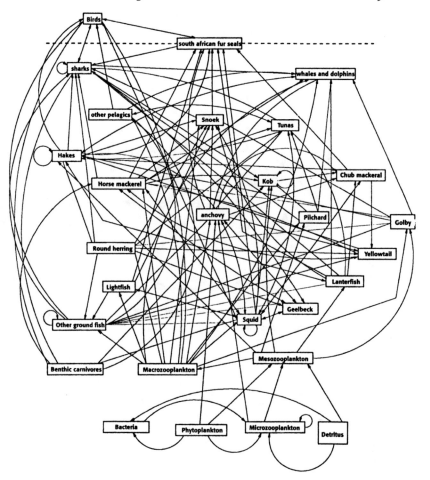

FIGURE 3.9.   Interactions in a typical complex ecosystem.

From Stuart Kauffman, *Investigations.* Copyright 2000 by Oxford University Press, Inc. Used by permission of Oxford University Press.

(4) The role of nested hierarchies

A final layer of complexity is added in cases where the local–global structure forms a nested hierarchy. Such hierarchies are often represented using nested circles (see Figure 3.10). Nesting is one of the basic forms of combinatorial explosion. Such forms appear extensively in natural biological systems, as Stephen Wolfram has recently sought to show in his massive treatment of the subject.[29]

FIGURE 3.10.   Nested hierarchies in biological systems.
Frequently used image of embedding, redrawn by Ben Klocek.

Organisms achieve greater structural complexity, and hence increased chances of survival, as they incorporate discrete subsystems. Similarly, ecosystems complex enough to contain a number of discrete subsystems evidence greater plasticity in responding to destabilizing factors.

EMERGENCE IN EVOLUTION

In one sense, emergence in evolution is similar to the sorts of examples we have been considering. As Terrence Deacon notes, it consists of 'a collection of highly convoluted processes that produce a remarkably complex kind of combinatorial novelty'.[30] In another sense, however, biological evolution adds an importantly new dimension into the productive process that is natural history. Now for the first time causal agents emerge that include an element of 'memory', which is isolated by cellular membranes and transmitted, more or less intact, to their offspring via nucleic acids. These new structures make each organism a sort of hypothesis, a guess about what kind of structure might thrive in its particular environment. 'The result', comments Deacon, 'is that specific historical moments of higher-order regularity or of unique micro-causal configurations can exert *an additional cumulative influence* over the entire causal future of the system.'[31] With this new emergent level, natural selection is born.

The title of this section signals a crucial difference in approach between contemporary emergence theory and the British Emergentists of the early twentieth century. By working with the title 'emergent evolution', C. Lloyd Morgan and others implicitly claimed to have discovered a new *kind* of evolution. Does 'emergent evolution' not hold out the implicit promise that Morgan's theory of emergence will provide the tools to write a more adequate science of evolution? 'Emergence *in* evolution' backs away from such claims. Here the assumption is that one must work with the givens of contemporary evolutionary theory, with its data, theories, and methods. If contemporary biology needs to be modified and improved (and even its greatest advocates believe that it does), such changes will come, gradually or rapidly, on the basis of scientific criticisms that reveal areas where its explanations are inadequate—and only as better scientific explanations become available. Standard evolutionary theory will not be shown to be inadequate by the fact that a group dislikes this or that feature of the theories or some implication they seem to have. (Of course, what actually *are* the broader implications of evolutionary theory is frequently a philosophical question. Richard Dawkins is famous not for his science but for his philosophy.[32])

In short, 'emergence in evolution' suggests that, within the set of theories that we group under the heading of evolutionary biology, particular features can be discovered that are aptly described as 'emergent'. This approach looks to clarify those features and to show how and why the phenomenon of emergence is significant to an understanding of the biosphere. If this claim is sustained, one is justified in looking for analogies with the emergent features that characterize other phenomena within the natural world.

Transformations in evolutionary theory

The case for biological emergence is best made not by looking outside biology but by tracing trends in the understanding of evolution, and changes in the study of evolutionary systems, over the last fifty or so years. It is fair to say that the dominant perspective of the 'new synthesis' in biology in the mid–twentieth century was mechanistic.

The complicated appearances and behaviours of organisms and ecosystems could ultimately be explained at the biochemical level by gene reproduction and mutation. These processes upwardly determine the structures and functions of cells, organs, and organisms, which are then selected for or against by the environment. On this understanding biology will have completed its explanatory task when it has filled in the full explanatory story that runs from these random mutations through the process of selection and on to the current structure, functions, and behaviours of all biological organisms, including the functions and behaviours of human organisms. Even though the evidence now suggests that this model was overly ambitious in its claims and expectations, it must be said that it remains the (often unspoken) model of many working biologists today.

It is not hard to list the core features of model work within the new synthesis. As noted, it was mechanistic: one looked for the mechanisms that underlie and explain organismic behaviour. It was based on the assumption of the possibility of reduction to physical laws, and hence on the centrality of physics for biology. Although one assumed that explanations given in terms of physical laws alone would be far too complex to allow for explaining and predicting biological phenomena, it was assumed that translations of core biological explanatory principles into physical laws was still possible in principle. Above all, it was 'bottom-up': systems had to be explained in terms of their constituent parts and the laws governing the parts' behaviour; it would be unscientific to try to account for some particular phenomenon in terms of the broader system of which it was a part—unless, of course, that system had in turn been explained in terms of the parts and the laws that produced it.

Of course, the orthodoxy of the new synthesis within biology was not without its challengers. As Sydney Brenner wrote in 1974,

It is not good enough to answer [questions regarding biological development] by saying it is simply a matter of turning some genes on and others off at the right times. It is true that molecular biology provides numerous detailed precedents for mechanisms by which this can, in principle, be done, but we demand something more than these absolutely true, absolutely vacuous statements.[33]

Nor was the orthodoxy as strict as some have painted it: some of the leading formulators of the approach made suggestions that were incompatible with the characteristics just summarized. Thus, Dobzhansky advocated Teilhard de Chardin's notion of final causality for a time, until he was gradually criticized into silence. Throughout this period, the descriptive work of ethologists and environmental scientists represented a de facto break with the mainline approach. In addition to Dobzhansky's doubts, the famous paper by Gould and Lewontin in 1979 on the limits of adaptationism raised doubts about the new synthesis approach.[34]

A new series of suspicions about the dominant programme seems to have been unleashed by the theory of punctuated equilibrium of Eldridge and Gould.[35] The idea that evolution would take place through major jumps, followed by long periods of relative equilibrium and minimal change, is not intrinsically incompatible with the new synthesis. But it does introduce the possibility that there are empirical causal forces at work in evolutionary history that are not captured by genetics plus natural selection. Should broader environmental forces play the major role in determining the overall results of evolution, then the paradigm of upward determination from the level of genes must be incomplete. Additional doubts were raised by what should have been a major victory for the genetic programme: the completion of the Human Genome Project (HGP). The hype surrounding the HGP led many to believe that it would unlock the secrets of ontogenetic development. Yet the outcome of the project severely undercut such hopes: with only a few more than 30,000 genes to work with, it is simply impossible for the human genome to programme human traits in the level of detail that some had suggested. To the extent, for example, that E. O. Wilson's sociobiology[36] had depended on associating one particular gene with each inherited trait, his programme was curtailed by the unexpectedly small number of coding genes.

Thus it was not a long step to the development of epigenesis. Epigenesis was not new to the late twentieth century; Oscar Hertwig argued for epigenetic factors in embryogenesis in his 1900 book, *The Problem of Today: Preformation or Epigenesis?*, and the idea is found already in the philosophy of nature of Wilhelm von Humboldt. Of course, neither of the two positions covered in Hertwig's title gives a true account of embryogenesis: it is true neither that the individual develops simply by enlarging a preformed entity, nor that the zygote is completely unstructured, with all differentiation coming from outside. Today epigenesis has come to mean studies of individual development as the result of complex interactions between the individual organism's genes, its internal environment, and its external environment. The study of epigenetic causal factors over the last twenty-five years has produced a much fuller under-standing of the causal forces at work on embryogenesis beyond the mere unfolding of a pregiven pattern. Despite the fact that the com-bination of genetic and epigenetic factors is now a basic part of bio-logical theory, the self-understanding of biology as a 'bottom–up alone' discipline has not been completely dislodged by the shift.

One of the by-products of the renewed focus on epigenesis was a series of new breakthroughs in developmental biology. Gene-governed processes, it was now clear, cannot fully explain the empir-ical facts of ontogenesis. The development of individual organisms involves the emergence of and interaction between functioning systems at multiple levels. Yet, if genetic causation is only part of the story, why is it that functionally similar adult organisms often develop, despite the fact that vastly different environmental influ-ences may be impacting the ontogenetic process? Old debates between genetic preformation and epigenesis have been replaced by a new 'interactionist consensus' regarding development—the view, as Robert puts it, 'that neither genes nor environments, neither nature nor nurture, suffices for the production of phenotypes'.[37] There is now wide acceptance of the core premises of 'the new interactionism': genes and experience together, in their ongoing interaction, are responsible for the structure, functions, and behaviours of living organisms from cells to primates. Gone is the mono-linear causal story presupposed at the middle of the last century: 'Genomes, or even individual strands of DNA— the system's understudy—do not exist in isolation from natural environments except in the pristine artificiality of the lab; more-over, . . . there are good reasons to believe that even the structure (let alone the functions) of strands of DNA cannot be understood in isolation from their organismal context' (Robert, *Embryology*, 4). There are, for example, multiple ways in which environmental and intracellular factors influence the baseline cell processes of transcribing and translating DNA.[38]

Even if the new interactionism answers the age-old philosophical problem of *nature versus nurture* with a resounding 'both!' it is only the beginning of an immense programme of scientific research. Biologically the question is not whether environmental factors influence gene expression—the ability of the environment to switch genes on and off is already well established—but exactly how the process works to produce complex behaviours in organisms.[39] For example, environmental factors play a crucial role in altering transposons, which then influence cellular meiosis and gamete formation by introducing random variations into genetic sequences, producing 'genetic drift'. Buchanan *et al.* write that

data indicate that transpositions are influenced by developmental and perhaps environmental signals and may play a role in the temporal and spatial patterns of gene expression. The possibility that they exist as simply extraneous sequences is unlikely. Instead, they may act as a complement of the genome, increasing its diversity and adaptability.[40]

Although it is a matter of dispute which (if any) of the philosophers' theories of emergence correctly describe this process, it is clear that the framework of emergence better describes the present theoretical picture than any of the alternatives:

Developmental biologists almost uniformly hold that development is hierarchical, characterized by the emergence of structures and processes not entirely predictable (let alone explicable) from lower-level (e.g., genetic) properties of the embryo. ... Developmental biologists, therefore, hold to a kind of physicalist antireductionism, offering the methodological advice that we must engage in multi-leveled investigation of ontogeny in order not to miss key features at micro levels, meso levels, and macro levels. (Robert, *Embryology*, 14).

Systems biology

The interactions between parts and wholes that occur in biological systems mirror the features of emergence that we observed in chemical processes. Yet to the extent that the evolution of organisms and ecosystems evidences a 'combinatorial explosion',[41] compounded by factors such as the four just summarized, the causal role of the emergent wholes is greatly strengthened. Natural systems are made up of interacting complex systems and form a multi-levelled network of interdependency,[42] with each level contributing distinct elements to the overall explanation. For this reason the hope of explaining entire living systems in terms of simple laws now appears quixotic.

The new systems approach to biology, the Siamese twin of genetics, has begun to establish the key features of life's 'complexity pyramid'.[43] Construing cells as networks of genes and proteins, systems biologists distinguish four distinct levels: (1) the base functional organization (genome, transcriptome, proteome and metabolome); (2) the metabolic pathways built up out of these components; (3) larger functional modules responsible for major cell functions; and (4) the large-scale organization that arises from the nesting of the functional modules. Oltvai and Barabási conclude that '[the] integration of different organizational levels increasingly forces us to view cellular functions as distributed among groups of heterogeneous components that all interact within large networks'. Milo *et al.* have recently shown that a common set of 'network motifs' occurs in complex networks in fields as diverse as biochemistry, neurobiology and ecology. As they note, 'similar motifs were found in networks that perform information processing, even though they describe elements as different as biomolecules within a cell and synaptic connections between neurons in *Caenorhabditis elegans*'.[44]

'Information biology', much touted as a separate approach a decade or so ago, now seems to have been incorporated into the theoretical framework of systems biology.[45] At least one no longer finds articles in *Nature* and *Science* that treat information theory as a separate branch of biology; the information content of genes, cells, and other systems is naturally studied as as intrinsic component of those systems. Thus Leroy Hood, president of the Institute for Systems Biology in Seattle, Washington, stresses that integrating many different kinds of information, ranging from DNA to gene expression to proteins and beyond, is a key component of systems biology. The study of biological systems 'is global, hypothesis and discovery driven, quantitative, integrative. . . . and it is iterative. . . . If you just study the results of DNA arrays, you're not doing systems biology'.[46] In chapter 2 I identified the existence of irreducible laws and causal structures as the main criterion for separate levels within nature. Now one might add *distinct levels of information coding, storage, and retrieval* to the list of criteria.

When analysing recent developments in biology it is easy to fall into either simplistic or triumphalist judgements. Thus the fledgling discipline of systems biology is touted by some as a victory for holism in biology. After all, it is argued, does not the crucial role of the systems perspective for understanding empirical systems spell the end for bottom-up explanation in biology, the collapse of genetically based explanations at what should have been their moment of greatest victory: the mapping of the human genome? But this is not quite right. It is true that the success of systems-biological explanations spells the end of one sort of programme: the 'bottom-up' derivation of all structures and behaviours from the building blocks of all-determining genes. But systems biology is in fact an *outgrowth* of the revolution in microbiology, not its replacement. Only by understanding the influence of genes on cellular functioning have biologists been able to advance to a systems perspective. It turned out, not surprisingly, that genes activated by biochemical reactions form signalling pathways, which then organize into networks or pathways. An adequate cell biology requires understanding the complex movements both upwards and downwards: not only how the genes set in motion signalling pathways between cells, but also how the dynamics of the pathways and networks of pathways in turn play a causal role in gene expression.

Understanding complex cellular and intercellular behaviours as a product of the *combination* of these upward and downward forces offers, I will suggest, crucial insights into the role of downward causation in nature. The standard physics-based model of the natural world, which serves as the basis for the doctrine known as 'physicalism', emphasizes the role of parts in constituting the behaviours of larger objects. Observed macro-patterns are explained as the effect of micro-laws operating on large numbers of parts, and the dynamics of the resulting aggregate are reconstructed as the product of the dynamics of the parts. Systems theory undercuts the downwardly reductionist influence of this physicalist model. Because systems-based explanations analyse the emergent dynamics of systems of systems, they resist a privileging of some ultimately foundational level of the 'real phenomena' and the 'real causes'. As Csete and Doyle write, 'Convergent evolution in both domains [biology and advanced technologies] produces modular architectures that are composed of elaborate hierarchies of protocols and layers of feedback regulation'.[47] In this sense, systems theory is a natural ally for biologists. For standard-model physics the goal is to deconstruct complex structures into the smallest possible parts; in comparison to biology much less emphasis is placed on multiple structural layers that are irreducible to one another. Biological evolution, by contrast, is intrinsically about higher-order structures—organisms—which though existing in their own right are also composed of (or hosts to) myriads of other biological structures: organs, cells, viruses, bacteria. 'Doing justice to the data' in biology requires one to describe and explain these interacting structures without reducing them away.

Given this task and the nature of the biosphere, it is natural to think of an organism as a system, which is itself composed of a series of interacting systems, which themselves are composed of systems of systems, and so forth. The biological sciences attempt to reconstruct the dynamics of these interlocking systems and to find the most adequate explanatory tools and concepts for comprehending their evolutionary history and behaviour. Because survival and reproduction are the key biological goals, the robustness of systems and organisms becomes a key explanatory category. Csete and Doyle define robustness as 'the preservation of particular characteristics despite uncertainty in components or the environment' (pp. 1663–4). Systems biologists have been able to show how modular design—subcomponents of a system that have enough integrity to function as subsystems on their own—contributes to robustness. Modules are linked by means of *protocols*, 'rules designed to manage relationships and processes smoothly and effectively' (ibid. 1666). Gene regulation, covalent modification, membrane potentials, metabolic and signal transduction pathways, action potentials, and DNA replication all can be understood to function as protocols in this fashion. For example, the DNA regulatory network works alongside other equally complicated systems to control functioning at the level of cells and cell systems. There is no Laplacian temptation here: 'even from the first-stage model, which just states the interactions that occur at each node' of the system, write Davidson *et al.*, 'there emerge system properties that can only be perceived at the network level'.[48]

The network perspective offers a variety of specific tools for understanding the dynamics of systems.[49] When the complex topology of networks is mapped and modelled on computers, analysis of the network models reveals scale-free properties (properties that hold for systems regardless of the size of the system). According to Barabási and Albert, this fact 'indicates that the development of large networks is governed by robust self-organizing phenomena that go beyond the particulars of the individual systems'.[50] The same principles of self-organization hold for phenomena ranging from molecular biology to computer science; they have been used to model the dynamics of the world wide web, of academic publishing, and of 'social groups, where vertices are individuals or organizations and the edges are the social interactions between them' (ibid. 510).

Despite the apparent power of this explanatory framework for explaining a wide variety of natural phenomena, one should be somewhat cautious about the initial results. Systems biology is in its infancy; the interconnections are massively complex, requiring interdisciplinary research groups which are expensive to fund;

and the complexity of the systems involved makes neat predictions unlikely. Even Csete and Doyle admit that modelling biological systems involves 'multiple feedback signals, non-linear component dynamics, numerous uncertain parameters, stochastic noise models, parasitic dynamics, and other uncertainty models' (p. 1668). Nonetheless, as a theoretical perspective, systems biology offers the most sophisticated understanding of cell and organismic function yet available. As Kitano notes, 'a transition is occurring in biology from the molecular level to the system level that promises to revolutionize our understanding of complex biological regulatory systems and to provide major new opportunities for practical application of such knowledge.'[51] To understand biology at the system level, Kitano insists, 'we must examine the structure and dynamics of cellular and organismal function rather than the characteristics of isolated parts of a cell or organism.'

TOWARD AN EMERGENTIST PHILOSOPHY OF BIOLOGY

In these pages I have traced a variety of cases of increasing complexity across the natural sciences. The emergence of conductivity, the emergence of cellularity, and the emergence of foraging behaviours are not identical; the three cases cannot be subsumed under a single covering law. Still, we have found fascinating family resemblances connecting the various cases. In so far as the conceptual features explored in the first two chapters apply across a large number of empirical disciplines, there is increasing evidence that emergence represents a fruitful philosophical (meta-scientific) framework for comparing the relations between these diverse realms of the natural world.[52] According to this picture, the one world exhibits different kinds of laws or propensities at different levels, and different kinds of causation are at work at the various levels. As Neil Campbell notes,

With each upward step in the hierarchy of biological order, novel properties emerge that were not present at the simpler levels of organization. These emergent properties arise from interactions between the components. . . . Unique properties of organized matter arise from how the parts are arranged and interact. . . [W]e cannot fully explain a higher level of organization by breaking it down to its parts.[53]

Science is in some ways constitutionally opposed to differences in kind. The scientific response to claims such as 'Chemistry cannot explain life' or 'Thought is qualitatively different from the brain' is 'Well, let's find out. Let's see just how far we can get in accounting for higher-order patterns in terms of the constituent parts of the system.' Many of the tensions between philosophers and scientists can be traced back to this fact. Faced with the data that life is different from non-life and thought from non-thought, philosophers work to give adequate conceptual descriptions of the differences between the three orders of existence. Faced with the emergence of living structures, scientists try to reconstruct how they could have formed out of non-living materials—ideally, by discovering laws such that, given the initial conditions and enough time, the formation of living cells was all but inevitable.[54] Given these divergent goals, the philosophy of biology, understood as a genuine dialogue between the two fields, can represent a difficult undertaking.

A successful dialogue between biology and philosophy requires that one begin with the biology, as we have done; only when the facts are on the table can one reflect on their philosophical significance. Thus, for example, whether there is a very large number of distinct levels within the biosphere, with subtle gradations between them, or whether only a smaller number of basic levels exists, is a matter for empirical study. Still, biology raises conceptual or philosophical questions that are not utterly without interest to biologists. The nature of living systems certainly falls into this category.

Systems and entities: the whole–part structure of explanation in biology

It is unfortunate that in recent years the explosion of knowledge in molecular biology has caused all of biology to be painted with a reductionist brush. In explaining the organisms and behaviours that one finds in living systems, the drive to uncover the mechanisms of inheritance is balanced by acute observations concerning the interaction of organisms and their environments. Fully adequate explanations of biological phenomena require the constant interplay of both bottom–up and top–down accounts. Genotypes produce phenotypes, specific organisms, in interaction with the environment; but in the end it is the fate of the phenotype that determines the fate of the genes.

Organisms exhibit novel individual responses to a wide variety of internal and external stimuli. Behavioural responses can only be described in terms of the interaction of organism and environment. Since these behaviours cannot be defined in physical terms, it is unwarranted to say that they are physically deterministic. In his text on phenotypes, Rollo insists that 'it is the integration of biological systems that is most crucial to evolutionary success [and that] the aspect most relevant to this is the interaction among subcomponents. . . . An emphasis on holism and organizational evolution generates interesting ideas that cannot be derived from a genetic, reductionist view'.[55] Only higher-level studies can explain why damselflies are brightly coloured, why viceroy butterflies look like monarchs, why crickets sing, and why acacia trees grow hollow thorns (ibid. 13). The mechanism of sexual reproduction exists because the interplay of the environment and phenotypic differences greatly increases the top–down effects of the environment on the evolution of a species (pp. 144–62). Holistic factors such as appearance, smell, and mate availability, not to mention desires experienced by the organisms, are the driving forces in sexual selection.

But sexual reproduction is only one example of biological explanations that turn on phenotypic flexibility. Variations among organisms play a key role in niche variation and in responses to environmental cues (of which there may be thousands). One must conclude that

organisms are highly complex systems characterized by intricate interactions among parts, that the integration of features and subsystems is highly specific (e.g. precise signals may be emitted by one component that are received and interpreted in specific ways by other components of the coadapted system), and that this integration itself is a primary target of natural selection. As Thompson. . . . remarked, interactions, although less tangible, must be considered to be evolutionary products as concrete as morphologies. (p. 6)

Not only are organisms irreducible units in biological explanation; they in turn cannot be treated in abstraction from their environments. The static conception of organisms is actually a fiction; organisms are in continual flux, adapting to environmental stimuli and striving for homeostasis.[56] Ecosystems, for their part, consist of 'a set of interlinked, differently scaled processes'.[57] Like the most elementary systems in cell biology, ecosystems function as coordinated sets of factors, with interrelationships between variables complex enough that they often need to be treated as qualitative units rather than as aggregates of factors. As Allen and Hoekstra note in *Toward a Unified Ecology*, 'the ecosystem is a much richer concept than just some meteorology, soil, and animals, tacked onto patches of vegetation'.[58]

Over time the organism-in-conjunction-with-its-environment will evolve in a highly coordinated fashion, as in the case of Darwin's finches, whose beaks, feathers, and coloration adapted to the particular niche environment of the Galapagos.[59] The sometimes dramatic effects of speciation are due to the same forces of coevolution.[60] Consider the famous example of the evolution of tassel-eared squirrels at the Grand Canyon. Because of the size of the geologic rift, 'the tassel-eared squirrels evolved into two separate species (the North Rim is about 7500 ft. in elevation with a wetter climate and classic ponderosa pine stands, the South Rim is about 5500 ft. in elevation with a drier climate and pinon-juniper stands) over time, such that their morphologies, eating habits, breeding patterns, and appearance are now wholly distinct'.[61] In other cases 'keystone species' can radically alter their own ecosystems, as in rats who effect grassland species densities and proportions or deer who, in the absence of significant predators, can severely impact native pine forest forage densities.[62] Nor are the effects limited to other species: carp literally change the physical characteristics of a river, and *homo sapiens* is capable of transforming ecosystems beyond all recognition.

Even these few brief examples are sufficient to convey a sense of the mode of explanation that characterizes the broader study of biology. Every ethologist and field biologist confronts immensely complex interrelated systems, and she must describe their visible causal interactions qualitatively and holistically. Her goal then becomes to model the system as she observes it using the most precise mechanisms and predictors that she can derive. Success comes not by ignoring the actual interacting units but by moving continually back and forth between bottom–up mechanisms and top–down descriptions of actual behaviours. Organisms are not merely shorthand for lower-level forces; they are, as the theory of strong emergence maintains, causal forces in their own right. In the end the explanatory goal is met only when one has been able to fuse the various levels of explanation together into a single integrated account of the biological world.

Purpose in biology

The biosphere represents a fantastic increase in complexity from the physical components out of which it emerges. Life forms absorb physical energy and use it to build complicated structures: DNA strands, cell walls, nerve fibres, eyes, brains. These in turn become agents, carrying out complicated behaviours in interaction with their environments. Although the second law of thermodynamics always wins in the end—the net result is an increase of entropy in the universe—the principles of life function in the opposite direction; they make major inroads in the overall progression towards thermodynamic equilibrium. This fact is significant to our project because an anentropic process is one that accomplishes an *increase in order*, whereas the (thermodynamically) typical process results in greater disorder. Autopoietic or 'self-forming' processes, which allow systems to create themselves as it were, are dramatic examples of natural mechanisms that produce exponential increases in order.[63] When in addition internal changes in biological entities themselves become productive of complex behaviours, and in particular when they enhance the organism's prospects for survival and reproduction, we speak of them as purposive behaviours.

Biological evolution does not make use of purpose as an overarching explanatory category; one does not speak of evolution as such as having purposes. A theologian can say if she wishes (though of course not as a biological statement) that there is a God, a supernatural intentional agent, who brings about purposes *through* natural history. But one cannot say that *nature itself* possesses such purposes—at least not without negating the basic principles of the biological sciences. Why? Biology cannot explicitly introduce conscious purpose into the evolutionary process because its ontology does not include any entities (prior to the higher primates, who arrive rather late in the evolutionary process) concerning which there are biological reasons to postulate conscious intentional actions. But this does not prevent the ascription of *proto-purposiveness* to biological agents. We might call it a theory of *purposiveness without purpose* in the emergence and behaviour of organisms.[64] The behaviour of organisms represents a middle instance between the non-purposiveness of chemical emergence and the fully intentional purposive behaviour of conscious agents. More accurately, instead of *a* middle instance we should speak of an unbroken series of middle instances between the chemical level and the conscious level. Primitive organisms do not consciously carry out purposes in the way an intentional agent does. Yet the parts of an organism (or organ or cell or ecosystem) work together for its survival. Growth, nurturance, and reproduction function *so that* the chances of the organism's survival, and thus the survival of its genotype, are maximized.

Eventually, a level evolved at which entities within the natural world became capable of acting according to explicit conscious purposes. Gradually there emerged conscious persons who could be affected by and affect other conscious beings, in a manner fully consistent with, though also going beyond, the laws of physics. This evolutionary achievement rests on the shoulders of innumerable gradual developments, much as the eye with its exact presentation of a field of vision is built on the countless varieties of heat and light sensors that preceded it. Thus 'mind' as we know it in human experience and interaction has important precursors in animals' perception of their environment and especially in the signs of a rudimentary awareness of the other as other in some higher primates (call it proto-mentality).[65] The same holds true for virtually every other human capacity: each one was rehearsed, if you will, tried out in draft form and honed through environmental feedback. As the primates developed more and more complex central nervous systems in response to their environments, they also gradually developed capacities unmatched elsewhere in the biosphere.

If this account is carried through consistently, it allows us to speak of human thoughts and intentions, human symbolic interactions, as a genuinely new level of experience and behaviour. And yet, like pre-human forms of activity within the biosphere, human thought is *also* conditioned by the regularities of physical law and by the quasi-intentional level of biological drives. Human thought is removed from any simple identity with 'pure spirit' not only by its close correlation with human brain states but also by its location within an organism which is determined by the various and sundry forms of organismic striving that are part of its evolutionary prehistory. Traces of these various drives and urges remain in our involuntary reflexes, our immune and limbic systems, in the body's regulation of hormones, and in the release and uptake of neurotransmitters and inhibitors in every synapse of our brains. Much of this complex history of origination is reflected in human DNA, which serves both as a historical overview of how we got here and as a constant reminder that each human capacity is built on the foundations of the less advanced biological capacities of our ancestors.

What natural history—the immense diversity of life forms running from primitive cells to the staggering complexity of the central nervous system in higher primates—teaches us, then, is that philosophers from Plato to Descartes (and many of the religious traditions) were wrong: there is no absolute dividing line between mind and matter. Human cognitive behaviours, purposes, and goals are anticipated in the quasi-purposive behaviour of earlier organisms. Dualism, it now appears, is a flatlands philosophy, one that disregards the depth of understanding provided by natural history. Yet, it turns out, the physicalists are equally mistaken in prioritizing the theoretical framework of physics. Their error is the mirror-image of the dualists' blindness to natural history. If the one group overemphasizes the distinctiveness of human cognition, the other fails to recognize it in the first place as a distinct explanatory category.

From the standpoint of the philosophy of biology, emergence represents a *tertium quid* between physicalism and dualism. It suggests a different picture from either one. As new entities continuously evolved within the biosphere, they progressively exhibited new ways of functioning that could not have been predicted from the point of view of earlier stages of development. The lesson here is *gradualism*: anentropic living systems display purposive behaviour not found in more simple systems, then gradually manifest more complex internal feedback loops and higher degrees of self-monitoring. With increasing complexity the central nervous systems of animals are able to contain more complex internal representations of the surrounding environment, to the point that a primitive internal theory of other minds begins to evolve.[66] The internalized world of symbols and representations that is consciousness emerges not long afterwards.[67]

Of course, one may wish to speak of human thought in terms of a more robust account of mental causation and agency; I turn to this debate in the next chapter. In either case, the biology of emergence suggests one caveat, which must be emphasized here: if irreducibly mental causation exists, it can only be fully understood in terms of a developmental story that includes the role of physical laws, biological drives, and the increasing spontaneity of behaviour in more complex organisms—features both shared with other animals and distinguishing us from them. Let me put the point differently: as evolution proceeds, organisms come to enjoy a latitude of choice, which increasingly differentiates them from non-living systems. As organisms grow more complex, they manifest spontaneous behaviours of greater frequency and complexity, to the degree that one must finally acknowledge a qualitative difference. Human decision making manifests this range and quality of choice in a manner that is both continuous *and* discontinuous with the stages of development out of which it evolved. In this respect, as in many others, human 'mind' can be seen as an isolated peak in the evolutionary landscape[68]—rising out of the foothills below it and yet clearly higher in elevation than anything else around.

The contention of qualitative difference is hotly debated, in part because of the disciplinary differences between biologists and philosophers mentioned above. Thus critics have often argued that the compounding of complexity—perhaps in the form of system-level features of networks, the nodes of which are themselves complex systems—represents only a *quantitative* increase in complexity, in which nothing 'really new' emerges. This is the view often referred to as 'weak emergence'; it is ably defended by (*inter alia*) John Holland and Stephen Wolfram, whose work I examined above.

Yet, as Leon Kass notes in the context of evolutionary biology, it never occurred to Darwin that 'certain differences of degree—produced naturally, accumulated gradually (even incrementally), and inherited in an unbroken line of descent—might lead to a difference in kind...'[69]

CONCLUSION

In these pages I have made the case for emergence in the realm of the natural sciences. When the natural process of compounding complex systems leads to irreducibly complex systems, with structures, laws, and causal mechanisms of their own, then one has evidence that reductive physicalist explanations will be inadequate. Cases of emergent systems in the natural world suggest that the resources of micro-physics cannot, even in principle, serve as an adequate explanatory framework for these phenomena.

We found that the scientific examples support both weak and strong emergence. The cases that support strong emergence are those in which it is meaningful to speak of whole-to-part or systemic causation. By contrast, in the cases where laws allow an explanatory reduction of the emergent system to its subvening system (in simulated systems, via algorithms; in natural systems, via 'bridge laws') the weak emergence interpretation suffices.

For reasons mentioned at the outset, scientists will prefer weak to strong emergence if the data are neutral between them. The strong view only rises to prominence if there are instances where the data cannot be adequately described by means of the model of passive whole–part constraint as opposed to active causal influence. In these instances, especially where we have reason to think that such lower-level rules are impossible in principle, the strong emergence interpretation is to be preferred. This is the case in at least some of the instances examined here.

I turn next to the examination of mental events and mental properties in their relationship to the biological systems in which they arise. For reasons I will discuss, these cases compel the strong interpretation even more than the biological cases do. Strong emergence—that is, emergence with mental causation—thus represents the most viable response to the mind–body problem. It has the merit of preserving common-sense intuitions about mental causation, thereby corresponding to our everyday experience as agents in the world. Moreover, the evolution of mental events without causal force would represent an unacceptable anomaly within evolutionary history: why expend the organism's valuable resources to produce *qualia* or experiential qualities if they have no causal role to play? Epiphenomenalism makes no evolutionary sense.

The borderline cases in the present chapter should thus be reconsidered on the basis of the outcome of the chapter that follows. This makes the two segments of the overall argument interdependent, and indeed in both directions. The strong emergence of mental causation provides additional impetus to grant the strong interpretation in the case of certain biological phenomena. At the same time, the evolutionary story that I have told in these pages must represent the horizon of interpretation for philosophers of mind. To conclude that both reductive physicalism and dualism are mistaken is to maintain that mind emerges through an evolutionary process. However novel mental events may be, they will never be fully understood apart from the details of this process.

NOTES

1. See C. P. Snow's famous essay on science and the humanities, *The Two Cultures*, 2nd edn. (Cambridge: Cambridge University Press, 1964).
2. For more detail see Philip Clayton and Paul Davies (eds.), *The Re-emergence of Emergence* (Oxford: Oxford University Press, 2006).
3. See Robert B. Laughlin, 'Nobel Lecture: Fractional Quantization', *Reviews of Modern Physics*, 71 (1999), 863-74. Perhaps the seminal article on emergence in physics is Phil W. Anderson, 'More is Different: Broken Symmetry and the Nature of the Hierarchical Structure of Science', 177 (4 Aug 1972), 393-6).

4. Wojciech Zurek, 'Decoherence and the Transition from Quantum to Classical—Revisited', *Los Alamos Science*, 27 (2002), 14. Cf. Wojciech Zurek, 'Decoherence and the Transition from Quantum to Classical', *Physics Today*, 44/10 (Oct. 1991), 36–44.

5. The physics of snow crystal formation is beautifully described at www.snowcrystals.com, a site maintained by the California Institute of Technology; see http://www.its.caltech.edu/~atomic/snowcrystals/ (verified 22 Feb. 2004).

6. The mathematics of fractals has been used in modelling naturally occurring systems not only in physics but also in biology, chemistry, economics, and studies of human behaviour. The field now has its own journal, *Fractals*, and is nicely summarized by *World Scientific*; see http://www.worldscinet.com/fractals/fractals.shtml (verified 22 Feb. 2004).

7. See G. K. Batchelor, *An Introduction to Fluid Dynamics* (Cambridge: Cambridge University Press, 2000).

8. See Arthur Peacocke, *God and the New Biology* (Gloucester, Mass.: Peter Smith, 1994), 153.

9. John Holland, *Emergence: From Chaos to Order* (Cambridge, Mass.: Perseus Books, 1998), 138.

10. Ibid. 194.

11. See George Ellis, 'True Complexity and its Associated Ontology', in John Barrow, Paul Davies, and Charles Harper, Jr. (eds.), *Science and Ultimate Reality: Quantum Theory, Cosmology, and Complexity* (Cambridge: Cambridge University Press, 2004).

12. Stephen Wolfram, *A New Kind of Science* (Champaign, Ill.: Wolfram Media, 2002), 352.

13. Holland, *Emergence*, 102.

14. Deborah M. Gordon, *Ants at Work: How an Insect Society is Organized* (New York: W. W. Norton, 2000), 141.

15. Deborah M. Gordon disputes this claim, ibid. 168. 'One lesson from the ants is that to understand a system like theirs, it is not sufficient to take the system apart. The behavior of each unit is not encapsulated inside that unit but comes from its connections with the rest of the system.' I likewise break strongly with the aggregate model of emergence below.

16. Ilya Prigogine, *Order out of Chaos: Man's New Dialogue with Nature* (New York: Bantam Books, 1984), 134.

17. Ibid. 152.

18. Physical chemist Arthur Peacocke notes how sensitive the Belousov-Zhabotinsky reactions are to the specific dimensions of the space in which they are confined: 'alter the size of the test-tube and all remains homogeneous!' (personal correspondence). For a detailed analysis of these and related phenomena, see Arthur Peacocke, *An Introduction to the Physical Chemistry of Biological Organization* (Oxford: Clarendon Press, 1983, 1989).

19. Stuart Kauffman, 'Whispers from Carnot: The Origins of Order and Principles of Adaptation in Complex Nonequilibrium Systems', in George Cowen,

David Pines, and David Meltzer (eds.), *Complexity: Metaphors, Models, and Reality* (Boulder, Colo.: Perseus Book Group, 1999), 90.

20. Prigogine, *Order out of Chaos*, 156.

21. Cyclic AMP also plays a crucial role as a precursor molecule that contributes to the process of the up or down-regulation of gene transcription. In this case cAMP, in combination with other enzymes, signals the cell to initiate transcription of phosphodiesterase, which is responsible for the conversion of cAMP into AMP. cAMP breakdown thus contributes to the inhibition of gene transcription. See James D. Watson *et al.*, *Molecular Biology of the Gene*, 4th edn. (Menlo Park, Calif.: Benjamin/Cummings, 1987), 478, and Gerhard Michal (ed.), *Biochemical Pathways: An Atlas of Biochemistry and Molecular Biology* (New York: John Wiley & Sons, 1999), 131.

22. See Stuart Kauffman, *Investigations* (New York: Oxford University Press, 2000); Kauffman, *At Home in the Universe: The Search for Laws of Self-Organization and Complexity* (New York: Oxford University Press, 1996); Brian Goodwin, *How the Leopard Changed its Spots: The Evolution of Complexity* (Princeton, N.J.: Princeton University Press, 2001); Christian de Duve, *Vital Dust* (New York: Basic Books, 1995); Murray Gell-Mann, *The Quark and the Jaguar: Adventures in the Simple and the Complex* (New York: W. H. Freeman & Co., 1994), and Simon Conway Morris, *Life's Solution: Inevitable Humans in a Lonely Universe* (Cambridge: Cambridge University Press, 2003). See also Cowen *et al.*, *Complexity*, along with other works in the same series.

23. Kauffman, *Investigations*, 35.

24. Holland, *Emergence*, 201.

25. Roger Lewin, *Complexity: Life at the Edge of Chaos*, 2nd edn. (Chicago: University of Chicago Press, 1999), 13.

26. Kauffman, *Investigations*, 191.

27. Wayne G. Landis and Ming-Ho Yu, *Introduction to Environmental Toxicology*, 3rd edn. (New York: Lewis Publishers, 2004), 381.

28. Rupert Sheldrake, *A New Science of Life: The Hypothesis of Morphic Resonance* (Rochester, Vt.: Park Street Press, 1981, 1995).

29. Wolfram, *New Kind of Science*, 357–60; see his index for dozens of further examples of nesting.

30. See Terrence Deacon, 'The Hierarchic Logic of Emergence: Untangling the Interdependence of Evolution and Self-Organization', in Bruce H. Weber and David J. Depew (eds.), *Evolution and Learning: The Darwin Effect Reconsidered* (Cambridge, Mass.: MIT Press, 2003), 273–308.

31. Ibid. 297, emphasis added.

32. The philosophical, even metaphysical, preoccupation of Dawkins's work is clear from his titles: *The Blind Watchmaker: Why the Evidence of Evolution Reveals a Universe without Design* (New York: Norton, 1987); *A Devil's Chaplain: Reflections on Hope, Lies, Science, and Love* (Boston: Houghton Mifflin Co., 2003).

33. Quoted in Jason Scott Robert, *Embryology, Epigenesis, and Evolution: Taking Development Seriously* (Cambridge: Cambridge University Press, 2004), 1. See esp. ch. 4, 'Constitutive Epigenetics'.

34. Stephen J. Gould and R. C. Lewontin, 'The Spandrels of San Marco and the Panglossian Paradigm: A Critique of the Adaptationist Programme', in *Proceedings of the Royal Society of London*, Series B, *Biological Sciences* ('The Evolution of Adaptation by Natural Selection'), 205 (1979), 581–98.

35. See Niles Eldridge and Stephen J. Gould, 'Punctuated Equilibria: An Alternative to Phyletic Gradualism', in T. J. M. Schopf (ed.), *Models in Paleobiology* (San Francisco, CA: W. H. Freeman, Cooper 1972).

36. See E. O. Wilson, *Sociobiology: The New Synthesis* (Cambridge, Mass.: Harvard University Press, 1975).

37. Robert, *Embryology*, 2.

38. See Watson *et al.*, *Molecular Biology*, 519–22. These epigenetic effects include DNA transcriptional modifications and/or activation/suppression, mRNA modification, tRNA modification, or genetic excising (cutting the gene into parts). Most involve the action of multiple independent enzymatic processes, which require the activity of other catalytic enzymes as well as their own genetic controls. Michal, *Biochemical Pathways*, 150, lists ten different repressor and promoter elements in the human genome which function as responses to environmental conditions.

39. See Matt Ridley, *Nature via Nurture: Genes, Experience, and What makes us Human* (New York: HarperCollins, 2003), and the review by Kevin N. Laland, 'The New Interactionism', *Science*, 300 (20 June 2003), 1879–80.

40. Bob Buchanan, Wilhelm Gruissem, and Russell Jones, *Biochemistry and Molecular Biology of Plants* (Somerset, NJ: John Wiley & Sons, 2000), 337.

41. Harold Morowitz, *The Emergence of Everything: How the World Became Complex* (New York: Oxford University Press, 2002).

42. Cf. Niels Henrik Gregersen (ed.), 'From Anthropic Design to Self-Organized Complexity', in *Complexity to Life: On the Emergence of Life and Meaning* (Oxford: Oxford University Press, 2003).

43. Zoltán Oltvai and Albert-László Barabási, 'Life's Complexity Pyramid', *Science*, 298 (2002), 763-4; for a popularized presentation see Albert-László Barabási, *Linked: The New Science of Networks* (Cambridge, Mass.: Perseus Books, 2002).

44. R. Milo *et al.*, 'Network Motifs: Simple Building Blocks of Complex Networks', *Science*, 298 (2002), 824–7.

45. See Hubert Yockey, *Information Theory and Molecular Biology* (Cambridge: Cambridge University Press, 1992). This is not to say that discussions of the nature of biological information have become less important. For a sample of the recent discussion, see Werner Loewenstein, *The Touchstone of Life: Molecular Information, Cell Communication, and the Foundations of Life* (New York: Oxford University Press, 1999); Mike Holcombe and Ray Paton (eds.) *Information Processing in Cells and Tissues* (New York: Plenum Press, 1998); Susan Oyama, *The Ontogeny of Information: Developmental Systems and Evolution*, 2nd edn. (Durham NC: Duke University Press, 2000); and Roland Baddeley, Peter Hancock, and Peter Földiák (eds.), *Information Theory and the Brain* (Cambridge: Cambridge University Press, 2000).

46. Mignon Fogarty, 'Systems Biology has its Backers and Attackers', *The Scientist*, (6 October 2003); http://www.the-scientist.com/yr2003/oct/research3_031006.html, verified 20 Jan 2004. Hood speaks of 'all these people who say they've been doing systems biology for years and years'. In one sense, this is true: biological research has been as global as the technologies have allowed. But, Hood complains, many researchers claiming to have done systems biology have in fact looked closely at the interactions between small numbers of genes, or they have used arrays to look broadly at one-dimensional information such as genes or proteins.

47. Marie E. Csete and John C. Doyle, 'Reverse Engineering of Biological Complexity', *Science*, 295 (1 Mar 2002), 1664–9, p. 1664.

48. Eric H. Davidson *et al.*, 'A Genomic Regulatory Network for Development', *Science*, 295 (1 Mar 2002), 1669–78, p. 1677.

49. In many ways network theory has replaced the older theory of hierarchies; see Howard H. Pattee (ed.), *Hierarchy Theory: The Challenge of Complex Systems* (New York: George Braziller, 1973).

50. Albert-László Barabási and Reka Albert, 'Emergence of Scaling in Random Networks', *Science*, 286 (15 Oct 1999), 509–12, p. 509.

51. Hiroaki Kitano, 'Systems Biology: A Brief Overview', *Science*, 295 (1 Mar 2002), 1662–4. Cf. Hiroaki Kitano, *Foundations of Systems Biology* (Cambridge, Mass.: MIT Press, 2001).

52. I am indebted to Steven Knapp for discussions that influenced the argument and some of the formulations that follow.

53. Neil Campbell, *Biology* (Redwood City, Calif.: Benjamin Cummings, 1991), 2–3, quoted in George Ellis's contribution to Robert J. Russell, Nancey Murphy, and Arthur Peacocke (eds.), *Chaos and Complexity* (Vatican City: Vatican Observatory Publications, 1995), 362. Ellis comments, 'Indeed, not only are such different levels of description permitted, they are required in order to make sense of what is going on' (ibid.).

54. See David W. Deamer and Gail R. Fleischaker, *Origins of Life: The Central Concepts* (Boston: Jones & Bartlett, 1994).

55. C. David Rollo, *Phenotypes: Their Epigenetics, Ecology, and Evolution* (London: Chapman & Hall, 1995), 397–8.

56. See J. Baird Callicot, 'From the Balance of Nature to the Flux of Nature', in Richard L. Knight and Suzanne Riedel (eds.), *Aldo Leopold and the Ecological Conscience* (Oxford: Oxford University Press, 2002), 90–105.

57. T. F. H. Allen and T. W. Hoekstra, *Toward a Unified Ecology* (New York: Columbia University Press, 1992), 98–100, quoted in Callicott, 'Balance of Nature', 101.

58. Ibid.

59. See Everett C. Olson and Jane Robinson, *Concepts of Evolution* (Columbus, Ohio: Charles E. Merrill, 1975), 138–40. The Manchester moths (148–50) are an equally famous example.

60. Andrew Cockburn, *An Introduction to Evolutionary Ecology* (Oxford: Blackwell Scientific Publications, 1991), e.g. 234–46.

61. Zachary Simpson, personal communication. Simpson notes that most ecologists conceive of nature 'as a stochastic system with multiple asymptotic and irreducible variables which together constitute a whole that is greater than the parts'.

62. For further examples see Ernst-Detlef Schulze and Harold A. Mooney (eds.), *Biodiversity and Ecosystem Function* (Berlin: Springer-Verlag, 1994), 237–47.

63. See Milan Zeleny (ed.), *Autopoiesis: Dissipative Structures, and Spontaneous Social Orders* (Boulder, Colo.: Westview Press, 1980); John Mingers, *Self-Producing Systems: Implications and Applications of Autopoiesis* (New York: Plenum Press, 1995); Humberto Maturana, *Autopoiesis and Cognition: The Realization of the Living* (Dordrecht: D. Reidel, 1980). See also Niels Henrik Gregersen, 'The Idea of Creation and the Theory of Autopoietic Processes', *Zygon*, 33 (1998), 333–68; Gregersen, 'Autopoiesis: Less than Self-Constitution, More than Self-Organization: Reply to Gilkey, McClelland and Deltete, and Brun', *Zygon*, 34 (1999), 117–38.

64. One increasingly finds theorists who do not shy away from invoking the category of purpose in explaining animal behaviours. See Colin Allen, Marc Bekoff, and George Lauder (eds.), *Nature's Purposes: Analyses of Function and Design in Biology* (Cambridge, Mass.: MIT Press, 1998) and Michael Denton, *Nature's Destiny: How the Laws of Biology Reveal Purpose in the Universe* (New York: Free Press, 1998). But see also Michael Ruse, *Darwin and Design: Does Evolution have Purpose?* (Cambridge, Mass.: Harvard University Press, 2003): purposes must not be ascribed to evolution as such, but only to organisms within the biological world.

65. For a summary see John Cartwright, *Evolution and Human Behavior* (Cambridge Mass.: MIT Press, 2000).

66. See R. Byrne, *The Thinking Ape* (Oxford: Oxford University Press, 1995); cf. Cartwright, *Evolution and Human Behavior*, 178–83.

67. See Terrence Deacon, *The Symbolic Species: The Co-evolution of Language and the Brain* (New York: W. W. Norton, 1997).

68. Human mental and affective experience is isolated by the conditions of natural law and biological drive, and perhaps also by human free agency.

69. Leon Kass, *The Hungry Soul: Eating and the Perfecting of Our Nature* (Chicago: University of Chicago Press, 1999), 62.

4

Emergence and Mind

It is not possible to engage in reflection on the relationship of mind and brain without considering the evolutionary history that produced brains in the first place. Or rather, it is certainly possible, since many have written treatises in the philosophy of mind without considering evolution. A dualist might well conclude that she is not required to consider evolution since, however the brain got here, thought is something qualitatively different from it, being only contingently dependent (at most) on brain states. Strictly speaking, a physicalist philosopher might also think that he can dispense with evolutionary history, since the details of the brain as a biological system are of only contingent interest; what matters finally is to complete the structure of understanding upwards from its foundational microphysical laws and processes.

More accurately, then, I should have said: it is not possible to write an *emergence* theory of the mind–brain relation, understood as a position distinct from both dualism and physicalism, without simultaneously exploring the topic of other emergent structures in evolutionary history. If one holds that thought is the only causal force not reducible to physics that has emerged in the natural world, then one should be a dualist; and if one holds that there are no emergent causal forces in the world, one remains a physicalist. In brief, the distinctiveness of the emergentist thesis lies in its claim that the natural world exhibits a variety of levels at which distinct types of laws and causes can be recognized. The argument in the present chapter is therefore dependent on the success of the case made in the immediately preceding pages. Understanding the relationship between mind and brain—between consciousness and its neural correlates—requires understanding the multi-levelled structure of the natural world. On this view, the appearance of mental causes is, in one sense, just another case of emergence— just another case in which a complicated natural system gives rise to unexpected causal patterns and properties. Of course, these particular phenomena matter in a very personal sense to us humans; to us they don't seem to be 'just another level'. Indeed, that fact— that subjective experiences *matter*, and matter to us *as persons*—is a crucial datum that an adequate philosophy of mind dare not disregard.

In another sense, I will suggest, mind is not just another emergent phenomenon. In the previous chapter we found that some of the biological cases stand on the boundary between weak and strong emergence. I argued that the strong interpretation does better justice to biology as a whole, given that emergent systems are not just aggregates of microphysical states but cells and organisms—the agents that populate the biosphere and that serve as individualized objects of study for many biologists. Still, I had to admit that at least some of the scientific cases could be read either way. In the case of mental phenomena, I will now argue, the ambiguity disappears: one cannot make sense of mental causation except from the standpoint of strong emergence. If the strong emergence interpretation of mental causes is not correct, one should be an epiphenomenalist about mind, that is, one should hold that mind has no effect on the world. To the extent that one thinks that epiphenomenalism is a conclusion to be avoided, to that extent one has reason for endorsing strong emergence.

THE THREE LEVELS OF EMERGENCE

First, however, a recap. We have encountered a very wide range of emergent phenomena across the natural sciences. One would have to present and analyse a staggering range of empirical data in order fully to understand what is at work at each of these various stages of cosmic evolution. Is there any way to bring order into such an immense subject? The answer depends on what principle one uses in comparing the instances. The principle most often used in the literature—correlating emergence with increasing complexity (of structure, of behaviour, of language usage)—is indispensable, since it brings a metric, a quantitative measure, to the process (for example, we can measure linguistic complexity in terms of syntactic richness, vocabulary, etc.). At the same time, quantitative measures fail to explain the 'breaks' in the process at which qualitatively new behaviours or experiences arise. At least at first blush, success in establishing quantitative comparisons, to the extent that we achieve them, might seem to rule out a qualitative characterization of the results of the sort defended by the strong emergence thesis. Or, to put the concern differently, one might acknowledge many instances of emergence, but if each is *sui generis* no general theory of emergence will follow.

Beyond summarizing individual examples of emergence, then, I looked for broad patterns that would link together multiple instances of emergence within the natural world. Pursuing this strategy meant giving up the more rigorous criterion of a quantitative measure. At the same time, moving to a more qualitative analysis and a certain level of conceptual abstraction allowed for the recognition of broader similarities in the natural world. Two patterns stood out in particular.

First, the emergence of life used to be treated as a single distinct ontological change: at one point there were only inorganic materials, and at the next (distinct) moment, there were life forms. This construal of the living/nonliving distinction, we saw, has not stood up to recent results. Biochemists such as Gerald Joyce and Jeffrey Bada argue that, given the structure of the heavy elements, the arising of life, at least on earth, was not improbable. Bada argues that life began as a 'boundary-less soup of replicating molecules'; only later did the first membranes arise by chance. Joyce defines life as 'a self-sustain[ing] chemical system capable of undergoing Darwinian evolution'. If the biochemists are right, the boundary between living and nonliving things is much more porous than we thought in the past; the line between them is a hazy one, and motion across it can occur in a much more gradual fashion than we once thought.[1]

But even if the line of distinction is not completely clear—some characteristics of viruses link them more closely to the nonliving, other characteristics to the living world—there are still broad characteristics shared by organisms throughout the biosphere and throughout evolutionary history. Growth and development, homeostatis, reproduction, and controlled energy exchange with the environment are shared features of living organisms; equally fundamental is the fact that change over time is controlled by a process of evolutionary adaptation. These features are so basic that there is some temptation to call them *meta-emergent properties*. (However, since no firm conceptual or empirical distinctions can be drawn between emergent and meta-emergent properties, this locution should be used cautiously.) Empirically, following the lead of Morowitz, it may be more accurate to analyse life not in terms of a single moment of emergence, but rather as a sort of family resemblance that ties together a large number of individual emergent steps.

A second broad area of family resemblance had to do with self-awareness. Self-awareness in the biological sense involves not just the monitoring of the external environment (a function too easily confused with perception) but also the monitoring of the organism's own internal states and the modification of its behaviours as a result. The self-reflexivity of this feedback loop has been fruitfully explored by Terrence Deacon.[2] Some also distinguish reflective self-awareness from generic self-awareness as a separate area of family resemblance. As the name implies, reflective self-awareness requires the ability to monitor one's own self-monitoring. If the feedback loop of self-awareness is a second-order phenomenon, then, as several writers in the field have pointed out, reflective self-awareness becomes a third-order phenomenon: being aware of *how* you are aware. Using more strongly mental predicates, we could describe it as knowing that one is thinking, or knowing one's own thoughts, or knowing that one is experiencing certain *qualia* (felt experiences). This interpretation reflects the fact that sensation and knowing, at least in a pre-conscious sense, occur relatively early in biological development, with conscious knowing building upon them at a later stage. Thus Rodney Cotterill argues that the bacterium *E. gracilis* evidences cognition, since it modifies its behaviour based on what it discovers in its environment:

Indeed, one could say that it *knows* things about its environment, even though that knowing is unconscious knowing. This would be a more useful description of the situation because it would emphasize that knowing need not be conceptually linked to consciousness. One could then go on to speculate whether *consciousness requires the more sophisticated feat of knowing that one knows*. This, indeed, will be the line taken here.[3]

INTRODUCING THE PROBLEM OF CONSCIOUSNESS

It is unwise to dive into the tumultuous waters of the contemporary mind–body debate without first acknowledging how dangerous they are. (They may not be crocodile-infested, but they are certainly cluttered with the wreckage of previous constructive attempts.) Only through understanding the full severity of the problem can one begin to recognize clues that point towards the answer.

The first problem lies in the idea of mind itself. In a sense, of course, it is uncontentious that mental *properties* have emerged in the course of natural history; anyone who comprehends this sentence has already conceded the point. Yet asserting the existence of minds is clearly not the same as asserting the existence of cells. If someone asserts the existence of a thing called 'mind', has she not broken irrevocably with scientific method, with anything that a natural scientist could establish or verify? Yet if someone denies the existence of mind, has he not broken just as fatally with common sense?

The dilemma reveals how significant is the difference between conceiving mind as a property and mind as an object. Considering the mind as an object invites charges of dualism, since (as Descartes argued) an object that is non-physical, immaterial, not composed out of parts, and not located in space and time must be a different kind of thing altogether, which he called *res cogitans*. (The same is also true of that other type of dualism which is implied by the Aristotelian-Thomistic concept of the soul as the form of the body.) Given the greater, and perhaps insuperable, difficulties raised by talking about minds as things, at least in the context of the scientific study of the world—and given that it is already difficult enough to speak of mental properties without falling into epiphenomenalism—it is far preferable to limit our theory of the mental to mental properties: complex, emergent properties ascribed to the brain as their object. After all, we have no problem locating brains among the furniture of the universe and parsing them in terms of our knowledge of the physical world, whereas modern thought has been consistently stymied by the challenge of integrating mind-talk with the methods and results of science.

Yet limiting oneself to mental-talk as properties-talk doesn't remove all the tensions either. Mental properties are so radically different in kind, it appears, from the brains that are said to produce them that linking the two conceptually—or causally, for that matter—seems well nigh impossible. The initial scepticism about emergence often arises at this point. At the outset many assume that consciousness is an obvious example of an emergent phenomenon. Here if anywhere, it seems, nature has produced something irreducible: no matter how strong the biological dependence of conscious experiences on antecedent states of the central nervous system, the two could never be equivalent. To know everything there is to know about the progression of brain states is not to know what it is like to be you, to experience your joy, your pain, or your insights. No human researcher can know, as Thomas Nagel so famously argued, 'what it's like to be a bat'.[4]

Unfortunately, consciousness, however intimately familiar we may be with it on a personal level, remains an almost total mystery from a scientific perspective. Indeed, as Jerry Fodor once noted, 'Nobody has the slightest idea how anything material could be conscious. Nobody even knows what it would be like to have the slightest idea about how anything material could be conscious. So much for the philosophy of consciousness'.[5] Given the difficulty of the transition from brain states to consciousness, one might worry with Colin McGinn that we face here an irresolvable mystery.[6] The slide towards incommensurability begins even if consciousness is sufficiently different from the neural states with which it is said to correlate, and it may become insoluble if the consciousness as an emergent is qualitatively different from other cases of natural emergence.

THE NEURAL CORRELATES OF CONSCIOUSNESS

How far can the neurosciences go, even in principle, in explaining consciousness? Given the difficulties I have just reviewed, it is clear that the project faces two different dangers right from the outset. It must not accept a definitional equivalence between brain and mind, an identity of mental states with brain states, lest the difference of the mental as we experience it be lost ('consciousness explained away', to paraphrase Daniel Dennett's opponents); but nor can it make the difference between brain and mind too great, lest the obvious dependence of mental states on brain states go unexplained.

If one is attempting to begin with the neurosciences, yet with an eye to the question of consciousness, there is an obvious place to start: with those data and theories that have as their goal to understand *the neural correlates of consciousness* (NCC). Following this method, one presupposes—as seems hard to deny—that consciousness is associated with specific neural activities. These neural firings and action potentials, taking place in a brain with a particular structure and history, play a causal role in producing the phenomena of our first-person world: the experiences of pain or sadness or knowing that $6 \times 7 = 42$ or longing for world peace. Approaching the problem of consciousness via the study of NCC is no less plausible for the fact that the theorists working in this area often disagree radically on methods and results.

This focus allows us to explore some of the specific types of NCC scientists are now beginning to discover and to explain. It is an exciting time in the study of cognition and awareness. New brain-scanning techniques are providing data on NCC that was previously unavailable; one has the sense that the growing body of knowledge about awareness, especially visual awareness, is providing the building blocks for an empirical study of consciousness where once only philosophers' speculations reigned. With the prospect of increasing amounts of data, the current proliferation of theories about NCC need not be a matter of concern; they are (or: one hopes they will become) a series of testable hypotheses, or at least the outlines of research programmes that can be judged by their fruitfulness in explaining neuronal activity and conscious experience. The currently proliferating hypotheses involve studies of the specific properties and firing patterns of individual neurons (such as Koch's 'grandmother neurons'), of groups of neurons, and of broad integrated systems within the brain.

I limit my survey to nine important proposals, all of which (with the exception of Libet) have been advanced over the last ten years or so:

1. Benjamin Libet's early work first suggested that awareness was a later, emergent product of brain activity. In his well-known experiments, the thalamus of human subjects was stimulated, and the subject was asked to identify when the stimulus had occurred. Even when the stimulus was too brief for the subjects to be consciously aware of it, they could perform significantly better than chance when asked to 'guess', and then to signal, when the stimulus had occurred. By contrast, 'To become aware of the stimulus (even if this awareness was somewhat uncertain) required a significantly longer train. . . . Libet and his colleagues interpreted this as implying that a certain duration of the pulse train was needed for awareness.'[7] Awareness of touch and pain on the part of the subject, it turns out, emerges in a highly predictable fashion: 'In short, in the somatosensory system, a weak or brief signal can influence behavior without producing awareness, while a stronger or longer one of the same type can make awareness occur.'[8] Stephen Kosslyn nicely summarizes the result: 'Benjamin Libet and his colleagues find that conscious experiences reliably lag behind the brain events that

presumably evoke them. This finding suggests that the "chord" takes time to establish, even after all the "notes" are present.'[9]

2. Since Libet's experiments, a wealth of other instances of accurate perception below the threshold of awareness have been explored. Perhaps the most famous are the blindsight experiments. These involve cases of subjects with damage to the primary visual cortex (specifically in V1, the striate cortex). When the patients are asked to point to the location of a light that appeared in the damaged part of their perceptual field, they can do so with a high degree of accuracy, even though they have no conscious awareness of having perceived the light at all. In these cases, apparently, even though the damage is sufficient to inhibit awareness, the subject is still able to point reliably in the direction of the light source, since enough neural pathways remain intact for motor output to occur.[10]

3. Prosopagnosia, or the inability to recognize faces, serves as another example in this genre.[11] As Francis Crick reports, 'While hooked up to a lie detector and shown sets of both familiar and unfamiliar faces, the patients are unable to say which faces were familiar, yet the lie detector clearly showed that the brain was making such a distinction even though the patients were unaware of it. Here again we have a case where the brain can respond to a visual feature without awareness.'[12]

4. Crick hypothesizes that the neural activity responsible for awareness begins in the lower cortical layer, specifically layers 5 and 6. Perceptions and computations that are occurring in other regions of the brain cause firings in this region. These specific firings, he thinks, are the neural correlate of awareness. More controversially, Crick has suggested that a particular type of neuron, the large 'bursty' pyramidal cells in layer 5, which often project outside the cortical system altogether, may be the actual carriers of consciousness.[13] In other work, he has concentrated on thalamic connections, suggesting that reverberating circuits with a sufficient degree of projection (in cortical layers 4 and 6, he thinks) are the key correlates to consciousness.[14] As we come to understand attentional mechanisms and very short-term memory, he suggests, we will begin to understand the experience of awareness.

5. Christof Koch emphasizes that consciousness must have a biological function, or it would not have evolved as it has. Central for him is the planning function. Each major brain function (e.g. vision) projects into the prefrontal cortex, where the planning function is carried out. This particular suggestion by Koch for the

NCC is particularly intriguing because it moves beyond one-to-one correlations of neurons and consciousness, opting instead for a function-based account that involves, albeit implicitly, the broader process of emergence in natural history. Unfortunately, however, Koch has also sought to associate consciousness with very specific groups of neurons, on analogy with the famous (or notorious) concept of 'grandmother neurons', that is, neurons that fire only when presented with a very specific stimulus such as seeing one's own grandmother.[15]

6. Exploring the hypothesis of a specific region and function, Bernard Baars defends a position he calls 'global workspace theory'. According to this hypothesis, conscious and unconscious neural events are compared on a frequent basis in this posited 'workspace'. Baars uses workspace theory to account for binocular rivalry, blindsight, selective visual attention, and parietal neglect.[16]

7. Often, at least until recently, the literature seemed to divide into two opposing camps, the one arguing that consciousness is a holistic function of the brain, the other that it is the product of specific types of neurons, groups of neurons, or areas of the brain. With their theory of the 'unconscious homunculus' Crick and Koch have thrown down the gauntlet against the either/or. They build on a suggestion first made by Fred Attneave, whose article 'In Defense of Homunculi' had posited multiple processing systems in the brain: hierarchical sensory processing, an affect system, a motor system, and a system he labelled 'H' for 'homunculus'. As Crick and Koch summarize, this 'H' system 'is reciprocally connected to the perceptual machinery at various levels in the hierarchy, not merely the higher ones. It receives input from the affective centers and projects to the motor machinery.'[17] Attneave had located the homunculus system in a subcortical area such as the reticular formation. Crick and Koch's innovation is to imagine the homunculus to be unconscious, with only a partial representation in consciousness. This preserves its planning function, its integration function, and its decision function, while insisting that only some of these activities are represented in images and speech. This new proposal builds (as they admit) on the so-called intermediate-level theory of consciousness advanced by Ray Jackendoff. Not long ago Jackendoff postulated three different cognitive domains: the brain, the computational mind, and the phenomenological mind. Likewise, Crick and Koch's view allows for computations and even planning to be carried out in a largely unconscious fashion, with only partial

representations of these activities making it into consciousness. If they are right, our entire subjective experience may be the product of only a relatively small number of neurons—though, as they admit, 'how these act to produce the subjective world that is so dear to us is still a complete mystery' (p. 109).

8. Wolf Singer argues that the content of conscious experience is represented 'implicitly' by *dynamically associated assemblies*. He looks in particular at the synchronization of responses in groups of neurons, arguing that they are the brain phenomena most suitable for the occurrence of awareness.[18] Consider the list of Singer's assumptions, which are widely shared by neuroscientists publishing in this field—at least until he begins to try to explain exactly *how* assemblies of neurons would have to function together if they are to produce awareness (I omit the later assumptions in his list, since they would win even less unanimity):

(a) phenomenal awareness necessitates and emerges from the formation of metarepresentations; (b) the latter are realized by the addition of cortical areas of higher order that process the output of lower-order areas in the same way as the latter process their respective input; (c) in order to account for the required combinatorial flexibility, these metarepresentations are implemented by the dynamic association of distributed neurons into functionally coherent assemblies rather than by individual specialized cells; (d) the binding mechanism that groups neurons into assemblies and labels their responses as related is the transient synchronization of discharges with a precision in the millisecond range . . .[19]

9. Further progress towards understanding has been made in a series of recent publications by Edelman and Tononi. They accept a fundamentally emergentist view of consciousness, with a stress on its holistic features: 'each conscious state is an indivisible whole' and 'each person can choose among an immense number of different conscious states'.[20] But—especially as they develop the position in their article 'Consciousness and Complexity'—it is a holism that results from increasing complexity. To attempt to derive conscious experience from a single (type of) neuron is a category mistake: consciousness is the wrong *kind* of property to associate with a single neuron firing.

What kind of a neurological property, then, is consciousness? Edelman and Tononi emphasize two of its features: 'conscious experience is integrated (each conscious scene is unified) and at the same time it is highly differentiated (within a short time, one can experience any of a huge number of different conscious states)'.[21]

But both integration and differentiation can be quantified. The authors develop two tools for measuring them: functional clustering for measuring integration, and neural complexity for measuring differentiation. The results of their detailed analysis are potentially significant: conscious states turn out to be the informationally most complex states, since they reflect 'the coexistence of a high degree of functional specialization and functional integration'.[22] What is surprising about their position is that it postulates a relatively small neural system, which they call the 'dynamic core', as responsible for consciousness, rather than construing consciousness as a correlate of much more global brain states.

CAN STUDIES OF NEURAL CORRELATES SOLVE THE PROBLEM OF CONSCIOUSNESS?

The goal of a successful theory of consciousness is to remove the apparent opposition between neuroscientific accounts and first-personal descriptions of conscious experience. Clearly, the empirical search for the neural correlates of consciousness that I have just been exploring is a step towards such a theory. But is it sufficient?

Any account of consciousness faces two major challenges. It must explain what role brain structures and processes play in higher order cognitive functions, and it must account for our own lived experience of the conscious life. The family of positions currently being debated under the heading of emergence theories responds to these challenges with the claim that *conscious phenomena are properties that emerge only through the functioning of increasingly complex neurological systems*. Now I am not certain that emergence theory would be falsified if awareness turns out to be correlated with one particular type of neuron or with a small group of neurons. But to the extent that emergence theories depend upon complex systemic phenomena, involving large brain regions or (some argue) the brain as a whole, the standard defence of the position would certainly be undercut by a non-holistic neuroscience of consciousness.

The classical expression of the emergentist view in neuroscience is found in the later work of Roger Sperry (see Chapter 1, above), which interpreted mind as an emergent property of the brain as a whole. This assumption that novel qualities emerge only from a system taken as a whole links Sperry's influential position to the whole–part framework that we repeatedly encountered in earlier chapters. Sperry's position amounts to the prediction that only when the brain is understood as a single integrated system—say, at the level of the sum total of the distributed systems that are relevant to a particular cognitive function—will we be able to give an adequate account of the nature of mind. To view a system as a whole does not negate the study of its individual parts, as some holistic, New Age theories of mind would have it. Rather, it directs attention to those systemic effects that apparently involve more than an aggregation of the effects of the system's parts.

The 'dynamical systems approach', for example, shifts attention from the neuronal level to broader brain systems as the physiological correlate for the emergence of mental states. This commitment connects it in theory to the recent work in systems biology that I examined in the previous chapter—a connection that has not yet been much explored in the literature. In one (admittedly speculative) reconstruction, Hardcastle writes:

> Hormones and neuropeptides impart data through the extracellular fluid more or less continuously in a process known as 'volume transmission'. What is important is that these additional ways of communicating among cells in the central nervous system mean that simple (or even complicated) linear or feedforward models are likely to be inaccurate. . . . Discovering the importance of global communication in the brain has led some to conclude that it is better to see our brain as a system that works together as a complex interactive whole for which any sort of reduction to lower levels of description means a loss of telling data.[23]

Broader dynamic systems allow for the kind of holistic effects that are typical in emergent systems throughout biology. Admittedly, neuroscience is nowhere close to understanding 'large-scale, complex electrophysiological or bioelectrical activity patterns involving millions of neurons and billions of synapses',[24] and this particular proposed mechanism may not stand up to closer scrutiny. But these are the *sorts* of processes that can be scientifically studied and that may yield to a more integrative understanding of the neural correlates of consciousness.

Israel Rosenfield posits an equally global point of contact, albeit with some scepticism about whether the difference between thought and brain state is thereby overcome. The closest area of comparison lies in their overall dynamics. The overall dynamics of the brain come closest to mirroring the dynamics of thought, whereas the individual components of these two dynamical systems—individual memories, say, on the thought side, and individual neural events on the brain side—evidence different logics that remain incommensurable. Rosenfield thus concludes:

Our perceptions are part of a 'stream of consciousness', part of a continuity of experience that the neuroscientific models and descriptions fail to capture; their categories of color, say, or smell, or sound, or motion are discrete entities independent of time. . . . A sense of consciousness comes precisely from the *flow* of perceptions, from the relations among them (both spatial and temporal), from the dynamic but constant relation to them as governed by one unique personal perspective sustained throughout a conscious life. . . . Compared to [this flow], units of 'knowledge' such as we can transmit or record in books or images are but instant snapshots taken in a dynamic flow of uncontainable, unrepeatable, and inexpressible experience. And it is an unwarranted mistake to associate these snapshots with material 'stored' in the brain.[25]

The more the study of NCC points in the direction of such dynamical, integrated systems, the closer it stands to emergence predictions. Thus Daniel Dennett, whose reductionism in *Consciousness Explained* is otherwise no friend to strong emergentists, does admit,

The consensus of cognitive science . . . is that *over there* we have the long-term memory . . . and *over here* we have the workspace or working memory, where the thinking happens. . . . And yet there are not two places in the brain to house these two facilities. The only place in the brain that is a plausible home for either of these separate functions is the whole cortex—not two places side by side but one large place.[26]

The emergence programme turns not just on the size of the region involved but also on the degree of complexity of the system. In neurological systems the level of complexity is a function of the degree of interconnection; it is increased exponentially, for example, to the extent that dynamic feedback and feedforward loops are involved. This is the sort of structure that Edelman describes: 'Nervous system behaviour is to some extent self-generated in loops; brain activity leads to movement, which leads to further sensation and perception and still further movement. The layers and loops . . . are dynamic; they continually change.'[27] In Edelman's treatment, the increasing complexity of dynamic feedback and feedforward loops *just is* awareness or consciousness. These processes can be studied objectively by neurophysiologists, or they can be experienced subjectively by individual agents; in the end, he thinks, they are just two different descriptions of a single dynamical process. His leanings towards this thesis incline Edelman towards the tradition of dual-aspect theory.[28]

And yet one senses that there is something missing in this response. No matter how complex, dynamic, or self-catalysing the neural structures may be, they remain physiological structures—structures that scientists must describe in third-person terms. As W. J. Clancey notes, on that view it is structures all the way down:

> each new perceptual categorization, conceptualization, and sensory-motor coordination brings 'hardware' components together in new ways, modifying the population of physical elements available for future activation and recombination. Crucially, this physical rearrangement of the brain is not produced by a software compilation process (translating from linguistic descriptions) [nor is it] isomorphic to linguistic names and semantic manipulations (our conventional idea of software). Different structures can produce the same result . . .[29]

Research into the neural correlates of consciousness—one of the most fruitful research areas in the study of consciousness today—can offer no more than its name promises. At most one will be able to establish a series of *correlations* between brain states and phenomenal experiences as reported by subjects. Such correlations are of immense empirical significance. But if the resulting explanations are given exclusively in neurological terms, they will by the nature of the case not be able to specify what are the phenomenal experiences or *qualia* that the subjects experience. Nor will the causal effects of conscious experiences, if they indeed exist, be recognizable by these means.

WHY CONSCIOUSNESS REMAINS THE 'HARD PROBLEM'

The problem with answers based on the neural correlates of consciousness, then, is not that they make the problem too hard, but rather that they make it too easy. They end the inquiry at a point where the dissatisfactions just begin to arise. Mental properties remain different enough from the physiological processes that give rise to them, so that merely linking the two leaves the hard problem unsolved.

Evolutionary studies show that the distinct features of human cognition depend on a quantitative increase in brain complexity, along with other functional capacities, *vis-à-vis* other higher primates. Yet at some point in evolution this particular quantitative increase gives rise to what appears as a qualitative change. As Terrence Deacon has shown in *The Symbolic Species*, even if the development of conscious awareness occurs gradually over the course of primate evolution, the end of that process (at least for now) confronts the scientist with something new and different: symbol-using beings whose existence with language is clearly distinct from those who preceded them.[30] Understanding consciousness as an emergent phenomenon in the natural world—that is, naturalistically, non-dualistically—requires a theory of thoughts, beliefs, and volition because these are the phenomena that humans encounter in their natural, everyday experience. Mental causes, intention-based actions, structures built up out of ideas—these are experiential givens that demand naturalistic explanation.

This is what David Chalmers has identified as 'the hard problem' of consciousness. In his seminal 'Facing up to the Problem of Consciousness', Chalmers showed, correctly in my opinion, that many of the 'answers' to the problem of consciousness are only answers to the 'easy' problems. Among the so-called easy problems of consciousness Chalmers identified the attempts to understand:

- the ability to discriminate, categorize, and react to environmental stimuli;
- the integration of information by a cognitive system;
- the reportability of mental states;
- the ability of a system to access its own internal states;
- the focus of attention;
- the deliberate control of behaviour;
- the difference between wakefulness and sleep.[31]

'Easy' may have been a bit of a misnomer: comprehending, say, the deliberate control of behaviour is an incredibly complicated neuroscientific challenge. Nonetheless, as difficult as these issues are to resolve empirically, they pale in significance compared to the hard problem:

The really hard problem of consciousness is the problem of *experience*. When we think and perceive, there is a whir of information-processing, but there is also a subjective aspect. As Nagel has put it, there is *something it is like* to be a conscious organism. This subjective aspect is experience. When we see, for example, we *experience* visual sensations: the felt quality of redness, the experience of dark and light, the quality of depth in a visual field. Other experiences go along with perception in different modalities: the sound of a clarinet, the smell of mothballs. Then there are bodily sensations, from pains to orgasms; mental images that are conjured up internally; the felt quality of emotion, and the experience of a stream of conscious thought. What unites all of these states is that there is something it is like to be in them. All of them are states of experience.[32]

Explaining experience in this sense is, I suggest, at least half of the hard problem. It does not seem to be the *kind* of thing that could be explained in terms of functions or structures, since one could completely know the structures or functions of some experience and still not know what it is to have that experience. So, for example, the famous thought experiment by Frank Jackson imagines a neuro-scientist named Mary who knows everything there is to be known about the experience of red, but who, having been kept in a black and white room her entire life, has never had the experience of red. No matter how complete Mary's neurophysiological knowledge, when she first walks out of her room and sees a red object, she will have an experience she had never had before and will know something—namely, what it is like to have that experience—that she had not known before. This is true even though, *ex hypothesi*, before her liberation she had known everything that could be known about the structure and function of red.

Jackson and Chalmers are right on this point. If they are right, it underscores how perplexing even the first half of the 'hard problem' of consciousness really is. What biology in general, and the neuro-sciences in particular, are able to do is to understand the structures and functions of cells, organs, brain regions, and organisms. Isn't this implicitly what we found above in the brief discussion of recent theories concerning the neural correlates of conscious experience? Medically, of course, this is all that matters: if you know that reduced blood flow in a specific region is associated with impairment of the cognitive functions associated with that region, and if you are able subsequently to increase blood flow so that no further loss of memory or recognition or motor functions occurs, then you have been medically successful; you have discharged your responsi-bilities as a doctor. But this still leaves us unsure what the conscious experience *is*. Not that there is a shortage of potential answers. Beyond explanations of consciousness in terms of standard bio-logical structures and functions, a number of theorists add an 'extra ingredient' of some sort or another into their account. And surely there is no shortage of extra ingredients to be had: 'Some propose an injection of chaos and nonlinear dynamics. Some think that the key lies in nonalgorithmic processing. Some appeal to future discoveries in neurophysiology. Some suppose that the key to the mystery will lie at the level of quantum mechanics.'[33]

The second half of the hard problem moves from what consciousness is to what it does. It is one thing to recognize the radically different qualities that characterize brain states on the one hand and *qualia* on the other; it is quite another to ask how the one type of state can influence the other. The discussion of consciousness has moved increasingly from the first type of question to the second. The latter question—the question of how mental states can have any effect at all in the world—is in some ways the more difficult one: many philosophers acknowledge the existence of mental states but are epiphenomenalists when it comes to what they do. Strong emergence represents the contention that the epiphenomenalist response is mistaken.

The exploration of NCCs and the hard problem brings at least two dangers to light. First, it is crucial not to confuse testable hypotheses about mind with philosophical speculation about its nature; the latter is important but, like the Owl of Minerva, comes only after careful scientific examination (see Chapter 5 below). The danger with the 'extra ingredient' theories is that they are often put forward as if they were *scientific* answers to the question of consciousness. Second, when the 'extra ingredient' theories are (correctly) relocated to the category of philosophical theories about the nature of mind, they must be assessed on how well they do at accounting for what is different about mental causality as well as what ties it to other types of causal influence.

Chalmers's own answer to the problem of consciousness in the article cited above—whatever other inadequacies it may have—does seek to explain what is different about the experiential states that persons have. What he elsewhere calls 'naturalistic dualism'[34] is the right *sort* of answer to the hard problem, although I do not believe that Chalmers's combination of dualism and panpsychism (naturalistic or otherwise) offers the right set of resources for adequately linking the development of mind to natural history. The panpsychism he speculates about is, after all, an atemporal position, one that makes no reference to the evolutionary process. Yet it is a fundamental assumption of the biological sciences that the evolutionary process was responsible both for increased brain capacity (at the genetic level) and for the behaviours produced by brains (which is the level on which selection pressures operate).

WEAK SUPERVENIENCE AND THE EMERGENCE OF
MENTAL PROPERTIES

Before beginning the attempt to formulate a better response to the problem, it is necessary to clearly state some background assumptions and to appropriate (albeit with modifications) some important tools from recent debates in the philosophy of mind. First, three assumptions:

- On the one hand, strongly dualist theories of human nature, and in particular substantival theories of the soul, have become problematic in an age of science. The metaphysics of soul stands in serious tension with much contemporary metaphysics, with modern science, and with the epistemologies that are able to incorporate them.
- On the other hand, many aspects of our ordinary experience as actors in the world conflict with physicalist accounts of personhood.[35] Reductive physicalist accounts are not able to do justice to the first person/third person distinction—to what it is like to see red or listen to Beethoven or love another person or use language symbolically. Making sense of representational or truth-seeking language, of intentionality, and of 'raw feels' may require a richer semantics than physicalism can provide.
- Recent criticisms of non-reductive physicalism, particularly those advanced by Jaegwon Kim,[36] raise serious doubts whether *any* version of physicalism other than reductivist physicalism is in the end coherent.

Supervenience theory is helpful for formulating some of the requirements on a theory of mind today and for drawing attention to where the strengths and weaknesses of physicalism lie. Supervenience is not the same as emergence, but it can play a role in developing an emergentist theory of mind. Its contributions fall in three major areas:

First, in the most general terms, supervenience means that one level of phenomena or type of property (in this case, the mental) is dependent upon another level (in this case, the biological or neurophysiological), while at the same time not being reducible to it. I have used the term *weak supervenience*, adapted from Jaegwon Kim, as a way of expressing this minimal position. *Strong supervenience* positions by contrast—and these are admittedly the most common versions of the theory—generally argue for a *determination* of supervenient phenomena by the subvenient level. This would mean, for example, that mental phenomena are fully determined by their neural substrate. Since any difference in the supervenient level, no matter how small (having a different thought, for instance) would be the result of some difference in the subvenient systems (here, a different state of the brain and central nervous system), the 'strong' theory has to say that the subvenient level provides the real explanation for the phenomena in question.

Second, as long as supervenience is understood to be a *token–token* relationship—any individual instance of a mental property directly supervenes on some specific brain state—then, according to most standard presentations of the theory, there is no real place for mental causation. For in each case the mental event will be fully determined by its corresponding physical event, which means that the causal-explanatory story has to be told in terms of physical events alone (in this case, neurons firing). One can *say* that a mental input should be added to the chain of brain states causing other brain states, as in Figure 4.1: but it is not clear why the imagined mental cause would not be redundant in this case. Although strong supervenience, unlike eliminitivist theories of mind, appears to admit the existence of mental events (thoughts, feelings, and the like), there seems to be nothing left for them to do; the 'real' explanatory story has been told in terms of physical events alone. One must conclude, the rhetoric of some philosophers notwithstanding, that strong supervenience theories actually amount to a de facto epiphenomenalism (the view that mind exists but has no

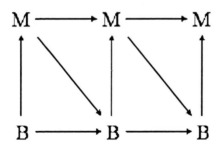

Downward Causation

FIGURE 4.1. The problem of supervenient mental causes.

causal effect in the world). Supervenience does not yet give an account of how our ideas might play a causal role in influencing the actions of our bodies.

Third, supplementing supervenience with emergence involves a shift from token–token to type–type comparisons of the mental and the physical. That is, on the latter view the mental and the physical represent two types of events in the world, and the relationship between them must be specified by explaining in more general terms how events of the one type are related to events of the other type. From the perspective of emergence, mental events manifest a type of property, one whose existence depends on another type of property, the neurophysiological states of the organism.

Jaegwon Kim and others have constructed arguments based on the notion of 'multiple realizability' which I believe strengthen the case for this *type–type* understanding of the relationship between the mental and the physical. For a mental property to be multiply realizable means that a number of different biological systems, or even nonbiological ones, might have produced the same property. 'Take pain', writes John Heil. 'Many different kinds of creature could be in pain. When we look at the possibilities, it appears unlikely that these creatures share a unique physical property in virtue of which it is true that they are in pain. This tells against "type identity," the view that the pain property could be identified with some physical property.'[37] The fact of multiple realizability weakens the claim that mental properties are really of the same type as physical properties, as 'type-identity' theories hold. Thus pain is a different type of property than the chemical properties of a given neuronal synapse. It is theoretically possible, for example, that in the future a team of scientists might build an electronic model of a human brain that would evidence something like the mental properties we experience. In such a case, analogs to our mental and physical properties would still be present, even though the *tokens* (the specific mental and physical events) would be massively different.

Type–type comparisons still leave weak supervenience (as defined above) intact. Mental properties are a type of property which evidences a dependence relation on neurophysiological properties or states of the organism. For example, pain phenomena are still dependent in some way on states of the nervous system— anaesthetize the nerves in an injured limb, and the patient will generally report a decrease or disappearance of the pain. This approach also makes evolution central. To explain the emergence of this new type of phenomenon it is necessary to trace the natural history of the central nervous system from its biological origins to the form it presently takes in humans. Whereas emergence theories draw primarily on the history of evolution, those who define the problem in terms of token–token relations—this mental event is produced by this particular physical state of the brain—generally emphasize the physical laws and presently occurring microphysical events as determinative for the understanding of consciousness. This may be good physics, but it is bad biology.

I suggest that the evolutionary study of the emergence of brains and the accompanying mental phenomena represents the most natural scientific approach to the topic. After all, neurophysiology involves the study of biological structures and functions in the higher primates, and all biological studies presuppose evolution as their primary theoretical framework (even when it remains in the background). Explaining the supervenience of the mental on the physical, understood as an example of evolutionary emergence, therefore requires a diachronic as well as a synchronic perspective. Mental properties depend upon the entire natural history that caused increasingly complex brains and central nervous systems to evolve, as well as on the physical state of the organism at a particular time. (To the best of our knowledge, corpses don't have *qualia*.) This evolutionary dependency is neither logical nor metaphysical—two requirements often associated with supervenience relations in the philosophy of mind. Rather, the assertion of both a diachronic and a synchronic dependence of mental properties is our best reconstruction of the highly contingent natural history that produced organisms like *homo sapiens*. Therefore we might best label the resulting position *emergentist supervenience.*

Understanding the dependence relation from the perspective of natural history represents a firm break with dualist theories of mind, which have generally denied that mind is essentially dependent on the history of biological systems. Focusing on the evolutionary origins of mind is therefore part of what distinguishes the emergence approach as a separate ontological option in the debate. At the same time, the dependent type–type relationship between the mental and the physical also allows one to give a more robust account of the nonreducibility of the mental than the competing accounts provide. Wherein, then, does this nonreducibility lie, and how can it best be characterized? Much turns on this question.

In discussing biological emergence in the previous chapter I noted how each emergent level of complexity helps to set the stage for introducing and understanding the next. This is true, for example, of each of the twenty-eight levels identified in the recent book by the George Mason biophysicist Harold Morowitz.[38] Thus it seems to be a general feature of the ladder of natural history that one's understanding of later stages will be strongly influenced, albeit not fully determined, by one's knowledge of the earlier stages. Or—to put it more colloquially—knowing where you are depends in large measure on knowing how you got there.

TOWARD AN EMERGENTIST THEORY OF MIND

On the view I am defending, consciousness is one more emergent property of this natural universe. Call this view *emergentist monism*. The position would be falsified if it turned out that, in the course of universal evolution, only one strongly emergent property had appeared. In that case one would have to accept some sort of temporalized dualism: the universe was fundamentally physical up to some point, and then mental states arose, and after that the universe (or at least some portion of it) was both physical and mental. By contrast, emergentist monism is supported if—as seems in fact to be the case—natural history produces entities that evidence a range of hierarchically ordered emergent qualities. The previous chapters have gone a long way towards specifying the content of this claim. It is time now to see what sort of theory of mind is suggested by this view.

The challenge is clear: can an emergentist theory of mind be formulated which is sufficiently attuned to the power of neuroscientific explanations, yet which addresses the hard problem: the distinctive nature of the causal influence of mental states? There is a certain dynamic to the quest for such a theory that is somewhat akin to riding a see-saw. If you push off too hard from the mental side, you descend into the morasses of neurophysiological detail, and no mental causes are to be found. If however you push off too hard from the physical side, you end up in the world of purely mental terms, and no connection with the brain remains. The balance that we seek conceives mind as a type of property that emerges from the brain, which though different from remains continually dependent on its subvenient base (hence the term emergentist supervenience). An outcome of evolutionary history, mental events as we know them are nonetheless not reducible to the neurological systems that produce them, in part because they play a causal role that is more than the sum of the physical events on which they depend.

To the extent that this position tries to do justice to the first-person experience of mental phenomena, some will accuse it of not being physicalist enough about consciousness. There is no reason, they will argue, to speak of conscious states as representing the emergence of a new kind of event, and especially not one with causal powers of its own. Yet to the extent that the theory construes mind as a natural product of evolutionary history, others will accuse it of selling out, reducing consciousness to materialism. Between Scylla and Charybdis we set our sails (or, to be truer to Homer, row for all we're worth).

Navigating between the shipwrecks

Debating the nature of mind presents the reader with a number of decision points, and each decision leads her to a new set of alternatives. One's course can be charted by the shipwrecks left behind by philosophers who have previously made this journey. Rather than presenting a dry survey of the alternatives, I propose to orient the discussion in terms of the major decision points, noting in each case how emergence theorists would respond and why that response is to be preferred.

So you want to be an emergentist; what are your options? There are certain decisions you must make before you can take even the first steps towards an emergence theory of the person. You must, for example, have rejected reductionist physicalism, the belief that all adequate explanations will finally be given in the terms of contemporary physics. On the other side, you must have rejected substance dualism, the view that there are two distinct kinds of substances (e.g. in the substance dualism of Descartes, *res cogitans* and *res extensa*, thinking and extended substance).

Of course there are other options besides emergence theory available to those who wish to avoid both reductionist physicalism and substance dualism. Among other things, you might be tempted towards dual-aspect monism, which maintains that there is just one kind or level of reality, even though it is sometimes apprehended in the mode of mind and sometimes in the mode of body. This originally Spinozistic view makes the mind–body problem a matter of perspective. Thus Max Velmans argues that 'neither the third-person physical facts nor the first-person subjective facts are ultimately real'; nonetheless, one can *choose* to view 'the underlying bedrock of reality' in four different ways: as 'operations of mind viewed from a purely external observer's perspective (P→P), operations of mind viewed from a purely first-person perspective (M→M), and mixed-perspective accounts involving perspectival switching (P→M; M→P)'.[39] Note that, strictly speaking, Velmans's account makes both physicalist and mentalist positions false: the two positions may be useful, but they do not actually reflect the world as it 'ultimately' is. For this reason one wonders why he thinks he is entitled to refer to the x that is viewed in these four different ways as 'operations of mind'; technically he should have said 'the neither-physical-nor-mental-underlying-reality', which is obviously not identical to 'operations of mind'. Moreover, one should be concerned that, on this view, mental states cannot be produced by the brain nor be causally affected by any neurological event. Gone, in that case, is any biological account of the evolution of mind. Is it enough to say that the mind–body problem boils down to a matter of perspective?

Or you might convert to panpsychism, believing that 'it's mind all the way down', that is, that every level of reality possesses some sort of mental experience.[40] Dual-aspect monism answers the question of the origination of mental events, one worries, by avoiding it, since it provides no account of how a biological structure such as the central nervous system might have produced mental events. Panpsychism, like dualism, makes a robustly metaphysical move, which unfortunately cuts it off from the evidential considerations that science could otherwise provide. Diving robustly into metaphysics in this way, while it does not show that the position is false, does create a certain incommensurability with its major competitors, making it difficult to assess its merits on empirical grounds. Finally, until relatively recently you might have thought that non-reductive physicalism was an attractive option. This position maintains that all things are ultimately physical but does not require that all explanations be given in physical terms. Whether or not all causes had to be physical causes turned out to be its Achilles' heel: say yes, and you seem to end up with a reductive physicalism; say no, and you aren't really a physicalist after all. I follow Jaegwon Kim, therefore, in holding that this view is an inherently unstable position rather than a useful halfway point between other options.[41]

But let us assume, for the sake of argument, that the earlier chapters have convinced you of the preferability of emergence to these particular competitors. What is the next decision to be made? The first decision point is between epistemic and ontological versions of the theory. According to epistemic versions, emergence has only to do with limitations of *our* knowledge of the physical order and/or with the particularities of how we come to know; ultimately, ontologically, all that exists are the physical systems whose behaviours are expressed by physical laws. This is the position that I dubbed *façon de parler* emergence in Chapter 2. Clearly, however, the more robust—and certainly the more ambitious—versions of emergence lie on the ontological side of the divide. According to these versions, emergence entails a genuinely new type of reality in the world. Again for the sake of argument, let us assume you are convinced that *façon de parler* emergence is really physicalism with a more lenient attitude towards as-yet-unexplained physical systems. If physicalism is unacceptable, *façon de parler* emergence does not solve its problems.

Ontological views, in turn, subdivide into those that accept only emergent properties and those that also accept emergent causal powers. The emergent-properties-without-causality view is consistent with believing that all that *actually* exists are physical objects controlled by physical laws. It is just that, on this view, very complicated physical objects like ourselves give rise to some rather unusual properties, such as thinking of world peace, liking chocolate ice cream, or intending to play rugby tomorrow. Such mental properties, although they exist, do not themselves *do* anything; all the 'doing' occurs at the level of the physical processes of which we are constituted.

Mental causation is therefore the linchpin of the debate. On this view, that structured part of the natural world which is your mental activity plays a causal role in influencing other mental occurrences—and presumably, therefore, also bodily behaviour. Michael Silberstein is thus right to define emergent properties in terms of the causal question. They are

qualitatively new properties of systems or wholes that possess causal capacities that are not reducible to any of the causal capacities of the most basic parts; such properties are potentially not even reducible to the relations between the most basic parts. Emergent properties are properties of a system taken as a whole; such properties either subsume the intrinsic properties of the basic parts or exert causal influence on the basic parts consistent with but distinct from the causal capacities of the basic parts themselves.[42]

Note that granting causal influence to emergent properties must have some effect on one's ontology. These properties must, after all, exist in a somewhat more robust sense if we have to ascribe a causal role to them than if they are epiphenomenal.

Those who accept the existence of emergent powers have to choose between stronger and weaker claims on their behalf. Much of the theory of mind one finally accepts will depend on how strong an account you give of emergent causal powers. The weakest form of emergent causality one can defend (Van Gulick's 'specific value emergence') is to insist that wholes and parts must have features of the same kind but may have different subtypes or values of that kind. Thus, for example, both the car and its parts have weight, but the car has more of it. A stronger version (Van Gulick's 'modest kind emergence') would allow wholes to have features that are different in kind from those of its parts. This is the view of emergence that I examined in Chapter 2 under the heading of 'whole–part constraint'. The most ambitious form of mental causality, however, which I have called *strong emergence*, adds that the holistic features of a complex system are not necessitated by the sum total of facts about the parts. Van Gulick calls this position 'radical kind emergence'.[43] He notes that to accept radical kind emergence is to hold 'that there are real features of the world that exist at the system or composite level that are not determined by the law-like regularities that govern the interactions of the parts of such systems and their features' (p. 18).

Challenges to mental causation

Now one may well have wished for a yet stronger statement regarding the uniqueness of mind. You may, for instance, want to conceive human persons as fundamental to the fabric of the universe. We want our intentions and goals to matter; we want our thoughts and feelings to be causally efficacious; we want the things that we find meaningful (or: the things that we *want* to be meaningful) really to *be* meaningful. In the next chapter I will look at more metaphysical theories of the existence of agents as qualitatively unique. But first it is necessary to step back and take stock of the difficulties that are raised by even a more minimal theory of mental causation.

What are the costs of strong emergence (radical kind emergence), with its assertion of downward mental causation? One cost involves the danger of negating scientific study and scientific method; another concerns not being able to specify the evolution of neural states; and a third involves not being able to explain where mental causation takes hold and why it does so when it does. Let us consider the three in turn.

Recall Van Gulick's observation that, for radical kind emergence, 'there are real features of the world that exist at the system or composite level that are not determined by the law-like regularities that govern the interactions of the parts of such systems' (p. 18). Prima facie, this fact would seem to raise a problem for the scientific study of human organisms and their brains. It is basic to the scientific method as standardly applied in studies of the brain to assume that the macro-properties of a system, whatever they are, are ultimately determined by the sum total of relations between the micro-properties of that system. To know the state of all the registers in your computer when it is running a programme *just is* to know the state of the system, and no fact about what the programme signifies—imagine it is processing an image of the Mona Lisa—is causally relevant to the computer's functioning. Are matters not analogous for the human brain?

The problem is a serious one. The neurobiologist William Newsome has recently challenged the view that mental events could give rise to new brain events without there being a full causal story told in terms of *prior* brain events. He writes:

I do not buy into the notion of high-level causation without accompanying low-level causation. In the neural network example . . . I am perfectly willing to argue for the reality of higher functional levels that cannot be understood simply in terms of the lower levels. But any higher level causality in the network is *mediated* through lower level causal mechanisms. Whatever algorithm the network 'discovers' is both 'real' and essential for our understanding of the network. But this algorithm does not manifest itself within the network through any mysterious forces that pull and tug on the computer chips. It is mediated entirely through standard physical forces. What is the evidence for a high-level causal arrow that controls events in the absence of low-level causal arrows?[44]

Any theory of mental causation must address Newsome's challenge. It seems clear that the answer must be given in terms of emergent effects of a highly complex integrated system that pertain to the system as a whole but not to its parts taken in isolation. Less plausible are accounts that make a place for mental influences only at the level of subcomponents in the brain. Where, for example, would be the point of contact: would 'mind' affect the outcome of quantum mechanical indeterminacies in the physics of the brain, as Nancey Murphy and Thomas Tracy have argued in a theological context?[45] Would it change the chemical composition at specific synapses? Or would it exercise its causality only at the level of 'the brain as a whole', as Roger Sperry believed? At one point, quantum indeterminacies seemed to offer the ideal opening for mental causation.[46] Unfortunately, contemporary evidence suggests that quantum effects (say, superimposed quantum states prior to decoherence) would be eliminated well before one reached the level of the neurochemical processes that are basic to brain functioning.[47]

As Michael Silberstein has shown, a number of standard scientific tools help to explain whole–part influences of this sort, including non-linear dynamics, chaos theory, and the field of complexity studies.[48] Although the role of 'strange attractors' and the sensitive dependence on initial conditions in these systems show some analogies to mental causation, there must also be features unique to the brain that play an ineliminable explanatory role.[49] The crucial feature in the account is the denial of decomposability: mental events cannot be merely a shorthand for some aggregate of individual neuron-firing potentials. Just as answering the 'binding problem'—the question of how multiple records are bound together to retain a unified image or experience in memory—turns on discovering some feature that makes them into a single system, so the question of mental causality requires an answer at a sufficiently systematic level.

A minimalist response: semiotic representation without mental causation

There is a minimalist response to this challenge. One can look within biological systems for the closest available analogs to cognitive functions such as learning, perceiving, or representing. This school of thought is functionalist in orientation: if sufficiently strong analogies can be established between human cognitive functions and some particular biological system, then (it is claimed) one is justified in maintaining that the biological system engages in the cognitive activity in question. So, for example, non-human complex adaptive systems might be said to 'learn', as long as one defines learning as 'a combination of exploration of the environment and improvement of performance through adaptive change'.[50] Obviously, systems from primitive organisms to primate brains record information from their environment and use it to adjust future responses to that environment. It would follow that learning is far more common in the biosphere, and occurs far earlier, than the standard psychological accounts have acknowledged.[51]

Within the philosophy of mind, Max Velmans has offered a sophisticated version of the minimalist response. Velmans asks why the brain cannot be understood as a representational system— not because it produces mental representations, but because it stands (or, more accurately, particular brain states stand) in a particular functional relation to the external world which we can call representation. If there are morphological similarities between the internal brain states and some part of the external world, and if these internal states function for the organism as a picture of that world, then (he claims) the brain itself can be construed as a representational system. Velmans maintains, for example, that the representation of visual images in the brain, which was classically considered a mental phenomenon, can be conceived without recourse to mentality. Consider Max Velmans's schema in Figure 4.2.[52] Here the cat-in-the-world and the neural representation of the

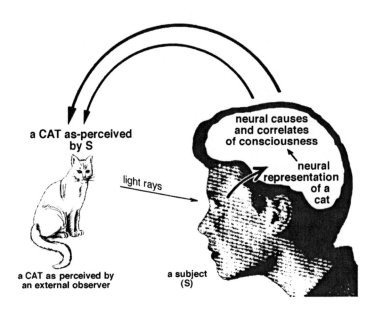

FIGURE 4.2. Neural representations of objects in the world.
From Max Velmans, *Understanding Consciousness*. Used by permission of the author.

cat are both parts of a natural system; no non-scientific mental 'things' like ideas or forms need to be introduced. In principle, the occurrence of these brain representations could count as merely a more complicated form of the feedback loop between a plant and its environment considered in the preceding chapter. This would provide something like the 'natural account of phenomenal consciousness' defended by Velmans,[53] but one in which no mental causes need be introduced (see Figure 4.3).

Now in fact Velmans chooses to interpret this model of representation within the context of dual-aspect theory. The 'ur reality', on

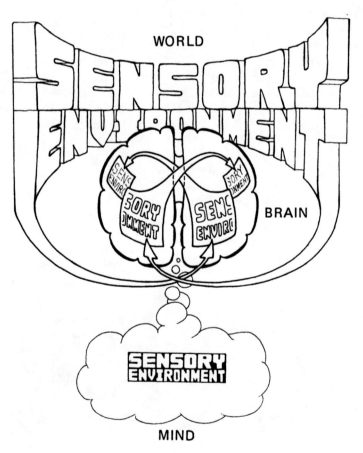

FIGURE 4.3.   'Mind' mirroring the sensory environment.
From Joseph LeDoux, *The Integrated Mind.* Used by permission of the author.

his view, is 'neither physical nor mental': 'Viewed from the outside, the operations of ur mind appear to be operations of brain. Viewed from a first-person perspective, the operations of ur mind appear to be conscious experiences.'[54] I considered some of the problems with dual-aspect theories above. For present purposes, however, note that the model just given does not *require* the dual-aspect interpretation; it could also pass as a physicalist recasting of the representation relation. That is, without emergence, the story of consciousness could be retold such that thoughts and intentions play no causal role. The diagram Velman uses (Figure 4.3) nicely expresses the challenge: if one limits the causal interactions to world and brains, mind will appear as a sort of thought-bubble outside the system.

Even more radical is the suggestion by Terrence Deacon that representation and intentional behaviour can be identified already at the level of the first self-reproducing cell.[55] As soon as an informational structure with the capacity to reproduce itself is contained with cell walls, it counts as a representation of the world for Deacon. It is—or one should better say: it functions as—a hypothesis about the world, the hypothesis namely that a structure of this type can reproduce successfully and thereby gain enough selective advantage to survive. According to Deacon one can rightly say that survival is the 'intention' of the unicellular organism. Of course, intentions and internal states grow massively more complex over the course of evolution, and more complicated structures can form internal structural-informational states (intentions) utterly beyond the purview of simple organisms, as in symbolic language use. But nothing new occurs ontologically, as it were, through the further increase in complexity. Representation, purposive behaviour, intentions—all of these are already present, albeit in rudimentary form, at the very earliest phases of biological evolution.[56]

Arguments such as these are hard to evaluate; they tend to produce two strong, and opposite, reactions. Proponents take it as a strength that features once associated with mentality such as representation and intentionality are here reconstructed without recourse to anything distinctively mental. Does that not prove the success of the endeavour? But critics locate the weakness of these conceptions in the same place: explanations tailored to earlier evolutionary stages, or to formal similarities between brain states and states of the world, though they reveal interesting analogies, do not capture what is particular to mental events. Beyond the similarities—in this case, similarities between the emergence of consciousness and previous examples of emergence in complex systems—lie the differences, which remain unexplained.

Velmans's conception, for example, allows for isomorphisms between physically distinct biological systems (the cat and the brain state produced by looking at the cat). But if one is to preserve mental agency, the isomorphism is not enough; there must be a place not only for the correlation ('knowing') but also for knowing that one knows, that is, for the awareness of the relation. As E. J. Lowe has argued, mental events must have specific goals. One makes the mental decision to buy a car, or to get out of bed, or to sing the *Krönungsmesse*; they are discrete decisions rather than intermingled states. Neural events, by contrast, are 'inextricably entangled'.[57] Physical actions are products of an interconnected web of brain events; there are no discrete groupings that represent the neural antecedents of 'deciding to open the door' or 'deciding to pick up your books'. Hence no physical account can be given that expresses the steps of the decision in neurological terms. Instead, 'we think of each decision as giving rise to just its "own" movement and without any contributions from decisions to perform other, independent movements; and to abandon this thought is effectively to abandon mental causation as common sense conceives of that phenomenon' (p. 640). We must either give up mental causation altogether, or we must understand it to be something more than a specific set of neural events.

The need for interpreted states appears also in the Chinese Room case (John Searle). In the example, one imagines a man locked inside a room who does not understand Chinese. He receives inputs from outside the room in the form of Chinese characters; he has rules for converting these symbols into other symbols; and he conveys those symbols to persons outside the room.[58] The Chinese-speaking agents outside the room understand their inputs to be questions, and they interpret his outputs as answers. But the poor man knows nothing of this; as far as he is concerned he is only 'manipulating uninterpreted formal symbols'.

As long as the symbols in the Chinese Room example lack an interpretation that makes them meaningful, they are merely syntactical structures standing in particular formal relations with other structures. Mental representation, by contrast, involves the semantic state of knowing that one thing (say, a thought) stands for another (say, an object in the world). The representation relation thus involves a level in the evolutionary process that is distinct from and irreducible to previous levels. At one point only formal or functional relations exist; at some later point individuals exist who are also aware of these relations, who interpret them consciously, and who are thus able to draw further inferences from them. At some point semiotics gives way to an interpreted or meaningful semantics. Is this particular emergent property more or less novel than properties that emerge earlier in evolutionary history? It is hard to say; judgements concerning novelty are notoriously slippery. Still, it is difficult to deny that these sorts of properties do exist (to deny it one must already have understood them, which appears to concede the point). They would not be experienced if certain types of neurophysiological structures did not exist, and yet they are not identical to the pre-semantic properties on which they depend.

ASSUMPTIONS AND A WAGER

In these last pages I have considered what is distinctive about the emergence of consciousness. I argued that strong emergence in this sense is consistent with the neuroscientific data and with the constraints on brain functioning. At the same time, it has the merit of conceiving of mental activity in terms of mental causation, which accords well with our own experience of mental agency.

Two assumptions have undergirded these results, and I should now lay them clearly on the table. I have assumed, on the one hand, that if a given account of mental influence is incompatible with natural science, that would be a telling argument against it. Aristotle's doctrine of entelechies, for example—of future, and thus merely potential, patterns pulling natural processes towards themselves—is incompatible with natural science in just this way. A theory holding that ideas directly change the chemical composition in a synaptic juncture would raise similar problems. Thus the theory of mental influence cannot mean interventions of mind into individual neurons. The neuroscientist Roger Sperry endorses a similar stipulation:

Higher-level phenomena in exerting downward control do *not disrupt* or *interv*ene in the causal relations of the lower-level component activity. Instead they *super*vene, in a way that leaves the micro interactions, per se, unaltered. These micro interactions and the interrelations of all the infra-structural components become embedded within, enveloped, and as a result are thereon moved and carried by the property dynamics of the larger overall system as a whole, in this case the wheel or the mind/brain process, that have their own irreducible higher-level forms of causal interaction.[59]

On the other hand, I have assumed that one should select among those philosophical theories that are compatible with the neuro-scientific results, based, in part, on whether they are able to preserve a place for mental causation . . . even if the result goes beyond the science we currently know.

These two assumptions amount to a sort of double wager. It is a wager, first, that the ultimately victorious account will not be forced to abandon a place for mental causation and, second, that the ultimately successful account will not invalidate the scientific study of the brain or make such study irrelevant. The second point is crucial: the more untestable a theory of mind becomes, the more it becomes an affront to science; and, I am assuming, the fact that a given theory of mind is an affront to science represents at least prima facie reason to reject it. Accepting the double wager explains why most philosophers today reject Cartesian dualism. In so far as Cartesian mental substance has nothing whatsoever to do with the physical world (for it belongs to another world altogether), brain science could never tell us anything about the nature of Cartesian mind. Conversely, accounts based on the stochastic regularities of neural firings alone can never explain thought because they leave no place for ideas to have a causal effect on the brain and central nervous system—and thus on one's actions in the world.

THE SCIENCE AND PHENOMENOLOGY OF AGENT CAUSATION

Philosophers who have sought to defend the irreducibility of mind have sometimes begun with rather ambitious theories of what an agent must be. For instance, William Rowe has championed the requirements for agent causation formulated by Thomas Reid: '(1) X is a *substance* that had *power* to bring about e; (2) X *exerted* its power to bring about x; (3) X had the *power* to refrain from bringing about e'.[60] The robust metaphysics that is built into such accounts makes serious conversation with the sciences difficult if not impossible. Any adequate approach must tarry much longer with the data from the natural and social sciences that bear on the theory of mental experience. Phenomenology, for example, provides a type of analysis that is committed to providing data on mental causation without heavy imports of ontology.

Numerous studies have been devoted to the phenomenological study of the mental in irreducibly mental terms, going back at least to William James's *Briefer Course in Psychology*.[61] James places great emphasis on the flow of consciousness, which is the particular form in which *attention* is manifested at the human level. In individual chapters he also considers the effects of will, habit, and thought, among other phenomena. Some interesting recent neuroscientific work involves the use of real-time brain imaging on meditators trained in introspection and in giving phenomenological reports (e.g. in the case of Richard Davidson's work, Tibetan Buddhist monks).[62] Early work by Maturana and Varela set the stage for such research by describing the 'structural couplings' between an organism and its surroundings, without seeking to explain away the mental side of the relationship,[63] and Varela's later work turned this approach into a major research programme.[64] A full analysis of the interacting levels of mind and brain will have to include practised phenomenological reports on the mental experiences that result from stimulation of the central nervous system, as well as real-time brain scans of practitioners who first place themselves into a particular mental state. The phenomenological method as utilized in these studies is especially useful for scientific research because of its ontological minimalism. Experienced conscious qualities are correlated with changes in brain states with minimal a priori interpretation; the correlations themselves then lead to theorizing about the nature of the relationship.

Let us assume for the moment that the emergence of such irreducibly mental states is granted, and that they are not taken to need grounding in a different kind of substance such as a soul. One then wants to know, how are these phenomenological predicates to be understood? Assuming they are not just epiphenomenal but have some sort of causal influence, what kind of causality do they represent? Following a long tradition, I would summarize the various forms of causality that come to light through phenomeno-logical studies of this sort under the heading of *agent causation*. That is, there is a type of emergent causation associated with the phenomenological level of experienced causation that is not identical to other forms of physical or biological causation.

By introducing agent causation in this context, I mean to focus on a set of qualities or mental properties to which we tend to ascribe a unified identity, rather than presupposing from the outset a particular substance with certain essential properties.[65] The latter approach tends to favour top–down explanations of mental phenomena based on the pregiven nature of the agent (or agents in general), which raises a much greater barrier to integration with the neurosciences than do the phenomenological studies just summarized. For example, the conceptual demands of the free will debate on the one hand, and the metaphysical presuppositions of substance-based approaches on the other, inevitably draw attention away from the empirical considerations on which a science-based theory of emergence must rest. In contrast to these approaches, the present approach compels one to focus on individual mental qualities that might be involved in causal interactions with the subvenient neurophysiological level.

The question 'wherein lies the unity of these various qualities?' has to be deferred, since speculations regarding the metaphysical status of agents have a different epistemic status. (I return to such questions in the next chapter.) Only an approach to agents that is metaphysically minimalist can maintain contact with scientific data and modes of study. Events and natural states can be studied in this fashion; statements about substances cannot. In short, the methodological assumption becomes: 'there *is* no agent apart from the act-ing, no subject of change without the chang-ing, no unity apart from the process of unify-ing. The agent, the subject, and the unity are all to be conceived as emergent from the dynamic interrelatedness of antecedent physical events'.[66]

The combination of science and phenomenology in the context of an emergentist research programme allows for (and requires) this sort of open-ended study of human agency. For example, one can explore parallels between the ontogenetic studies of the biologist and the developmental studies of psychologists:

An infant's haphazard encounters with his world can lead to recurrent gross-motor or fine-motor skills. These in turn expand the range of his universe, and experimentation with sound making can lead to meaning making. Cognitive skills eventually develop and the physical autonomy of the two-year-old becomes the intellectual autonomy of the adolescent. The schemes of recurrence in the human person are what we call habits: recurrent operations that at first are haphazard, then are consciously practiced, and eventually become routine.[67]

The key to the approach is not to set the study of persons in competition with scientific study. As Wilfrid Sellars wrote in a classic essay:

The conceptual framework of person is not something that needs to be *reconciled with* the scientific image, but rather something to be *joined* to it. Thus to complete the scientific image we need to enrich it *not* with more ways of saying what is the case, but with the language of community and individual intentions, so that by construing the actions we intend to do and the circumstances in which we intend them in scientific terms, we *directly* relate the world as conceived by scientific theory to our purposes, and make it *our* world . . .[68]

In what direction does an emergentist theory of agent causation point? The study of the human person involves not only all the knowledge we can glean about the brain and its workings, but also study of the emergent level of thought, *described and explained not only in terms of its physical inputs and nature, but also in terms intrinsic to itself.* Biological systems are already 'end-governed propensities to perform certain behaviours', either learned or genetically based.[69] On this base-level system is built a second-level motivational system, which is composed of 'beliefs and desires about actions to be performed'. The motivational and habitual systems are in turn influenced by a reflective level involving higher-order cognitive processes.[70] Each level plays a necessary role in explaining the phenomena of personal existence, and the role of the one cannot be superseded by the contributions of the others.

The emergentist anthropology that results begins with the notion of human persons as *psycho-somatic entities.* Humans are both body and mind, in the sense that we manifest both biological and mental causal features, and both in an interconnected manner. The mental characteristics depend on the physical, in a manner analogous to other dependency relations of emergent phenomena throughout the biosphere. At the same time, like earlier examples of emergence, they are different in kind from properties at lower levels, exercising a type of causal influence manifested only at the level of mentality.

Note that this debate concerns not only explanatory adequacy; it is also about ontology—about (at least) what sorts of properties one is willing to countenance in one's description of the world. The debate between physicalist and non-physicalist views of the person, after all, is not only about science; it is also about what actually or really or finally exists. One must ask: are the properties countenanced by physicalists—physicalism, after all, must mean 'of or pertaining to the methods of physics'—the only sorts of properties that humans have? In debating the issue it is important to distinguish the ontology of the phenomena (i.e. of the world as we experience it) from the ontology of the *best explanation* of the phenomena. A cultural anthropologist, for example, might note that the subjects she is studying tell her about discussions with the spirits of animals and give explanations of her arrival in their village that conflict with the world as she experiences it; perhaps they take her to be in contact with the spirit of one of their ancestors. In *describing* their beliefs, she suspends judgement on the truth of their beliefs, attempting to be as accurate as possible in re-presenting the world as they see it. In her explanations, however, she will feel free—indeed, it is required of her—to offer explanations which use the ontology accepted by her fellow anthropologists, and which therefore implicitly evaluate her informants' beliefs, even though this ontology may diverge widely from that of the subjects under study.

An analogous question is raised in explanations of agent causation. Here the key question under debate is how much of the content of thought and subjective experience is to be retained in one's account of the actual world, that is, how much of it plays a causal role in the correct explanations of human experience. Some theorists defend an explanatory ontology that consists exclusively of brains and other physical organs and their states. At the opposite end, others argue that both minds and bodies represent primitive substances, defined as radically different sorts of things (*res cogitans* and *res extensa*). Still other thinkers (e.g. social behaviourists) hold that both brains and their social contexts exist, that is, both brains and whatever things we are committed to by an account of social contexts. The emergentist view I have defended here holds that the correct explanatory ontology has to include multiple levels of 'really existing properties', since brains, mental properties, and interpersonal structures all exercise causal agency.

PERSON-BASED EXPLANATIONS AND THE SOCIAL SCIENCES

Let us suppose for the moment that a sufficient case has been made for mental causation and that no conceptual roadblocks stand in its way. One now wants to know: what is the organizing principle for the study of mental causes? Since neuroscientific and phenomenological studies played a role in making the case, they are obviously to be included. But it is, more generally, the notion of person-based explanations that ties together the various pieces.

It is not difficult to describe what is normally connoted by the word 'person'. A person is one who is able to enter into human social interaction: praising your tennis partner, planning your dinner party for next Friday, carrying out your intention to graduate from college by next May—and being aware of (at least some) other humans as moral agents who have value and rights equal to your own. These are concepts of personhood that are basic to research in the social sciences (psychology, sociology, and cultural anthropology); they are reflected in the literature of various cultures around the world, as well as in multiple religious traditions. If emergence is visible in the evolution of life, how much more evident is it in the evolution of culture—in human thought; in the explosion of technology; in changes in language, belief, and fashion?

Of course, there are many questions that still leave us unsure. When does personhood start? Does it demand a metaphysical basis, such as the introduction of the soul or person-substance? Does it develop and end gradually? Can it be effaced within a human being? Is it a legal or social fiction, or an enduring reality? Such broader philosophical questions are crucial to the complete definition of personhood and hence part of the discussion that neuroscientists, philosophers, and theologians must have if they are to find any common ground at all.

Personhood is therefore a level of analysis that has no complete translation into a state of the body or brain—no matter how complete our neuroscience might be. Of course, it presupposes such states; yet personhood represents an explanatory level that is distinct from explanations at the level of our 'hardware'. As Brian Cantwell Smith writes:

First, you and I do not exist in [physical explanations]—*qua people*. We may be material, divine, social, embodied, whatever—but we don't figure *as people* in any physicist's equation. What we are—or rather what our lives are, in this picture—is a group of roughly aligned not-terribly-well delineated very slightly wiggling four-dimensional worms or noodles: massively longer temporally than spatially. We care tremendously about these noodles. But physics does not: it does nothing to identify them, either as personal, or as unitary, or as distinct from the boundless number of other worms that could be inscribed on the physical plenum . . .[71]

The language of physics or biology and the language of personhood only partly overlap; one cannot do justice to the one using only the tools of the other. To give a purely biology-based account of the person is like saying that, because a club or church cannot survive without being financially viable (e.g. receiving income from some source), it *just is* the economic unit which economists describe in terms of income and expenditures. The confusion, one might say, is a confusion of necessary and sufficient conditions. A living body and a functioning brain are necessary conditions for personhood, yet the wide discrepancy in the 'logic' of the vocabularies suggests that they are not sufficient conditions. Personhood is not fully translatable into 'lower-level' terms; persons experience causal and phenomenological properties (*qualia*) that are uniquely personal. Yet more extensive ontologies are of course available, such as those involving the real existence of ethical predicates, religious predicates, and various substantival accounts of persons, selves, subjects, and spirits; we return to these in the following chapter. But nothing in the present theory immediately commits one to going beyond the mental and the types of explanation (e.g. personal and social explanations) with which this level is associated.

The point is important enough to bear underscoring. An agent-based explanation posits that an agent intends to bring about a certain result or goal, has (conscious or unconscious) reasons to think that certain actions will serve as means for achieving the goal, and for this reason engages in the actions. Agent-based explanations are therefore intentional and teleological. As von Wright notes, 'The *explanandum* of a teleological explanation is an action, that of a causal explanation an intentionalistically noninterpreted item of behavior, that is, some bodily movement or state'.[72] Beyond this minimal framework, the notion of personal agent *as such* does not need to import metaphysical baggage that conflicts with science—notwithstanding the claims of some philosophers.[73] For example, it is possible to employ explanations using agent causation without asserting metaphysical ('libertarian') free will; agent-based explanations are compatible, at least in principle, with the determining influence of biological causes.[74] It is sufficient that agent-caused behaviour is

brought about by the behaver for reasons which make reasonable the sort of behaviour he takes it to be. We may call such accounts *intentional explanations*. There is a clear difference between justifying the reasonableness of a person's behaviour given his attitudes, and explaining it as the outcome of his reasoning from those attitudes. The existence of a broadly causal element in intentional action must thus be acknowledged.[75]

The point is not that metaphysical minimalism about persons is the only or the final answer; in fact, in the next chapter I offer reasons for thinking that it is not. Rather the point is that a minimalist account of personal agency is sufficient (and necessary) for the scientific study of humans in the world. One's theory can now draw freely not only on the neurosciences and cognitive psychology, but also on the whole range of the social sciences: psychology, sociology, cultural anthropology, and so on. Indeed, given the universality of religious rites, rituals, and beliefs across human cultures, a full understanding of the human person would presumably also have to incorporate some sort of religious dimension of experience and those social scientific disciplines that address it.

The ongoing debate about the nature and methodology of the social sciences recapitulates (and sheds some helpful new light on) this discussion. The two opposing camps appeal to the two warring fathers of modern social science, Auguste Comte and Wilhelm Dilthey. Comteans argue for a predominantly natural scientific approach to the social sciences, allowing no in-principle gap between them and the natural scientific study of the human organism.[76] Present-day Diltheyans maintain that the object of study to which the human sciences are devoted is significantly different from the natural world. The natural world can be grasped using *causal* patterns of explanation, because such events really are the product of a series of causes. But human actions require the method of *Verstehen* or *empathetic understanding*, for human beings are subjects who are engaged in the project of making sense of their own world. Intentional actions can be understood only in terms of the logic of intentionality: wishing, judging, believing, hoping.[77]

The battle continues. A new round was launched by the successes of behaviourist social science, by Abel's oft-cited Comtean manifesto for positivism in the social sciences,[78] and more recently by the rapid advance of the neurosciences; shots were then returned by humanist psychologists and by more hermeneutically inclined theorists.[79] At the same time, analytic thinkers have carefully stressed the difference between explanations of human intentional actions and causal explanations of occurrences in the world, as in Georg Henrik von Wright's detailed defence of the logic of intentional explanations.[80] Whereas Carl Hempel tried to subsume the explanation of human actions under his general model of deductive-nomological explanation,[81] other leading philosophers of science such as Ernst Nagel underscored the unique nature of explanations of social action.[82] The net result is a clearer sense of what it is that sets person-based explanations of individual and social action apart from causally based explanations, which Anthony Giddens describes as the 'double hermeneutic'.[83] Explaining human behaviour involves a constructive interpretation on the part of the researcher, as is also the case in the natural sciences. But at the same time the subject of research is *also* interpreting the experimental situation from her own perspective—which to our knowledge atoms and cells do not do—and her interpretation invariably affects how she responds to the research situation or questions.

CONCLUSION

With some 10^{14} neural connections, the human brain is the most complex interconnected system we are aware of in the universe. This object has some *very* strange properties that we call 'mental' properties—properties such as being afraid of a stock market crash, or wishing for peace in the Middle East, or believing in divine revelation. To suppose that these features will be fully understood in biological terms is precisely that: a supposition, an assumption, a wager on a future outcome. A deep commitment to the study and understanding of the natural world does not necessitate taking a purely biological approach to the human person; even less does it require that the actions of persons must be explained through a series of explanatory sciences reaching down (finally) to physics, or, more simply, that all causes are ultimately physical causes.

To say that the human person is a *psycho-somatic unity* is to say that the person is a complexly patterned entity within the world, one with diverse sets of naturally occurring properties, each of which needs to be understood *by a science appropriate to its own level of complexity*. We need multiple layers of explanatory accounts *because* the human person is a physical, biological, psychological, and (I believe also) spiritual reality, and because these aspects of its reality, though interdependent, are not mutually reducible. Call the existence of these multiple layers *ontological pluralism*, and call the need for multiple layers of explanation *explanatory pluralism*, and my thesis becomes clear: ontological pluralism begets explanatory pluralism. (Or, to put it differently: the best explanation for explanatory pluralism is ontological pluralism.)

What *emerges* in the human case is a particular psycho-somatic unity, an organism that can do things both mentally and physically. Although mental functions weakly supervene upon a physiological platform, the two sets of attributes are interconnected and exhibit causal influences in both directions. We therefore need sciences or modes of study that begin (as sciences must) with a theoretical structure adequate to this level of complexity. To defend an emergentist account of the self is not to turn science into metaphysics. Instead, it is to acknowledge that the one natural world is vastly more complicated and more subtle than physicalism can ever grasp. One can *wager* that the *real* things that exist in the world are physical or biological processes within organisms, and that everything else—intentions, free will, ideas like justice or the divine—are 'constructs', complicated manifestations of neural processes. But I have suggested that the better wager is on the other side. I wager that no level of explanation short of irreducibly psychological explanations will finally do an adequate job of accounting for the human person. And this means, I've argued, the real existence and causal efficacy of the conscious or mental dimension of human personhood.

NOTES

1. Research reported in *New Scientist* (13 July, 1998).

2. See, among other works, Bruce Weber and Terrence Deacon, 'Thermo-dynamic Cycles, Developmental Systems, and Emergence', *Cybernetics and Human Knowing*, 7 (2000), 21–43.

3. Rodney M. J. Cotterill, 'Evolution, Cognition and Consciousness', *Journal of Consciousness Studies*, 8 (2001), 3–17, pp. 5–6.

4. Thomas Nagel, 'What is it like to be a Bat?', in Ned Block (ed.), *Readings in Philosophy of Psychology*, 2 vols. (Cambridge, Mass.: Harvard University Press, 1980), i. 159–68.

5. Jerry Fodor, *Times Literary Supplement* (3 July 1992), 5–7.

6. Indeed, Colin McGinn has argued powerfully that solving this mystery will lie forever beyond the ken of philosophers. See McGinn, *The Mysterious Flame: Conscious Minds in a Material World* (New York: Basic Books, 1999); *The Making of a Philosopher: My Journey through Twentieth-Century Philosophy* (New York: Harper Collins, 2002); and *The Character of Mind: An Introduction to the Philosophy of Mind* (Oxford: Oxford University Press, 1997).

7. Francis Crick, *The Astonishing Hypothesis* (New York: Charles Scribner's Sons, 1994), 229.

8. Ibid. 229.

9. Stephen Kosslyn and Oliver Koenig, *Wet Mind: The New Cognitive Neuroscience* (New York: Free Press, 1992), 436.

10. Crick, *Astonishing Hypothesis*, 171–3.

11. For more examples, see V. S. Ramachandran and Sandra Blakeslee, *Phantoms in the Brain: Probing the Mysteries of the Human Mind* (New York: William Morrow, 1998).

12. Crick, *Astonishing Hypothesis*, 173.

13. Ibid. 251.

14. Ibid. 252.

15. See Christof Koch's discussion of the concept of 'grandmother neurons', defended in his talk to the ASSC in 1998. Proceedings from the conference are contained in Thomas Metzinger (ed.), *Neural Correlates of Consciousness: Empirical and Conceptual Questions* (Cambridge, Mass.: MIT Press, 2000).

16. Bernard Baars, *In the Theater of Consciousness: The Workspace of the Mind* (New York: Oxford University Press, 1997).

17. Francis Crick and Christof Koch, 'The Unconscious Homunculus', in Metzinger (ed.), *Neural Correlates*, 107.

18. Wolf Singer, 'Consciousness from a Neurobiological Perspective', in Metzinger (ed.), *Neural Correlates*, 124.

19. Ibid. 134. I have substituted letters for his numbers.

20. See Gerald M. Edelman and Giulio Tononi, 'Reentry and the Dynamic Core: Neural Correlates of Conscious Experience', ibid. 139–51, p. 139.

21. See Giulio Tononi and Gerald M. Edelman, 'Consciousness and Complexity', *Science*, 282 (1998), 1846–51. The authors build on their earlier conclusion that 'a key neural mechanism underlying conscious experience are the reentrant interactions between posterior thalamocortical areas involved in perceptual categorization and anterior areas related to memory, value, and planning for action'.

22. What is remarkable about the dynamic core proposal is that it suggests measures of neural integration and complexity which should lead to testable predictions. The predictions include that the complexity of the dynamic core should correlate with the conscious state of the subject. 'Neural processes underlying automatic behaviours, no matter how sophisticated, should have lower complexity than neural processes underlying consciously controlled behaviours. Another prediction is that a systematic increase in the complexity of coherent neural processes is expected to accompany cognitive development.' See the *ScienceWeek* Focus Report, 'Neurobiology: Substrates of Conscious Experience', at <http://scienceweek.com/swf077.htm, verified 28 Feb. 2004. In the article Edelman and Tononi conclude, 'The evidence available so far supports the belief that a scientific explanation of consciousness is becoming increasingly feasible'. See also their *A Universe of Consciousness: How Matter becomes Imagination* (New York: Basic Books, 2001) and their joint contribution to H. Jasper, L. Descarries, V. Castellucci, and S. Rossignol (eds.), *Consciousness* (Philadelphia: Lippencott-Raven, 1998), 245–80.

23. See V. Hardcastle, *The Myth of Pain* (Boston: MIT Press, 1999), 78-82, quoted in Michael Silberstein, 'Converging on Emergence: Consciousness,

Causation and Explanation', *Journal of Consciousness Studies*, 8 (2001), 61–98, p. 82.

24. Ibid. 82.

25. Israel Rosenfeld, *The Strange, Familiar, and Forgotten: An Anatomy of Consciousness* (New York: Alfred A. Knopf, 1992), 6.

26. Daniel Dennett, *Consciousness Explained* (Boston: Little, Brown, & Co., 1991), 270–1.

27. Gerald M. Edelman, *Bright Air, Brilliant Fire: On the Matter of the Mind* (New York: Basic Books, 1992), 29.

28. See Brian O'Shaughnessy, *The Will: A Dual Aspect Theory* (New York: Cambridge University Press, 1980); Jose Luis Diaz, 'Mind–Body Unity, Dual Aspect, and the Emergence of Consciousness', *Philosophical Psychology*, 13 (Spring 2000), 393–403; Dennis M. Senchuk, 'Consciousness Naturalized: Supervenience without Physical Determinism', *American Philosophical Quarterly*, 28 (1991), 37–47; Jack H. Ornstein, *The Mind and the Brain: A Multi-Aspect Interpretation* (The Hague: Nijhoff, 1972).

29. See W. J. Clancey, 'The Biology of Consciousness: Comparative Review of Israel Rosenfield, *The Strange, Familiar, and Forgotten: An Anatomy of Consciousness* and Gerald M. Edelman, *Bright Air, Brilliant Fire: On the Matter of the Mind, Artificial Intelligence*, 60 (1991), 313–56.

30. Terrence Deacon, *The Symbolic Species: The Co-Evolution of Language and the Brain* (New York: W. W. Norton, 1997).

31. David Chalmers, 'Facing up to the Problem of Consciousness', repr. in Jonathan Shear (ed.), *Explaining Consciousness: The 'Hard Problem'* (Cambridge, Mass.: MIT Press, 1997), 10.

32. Ibid. 10.

33. Ibid. 17.

34. See David Chalmers, *The Conscious Mind: In Search of a Fundamental Theory* (New York: Oxford University Press, 1996).

35. Clayton, 'Neuroscience, the Person and God: An Emergentist Account', *Zygon*, 35 (2000), 613–52. Originally in Robert J. Russell, Nancey Murphy, Theo Meyering, and Michael Arbib (eds.), *Neuroscience and the Person* (Vatican City State: Vatican Observatory Publications, 1999), 181–214.

36. See Jaegwon Kim, *Mind in a Physical World: An Essay on the Mind–Body Problem and Mental Causation* (Cambridge, Mass.: MIT Press, 1998).

37. John Heil, 'Multiply Realized Properties', in Sven Walter and Heinz-Dieter Heckmann (eds.), *Physicalism and Mental Causation: The Metaphysics of Mind and Action* (Exeter: Imprint Academic, 2003), 11–30, p. 14. Hilary Putnam and Jerry Fodor first formulated the multiple realizability argument against reductionism in the 1980s. For a helpful summary and discussion of their arguments see Elliott Sober, 'The Multiple Realizability Argument against Reductionism', *Philosophy of Science*, 66 (1999), 542–64.

38. See Harold Morowitz, *The Emergence of Everything: How the World became Complex* (New York: Oxford University Press, 2002).

39. Max Velmans, 'Making Sense of Causal Interactions between Consciousness and Brain', *Journal of Consciousness Studies*, 9 (2002), 69–95, p. 75. Velmans quotes the last phrase from his *Understanding Consciousness* (London: Routledge, 2000), 251. See also his target article, 'How could Conscious Experiences affect Brains', *Journal of Consciousness Studies*, 9 (2002), 3–29.

40. Following A. N. Whitehead, David Griffin advocates this view, which he calls *panexperientialism*. See *Unsnarling the World-Knot: Consciousness, Freedom, and the Mind–Body Problem* (Berkeley, Calif.: University of California Press, 1998), and *Reenchantment without Supernaturalism: A Process Philosophy of Religion* (Ithaca, NY: Cornell University Press, 2001), ch. 3. Chalmers was also tempted in the direction of panpsychism in *The Conscious Mind*.

41. See Kim, *Mind in a Physical World*. This work contains references to Kim's criticisms of non-reductive physicalism going back some eight years.

42. See Michael Silberstein, 'Explaining Consciousness: Convergence on Emergence', talk read at the 2000 consciousness conference, University of Arizona, Tucson; available at http://www.etown.edu/philosophy/pdf/verge-merg1.pdf (verified 26 Feb. 2004), 1. Cf. Silberstein, 'Emergence and the Mind–Body Problem', *Journal of Consciousness Studies*, 5 (1998), 464–82, esp. p. 468, and Silberstein and John McGreever, 'The Search for Ontological Emergence', *Philosophical Quarterly*, 49 (1999), 182–200.

43. See Robert Van Gulick, 'Reduction, Emergence and Other Recent Options on the Mind–Body Problem: A Philosophic Overview', *Journal of Consciousness Studies*, 8 (2001), 1–34.

44. William Newsome, Stanford University, personal communication.

45. See Nancey Murphy, 'Divine Action in the Natural Order: Buridan's Ass and Schrödinger's Cat', and Thomas F. Tracy, 'Particular Providence and the God of the Gaps', in Robert J. Russell, Nancey Murphy, and Arthur Peacocke (eds.), *Chaos and Complexity* (Vatican City: Vatican Observatory Publications, 1995). Clearly their reference is to the influence of transcendent mind, but presumably the same dynamics would in principle hold for natural mental causation.

46. See Henry Stapp, *Mind, Matter, and Quantum Mechanics* (Berlin: Springer-Verlag, 1993).

47. See e.g. C. Seife, 'Cold Numbers Unmake the Quantum Mind', *Science*, 287 (4 Feb 2000), and Max Tegmark, 'The Quantum Brain', *Physical Review E* (2000), 1–14. Against this view, the quantum physicist Henry Stapp has computed that the scale of microtubules is such that quantum effects associated with sodium ions could affect releases and thus the chemical composition of synapses (personal communication).

48. See the excellent presentation in Michael Silberstein, 'Converging on Emergence: Consciousness, Causation and Explanation', *Journal of Consciousness Studies*, 8 (2001), 61–98.

49. One must also raise the question of whether there is sufficient spontaneity or play or indeterminacy in the proposed systems for the mental event to be more than the sum of its (non-mental) parts.

50. Peter Schuster, 'How do RNA Molecules and Viruses Explore their Worlds', in George Cowen, David Pines, and David Meltzer (eds.), *Complexity: Metaphors, Models, and Reality* (Sante Fe Institute Studies in the Sciences of Complexity Proceedings, 19; Reading, Mass.: Addison-Wesley, 1990), 383–414. See also the collection of essays edited by Bruce H. Weber and David J. Depew, *Evolution and Learning: The Baldwin Effect Reconsidered* (Cambridge, Mass.: MIT Press, 2003).

51. See Maxine Sheets-Johnstone, 'Consciousness: A Natural History', *Journal of Consciousness Studies*, 5 (1998), 260–94, and Rodney M. J. Cotterill, 'Did Consciousness Evolve from Self-Paced Probing of the Environment, and Not from Reflexes', *Brain and Mind*, 1 (2000), 283–98.

52. Max Velmans, *Understanding Consciousness* (London: Routledge, 2000).

53. Ibid.

54. Velmans, 'Making Sense', 74.

55. Terrence Deacon, 'The Hierarchic Logic of Emergence: Untangling the Interdependence of Evolution and Self-Organization', in Weber and Depew (eds.), *Evolution and Learning*. But cf. also his *Symbolic Species*.

56. Deacon explicitly connects his conception with the semiotics of C. S. Peirce.

57. See E. J. Lowe, 'The Causal Autonomy of the Mental', *Mind*, 102, 408 (1993), 629–44.

58. John Searle, 'Minds, Brains, and Programs', *Behavioural and Brain Sciences*, 3 (1980), 417–24.

59. Roger Sperry, 'In Defense of Mentalism and Emergent Interaction', *Journal of Mind and Behaviour*, 12 (1991), 221–46, p. 230.

60. William L. Rowe, *Thomas Reid on Freedom and Morality* (Ithaca, NY: Cornell University Press, 1991), 49. See also Rowe, 'The Metaphysics of Freedom: Reid's Theory of Agent Causation', *American Catholic Philosophical Quarterly*, 74 (2000), 425–46.

61. Of course, the history goes back much further. A full historical treatment would have to include the work of Henri Bergson, before him Wilhelm Dilthey and Wilhelm Windelband, before them Friedrich Schleiermacher—continuing back ultimately to Augustine.

62. See Richard J. Davidson and Anne Harrington (eds.), *Visions of Compassion: Western Scientists and Tibetan Buddhists examine Human Nature* (Oxford: Oxford University Press, 2002). The conceptual background to this work includes Julian M. Davidson and Richard J. Davidson (eds.), *The Psychobiology of Consciousness* (New York: Plenum Press, 1980); and Paul Ekman and Richard J. Davidson (eds.), *The Nature of Emotion: Fundamental Questions* (New York: Oxford University Press, 1994).

63. Humberto Maturana and Francisco Varela, *The Tree of Knowledge: The Biological Roots of Human Understanding*, rev. edn., tr. Robert Paolucci (New York: Random House, 1992).

64. The programme is beautifully described in Francisco J. Varela and Jonathan Shear (eds.), *The View from Within: First-Person Approaches to the Study*

of Consciousness (Bowling Green, Ohio: Imprint Academic, 1999) and in Varela's last book, ed. with Natalie Depraz and Pierre Vermersch, *On Becoming Aware: A Pragmatics of Experiencing* (Amsterdam: J. Benjamins, 2003). Key elements of Varela's theoretical approach are described in his book with Humberto Maturana, *The Tree of Knowledge* and in Varela, Evan Thompson, and Eleanor Rosch, *The Embodied Mind: Cognitive Science and Human Experience* (Cambridge, Mass.: MIT Press, 1991). See also Evan Thompson (ed.), *Between Ourselves: Second-Person Issues in the Study of Consciousness* (Thorverton: Imprint Academic, 2001). Varela's early death a few years ago tragically cut short his contribution to this field.

65. One finds a certain tendency in this direction in William Hasker, *The Emergent Self* (Ithaca, NY: Cornell University Press, 1999). In other cases the debate about real agents seems motivated by the attempt to prove the metaphysical free will of the agent in opposition to compatibilism, as in some of the essays in Timothy O'Connor (ed.), *Agents, Causes, and Events: Essays on Indeterminism and Free Will* (New York: Oxford University Press, 1995), e.g. O'Connor's own essay, 'Agent Causation'.

66. Nancy Frankenberry, 'The Emergent Paradigm and Divine Causation', *Process Studies*, 13 (1983), 202–17, pp. 204–5.

67. Cynthia S. W. Crysdale, 'Revisioning Natural Law: From the Classicist Paradigm to Emergent Probability', *Theological Studies*, 56 (1995), 464–84, p. 474.

68. Wilfrid Sellars, *Science, Perception and Reality* (New York: Humanities Press, 1971), 40.

69. William A. Rottschaefer, *The Biology and Psychology of Moral Agency* (Cambridge: Cambridge University Press, 1998), 19.

70. Ibid. 20.

71. Brian Cantwell Smith, 'God, approximately', unpublished paper, 3. This paper provides a brief summary of the broader argument in Cantwell Smith's *On the Origin of Objects* (Cambridge, Mass.: MIT Press, 1996).

72. Georg Henrik von Wright, *Explanation and Understanding* (Ithaca, NY: Cornell University Press, 1971), 124.

73. The positions of Reid and Rowe have been mentioned above. But one finds a similar tendency in the extensive conceptual analyses of thinkers such as Richard Taylor, *Action and Purpose* (Atlantic Highlands, NJ: Humanities Press, 1973); Roderick M. Chisholm, *Person and Object* (La Salle, Ill.: Open Court, 1976); Chisholm, 'The Agent as Cause', in Myles Brand and Douglas Walton (eds.), *Action Theory* (Dordrecht: D. Reidel, 1976); and Randolph Clarke, 'Toward a Credible Agent-Causal Account of Free Will', *Nous*, 27 (1993), 191–203.

74. Sed Ned Markosian, 'A Compatibilist Version of the Theory of Agent Causation', *Pacific Philosophical Quarterly*, 80 (1999), 257–77.

75. John Bishop, 'Agent-Causation', *Mind*, NS 92 (1983), 61–79, p. 62.

76. See Auguste Comte, *Cours de philosophie positive*, tr. as *Introduction to Positive Philosophy*, ed. Frederick Ferré (Indianapolis: Hackett Pub. Co., 1988).

The debate is recapitulated in present-day discussions of the sufficiency of evolutionary psychology or the biology of human behaviour. For a good overview see John Cartwright, *Evolution and Human Behaviour: Darwinian Perspectives on Human Nature* (Cambridge Mass.: MIT Press, 2000). Against this insufficiently emergentist approach to the study of human behaviour I follow William Durham in focusing on the coevolution of biology and culture as the more adequate explanatory context; see Durham, *Coevolution: Genes, Culture, and Human Diversity* (Stanford, Calif.: Stanford University Press, 1991).

77. See Wilhelm Dilthey, *Hermeneutics and the Study of History*, eds. Rudolf Makkreel and Frithjof Rodi (Princeton: Princeton University Press, 1996); Dilthey, *Introduction to the Human Sciences*, eds. Rudolf Makkreel and Frithjof Rodi (Princeton: Princeton University Press, 1989). Dilthey used this argument as the basis for his broader theory of the social sciences. The debate was repeated in the work of Wilhelm Windelband and others; see Windelband's classic essay from 1894, 'History and Natural Science,' tr. Guy Oakes, *History and Theory*, 19/2 (1980), 165–85.

78. See Theodore F. Abel on explanation versus understanding in *The Foundation of Sociological Theory* (New York: Random House, 1970).

79. See e.g. Hans-Georg Gadamer, *Truth and Method*, ed. Garrett Barden and John Cumming (New York: Seabury Press, 1975).

80. Georg Henrik von Wright, *Explanation and Understanding*.

81. See Carl Hempel, 'Typological Methods in the Natural and the Social Sciences', in Hempel, *Aspects of Scientific Explanation and Other Essays in the Philosophy of Science* (New York: Free Press, 1965).

82. See Ernst Nagel, *The Structure of Science: Problems in the Logic of Scientific Explanation* (London: Routledge & Kegan Paul, 1961).

83. Anthony Giddens explains the difference between natural and social scientific explanations in terms of the 'double hermeneutics' that characterizes social explanations in *New Rules of Sociological Method: A Positive Critique of Interpretive Sociologies* (London: Hutchinson, 1976).

5

Emergence and Transcendence

INTRODUCTION

The previous chapters have sought to defend emergence theory on the basis of contemporary science. It is helpful to review the course of the argument to this point: the one natural world exhibits different kinds of properties at different levels, and different kinds of causation are at work at these various levels. There may be a very large number of such levels, with subtle gradations between them, or there may be a smaller number of basic levels. Mind or mental properties present us with an especially clear, albeit an especially difficult, example of emergence. Conscious states and experiences are not found in the individual neurons; they emerge out of the massively complex system that is the human brain. When we look at human persons and their qualities, we realize that the whole is indeed greater than the sum of the parts.

As I argued, one must be able to distinguish three or more levels of emergence for the emergence thesis to be correct. If the world contained only mental and physical causes, the difference between them (the critic would quickly point out) would represent exactly that 'great divide' that so stymied classical dualists such as Descartes. In order to circumvent this objection, I first studied a number of transitions in the natural sciences. Recognizing that the empirical details differed among the disciplines in our study, we nonetheless identified significant patterns across the various examples. Not all the transitions clearly favoured the strong over the weak interpretation of emergence. But in at least a significant number of cases, such as the evolution of organisms as causal agents, I was able to establish important analogs to the strong emergence of mental causes. When we encounter conscious phenomena in studying (and in being) human persons, it is therefore most natural to interpret consciousness as another evolutionary emergent—a product, albeit perhaps of a different sort, stemming initially from the same kinds of selection pressures that have produced other complex phenomena over the course of natural history.

Nonetheless, many find something worriesome in acknowledging the role of mental phenomena—which presumably explains the resistance among many scientists and philosophers to mental causation. Recognizing human agency as irreducibly personal means, for example, that the dynamics of cultural evolution have supplemented, and sometimes superseded, the selection pressures of biological evolution. Though the difference between conscious phenomena and other products of the evolutionary process seems hard to deny, it may account for some of the resistance to the strong emergence account of persons. Certainly the dynamics of cultural evolution—the evolution of ideas, institutions, languages, and art forms—diverge in numerous ways from the dynamics and laws of biological evolution. But there is another cause for resistance, one that is less often openly acknowledged and discussed.

MIND AND METAPHYSICS

The concept of mind is often viewed as inappropriate to scientific study. It is, we are told, a term that naturalists should use with caution, if not eschew altogether. Some of this fear is unfounded: we have discovered that there are perfectly respectable senses in which naturalists can and should include emergent mental properties in their explanatory accounts. And yet in the resistance also lies a kernel of truth. Although one can use 'mind' in the sense in which I have defended it without having to make any assumptions inconsistent with scientifically based naturalism, speaking of mind can also lead to importing a number of metaphysical assumptions. Rather than sweeping them under the rug or dismissing them with derogatory phrases, let us hold them up to the light in order to subject them to careful analysis.

What are some of the common connections between metaphysics and mind? It turns out that the position one defends on mind or consciousness in relation to the neurosciences will have significant effect on one's stance towards the classical metaphysical debates. For example, (i) if one takes microphysical phenomena (laws, energies, particles) to be fundamental, then mental states will have to be interpreted as epiphenomenal. This starting assumption is clearly uncongenial not only to mental causation but also to all more robust accounts of mind or personal causation.

Likewise, (ii) dual aspect theories tend to work against efforts to integrate first-person and third-person accounts of mind. Such theories link most naturally with monist ontologies such as Spinoza's (or Sankara's monism, or Ramanuja's qualified non-dualism, or Thomas Nagel's 'view from nowhere'). As is well known, dual aspect theories set the mental and the physical side by side, without expressing how or why they are related. This move claims to give a place to mind without really relating it in a causal sense to the physical world or natural history.

(iii) Emergentist monism makes mental properties strongly emergent out of a substrate that is neither 'physical' nor 'mental'. Emergent mental properties are dependent on the lower levels of the hierarchy, yet genuinely emergent from it. Hence thought is dependent on neurophysiology but not reducible to it. Critics of this view often argue that emergence theory comes closest to *property dualism*. Actually it would be better to say that it is a form of *property pluralism*: many different and intriguing properties emerge in the course of natural history, and conscious experience is only one of them.

(iv) Substance dualism was probably the dominant metaphysical view in Western history from Aristotle to Kant, although it came in a variety of shapes and sizes. One of the reasons was that it synthesized nicely with theological concerns. For dualists from the Patristics on, God was the absolute substance or perfect being (*ens perfectissimum*); but God also created a world of independently existing substances, which have their own existence even while they, being contingent, continue to depend on God as their necessary ground. Humans obviously have physical bodies; yet, being made in the image of God, each should also possess, or be, a soul (*psyché*) or spirit (*pneuma*).[1]

Finally, (v) a different metaphysical world opens up for those who endorse the more *idealist* positions on the relationship of consciousness and brain, positions such as panpsychism, panexperientialism, and proto-panpsychism. In metaphysical discussions, especially those informed by the metaphysical traditions of the East, such positions are much more attractive and harder to refute than in a science-dominated discussion of the sort pursued in the present work. Idealist positions, one might say, turn the hard problem 'upside down'; their challenge becomes to explain how physical reality (or the experience of the physical world) might arise from a reality that is fundamentally mental or spiritual—whether that foundation is universal spirit, *brahman*, or the God of pure Spirit.

Perhaps the difficulty of even the upside-down hard problem is revealed by the strength of the tendency to respond that the physical world must ultimately be illusion (*maya*).

One cannot read this list without noting that not all of these responses accept the framework of naturalism. It is one thing to concede that the most viable naturalistic theory of mind is not purely physicalist, in that it retains a causal role for mental properties; it is another thing to raise questions about the parameters of naturalism which have guided us through the treatment so far. Still, even to formulate the topic 'mind and metaphysics' is to raise the question of non-naturalistic theories of mind. Once named, it seems arbitrary to exclude the question from our analysis.

The quickest way to see what may lie behind the question is to consider some of the broader metaphysical frameworks within which the emergence of mind might be placed and interpreted. I limit the typology to four major options, which should be adequately representative for our purposes. First of all, perhaps such claims are just wrong. That would mean that this world is fundamentally physical in its nature and origins. As Paul Churchland puts the point, 'The important point about the standard evolutionary story is that the human species and all of its features are the wholly physical outcome of a purely physical process. . . . We are creatures of matter. And we should learn to live with that fact'.[2]

In this case the emergence of thinking inhabitants was a happy coincidence (at least for us); our consciousness, and the beliefs people tend to form about its origins and significance, reveal nothing about the world's origins, destiny, or essential nature. On the physicalist hypothesis, we hold beliefs about free will and values and rationality and conscious choices not because these beliefs are *true* but because there are biological advantages to our holding such beliefs. For example, perhaps holding them contributes in some way to human reproductive success; perhaps those who believe themselves free are more likely to mate with genetically desirable partners and to raise children who do the same. (Whether humans with metaphysical beliefs are generally more attractive to potential sexual partners is another question altogether.) Or perhaps metaphysical beliefs should be viewed in pleiotropic terms, as 'spandrels': by-products of evolution that do not themselves contribute to survival or reproduction, but are causally linked to processes that do.[3] In the end, though, human beliefs about non-empirical matters are to be explained in terms of their biological functions—or at least as by-products of processes that serve such functions—and not in terms of their truth value.

Second, it could be that some of the beliefs that humans form about the reality of mental causation are true. That is, it could be that these beliefs correspond to some fact about the world, as strong emergence claims, and hence that physicalism is wrong. But perhaps the reality of mental causation is a brute given of evolution, with no broader metaphysical implications or entailments. Recall from Chapter 1 that, according to Samuel Alexander, the emergence of mind is not the result of any divine creative intent that preceded the universe. Instead, the universe—whether by some unknown law of necessity or by accident—eventually produced conscious beings who possess mental attributes, who are motivated by rational and moral considerations, and who correctly view themselves as mental, rather than purely physical, beings. In this specific sense, the universe did become mental, and may even have taken on attributes of deity. But no broader metaphysical conclusions follow, such as that a God must have created the world.[4] Call it the doctrine of *contingent emergence*.

On this view, the evolutionary process from the big bang onward was not the product of conscious choice or design, since no conscious being existed at the time of the big bang. Hence one cannot make any predictions about the future of mind in the universe. Perhaps consciousness is destined to pervade the universe in a process of unending complexification, as Frank Tipler once speculated,[5] or perhaps our fate will be the colder one predicted by Friedrich Nietzsche:

Once upon a time, in a distant corner of this universe with its countless flickering solar systems, there was a planet, and on this planet some intelligent animals discovered knowledge. It was the most noble and most mendacious minute in the history of the universe—but only a minute. After Nature had breathed a few times their star burned out, and the intelligent animals had to die.[6]

On the present model, there is just no way of knowing which of these possibilities is true. Unlike physicalism, the metaphysics of contingent emergence endorses the reality of mind or mental causes. But mind is not an *intended* by-product of evolution; it is a naturally emergent one.

Third, one could deny that emergence is contingent and yet still provide a purely naturalistic account of its inevitability. A number of scientists in recent years have resisted the strong contingency view of what they call 'ultra-Darwinism', arguing that there is good reason to think that the emergence of life is necessary. John Wheeler argues that it was necessary for observers eventually to arise in order to transform quantum potentiality to actuality.[7] The 'fine-tuning' argument holds that the laws and constants of the universe in general, and the conditions on earth in particular, had to fall within such an extremely narrow range for life to emerge that the odds of this all happening by chance are astronomically small.[8] Many have argued that the randomness of evolution is many orders of magnitude lower than Darwinist accounts have granted. Thus Michael Denton has suggested that the limited range of protein structures highly constrains the possible outcomes of the evolutionary process; for example, if the whole history of evolution were rerun it is still likely that intelligent animals would arise on earth which had multiple digits on their hands, including an opposable thumb and forefinger.[9] In a recent book Simon Conway Morris has also argued that the emergence of life would inevitably lead to intelligence.[10] Others have more gently challenged Stephen J. Gould's famous contention that, were one to replay the history of evolution, radically different entities would emerge. Thus the treatment in *Life Evolving: Molecules, Mind, and Meaning* by Nobel laureate Christian de Duve details the constraints which chemistry places on the structures and functions of living forms.[11]

In all these examples the resistance to the contingency position is based on scientific factors that constrain the possible outcomes of evolution. None of these authors uses the existence of these constraints as proof that an intelligent designer must exist. Some happen to be theists, some are atheists, and some are agnostic with regard to all such metaphysical questions. This distinguishes them from the so-called intelligent design movement which is currently popular among conservative Christian scholars especially in the United States.[12] The intelligent design school uses scientific data concerning the constraints on evolution as proofs of the existence of God as cosmic designer, proofs that I do not find compelling. The key point here is thus to uncouple the question of the degree of contingency in evolution from the question of theism. The degree of contingency in evolution does not necessarily correlate with the probability of theism. One could hold for scientific reasons that evolution is highly constrained and remain an agnostic, or one could believe that the outcome of evolution is highly contingent and still be a theist.

This brings us to the fourth and final position. It is possible that the universe was created by a conscious being who intended (something like) the present outcome. Let us call this view *theism*, and let us call the being in whom theists believe *God*. Until recently, theists (in this sense of the term) believed that this God would have had to predetermine the outcome of the world process, in a manner not unlike the working of Laplace's demon. Laplace, travelling in Newton's orbit, imagined a demon who could know the location and momentum of all particles in the universe at all times. The demon, Lapace thought, would thus be able to predict any future state of affairs by creating the right particles in the right places at the right time with the right momenta, since past and future states would follow deterministically from that initial creative act. Recall Laplace's famous claim:

An intelligence which knows at a given instant all forces acting in nature, as well as the momentary positions of all things of which the universe consists, would be able to comprehend the motions of the largest bodies of the world and those of the smallest atoms in one single formula, provided it were powerful enough to subject all data to analysis. To it, nothing would be uncertain; both future and past would be present before its eyes.[13]

Unfortunately, much of the history of reflection in the theistic traditions presupposes something like Laplace's demon (although with more character).

To make a long story short, the world turned out not to work like this. Given present understandings of quantum physics and complex systems, we now know that even Laplace's demon could not set things up at the big bang such that George W. Bush would win the presidential election in the United States in the year 2000 CE. Given the limitations on the current scientific understanding of evolutionary emergence, we do not yet know *how much* control the God of theism could have. Perhaps the divine agent could construct the physical conditions at the outset such that first life, and later conscious life, would evolve with physical necessity within, say, fifteen billion years. Or perhaps this God could only exercise a continual creative pull towards conscious life while being unable to determine with certainty that life would emerge. Arthur Peacocke has written provocatively of God as a composer who writes the outlines of a composition but leaves it to living things to produce the actual music,[14] and the theologian Philip Hefner has introduced the idea of humans as 'created co-creators' who work together with God.[15] The influential metaphysical system of Alfred North Whitehead supports a correlational model of God and world, which among certain of his followers has led to the concept of a 'divine lure' that is arguably consistent with the theory of an emerging world.[16]

THE PRESUMPTION OF NATURALISM

I have presupposed that there is a certain presumption in favour of naturalism. That is, throughout the preceding chapters I have assumed that the scientific disciplines relevant to each particular area of study offer the most justified form of knowledge that we have about that area. This has not been a metaphysical claim. Thus one might accept it while insisting at the same time that, for example, when an object accelerates according to the inverse square law of gravity, it remains *metaphysically possible* that a divine being is causing the acceleration. Likewise, one can accept an epistemic presumption in favour of naturalistic explanations and still hold that it is metaphysically possible that, unbeknownst to us, the regularities of the natural world are occasionally, or perhaps frequently, broken by direct interventions of God. But, for reasons classically formulated by David Hume,[17] I assume that the initial presumption in both cases must favour explanations given in terms of natural regularities. (Whether this initial presumption is ever defeasible will concern us further below.)

It is worth pausing to spell out the motivations for this presumption. Among multiple reasons one could cite the fact that, if we do not make it, science as we know it would be impossible. Scientific activity presupposes that causal histories are reconstructible in principle, which they would not be if the cause of some specific phenomenon lay outside the natural order altogether. It is also true that, on multiple measures, the mathematical sciences offer the most rigorous form of knowledge that humans have ever possessed. The fact that extremely precise predictions can be made in advance and then verified or falsified by independent observers holds the exact sciences to standards that are inconceivable in other areas of study.

For similar reasons—though here things become a bit more complex—it is easier to conceive mental properties as features of the natural world than to conceive them as signs of the actual existence of a mental subject or soul. To conceive mind as an object invites dualism, since (as Descartes argued) an object that is non-physical, immaterial, not composed of parts, and not located in space and time must be a very different kind of thing altogether. As we noted above, something similar can be said of the different sense of 'dualism' connoted by the Aristotelian-Thomistic concept of the soul as the form of the body. In either case, introducing a radically different kind of thing into one's explanations brings with it knotty epistemic problems, not the least of which is the problem of specifying how the two kinds of things might interact (and how one would know it if they did).

Consequently, given the difficulties of reconciling dualism with the scientific study of the world, we found ourselves compelled in the previous chapter to speak primarily of mental *properties*: complex, emergent properties predicated of the brain (or individual persons or groups of persons) as their object. Introducing properties and actions, we found, is easier than introducing metaphysical agents. Certainly there is no problem locating brains among the furniture of the universe and spelling out their features and dynamics in the context of our overall knowledge of the physical world. Yet here's the rub: 'physicalizing mind' does not remove all the tensions either, because mental properties are so radically different in kind from the brain on which they are dependent that linking the two (brains and consciousness) remains the 'hard problem' of neuroscience.[18] The intractability of this problem leaves the presumption in favour of mental properties over mental entities—in this case, persons as a metaphysical unity of mind and body—less certain, more defeasible, than it would otherwise have been. We shall have cause to revisit this problem shortly.

Finally, for similar reasons it looks like one must acknowledge an initial presumption in favour of metaphysical naturalism—though here the presumption is once again weaker than before. By metaphysical naturalism I mean the view that there are no things, qualities, or causes other than those that might be qualities of the natural world itself or agents within it. Prima facie metaphysical naturalism confronts fewer epistemological problems, since it does not require one to know kinds of things different from natural objects in the world. That is, it avoids at the metaphysical level the dualism-related epistemic difficulties that Aristotelian forms and Cartesian mental substances have faced in the philosophy of mind. Further, such naturalism would seem to be more parsimonious than its supernaturalist counterparts, since it comprehends fewer types of entities within its ontology, its catalogue of the furniture of the world.

But parsimony arguments are a slippery matter. Most of us are convinced that the radical idealism of Bishop Berkeley is false (though I shall not argue for that conclusion here). Yet Berkeley's idealism is significantly more parsimonious than metaphysical naturalism, since it admits only the divine mind and some number of finite minds. It is no great virtue for an explanation to be both parsimonious and false (especially if it is false *because* it strives too hard to be parsimonious!). One should beware, in short, of infelicitious uses of Occam's razor. Perhaps it would be better to argue that metaphysical naturalism is to be preferred because it does not add entities that are *different in kind* from the natural world, making, at least in principle, for a more unitary ontology.

Certain considerations are sometimes claimed to support the extension of naturalism into the domain of metaphysics. But here the arguments are not decisive. Even though I have happily granted the presumption in favour of naturalism throughout the preceding chapters, I am forced to admit some weakening of the presumption when the task becomes to show the superiority of naturalism as a metaphysical position. I return to these difficulties in a moment.

IS THERE AN EMERGENT LEVEL AFTER MIND?

If the world around us, and the world of culture in which we live and move, are both pervasively emergent, then it is hard to avoid asking, could there be one or more further levels of emergence as well?

It is not unusual to find such speculations in recent writings on emergence. Barabási's popular book, *Linked*, for example, treats networks as a distinctive sort of emergent reality. Scale-free networks depend on principles and manifest properties not found in any previous science. They explain Stanley Milgram's famous discovery that there are on the average only 'six degrees of separation' between any two individuals in the United States.[19] As a form of reality, Barabási argues, networks are pervasive; complex networks describe the kind of reality behind 'sexual relationships between people, the wiring diagram of a computer chip. . . . the Internet, Hollywood, the World Wide Web, the web of scientists linked by coauthorships, and the intricate collaborative web behind the economy' (221). Hotmail.com became the provider for one-quarter of the world's email accounts and the Love Bug virus infected millions of computers on 8 May 2000 thanks to a type of emergent connectivity, the core principles of which we are only beginning to understand.

Some are suggesting that these emergent qualities are the harbingers of a distinct emergent level of reality beyond that of the individual. Just as James Lovelock's 'Gaia hypothesis' postulated that the planet as a whole could be viewed as a living system,[20] others are now arguing that the interlinking of intelligence and information is creating a new superorganism, a sort of 'global brain'. Thus John Stewart's *Evolution's Arrow* claims to detect signs of the emergence of larger and larger cooperative organizations over time,[21] and Robert Wright's *Non-Zero: The Logic of Human Destiny* predicts the global integration of humankind as a new achievement of human spirit.[22] After all, he notes, human history is one long process of forming ever new and larger intelligent networks. Marc Pesce argues similarly that the internet is 'a self-organizing system of intelligent parts coming together to create a whole. . . . The neogenesis of the Web represents a concrete physical manifestation of a force that . . . is directing us to its own ends.'[23] Even Steven Johnson, who generally writes in a more sceptical vein, is ready to speak of cities as emergent entities characterized by new forms of information exchange. 'To the extent that the Web has connected more sentient beings together than any technology before it', Johnson concedes, 'you can see it as a kind of global brain.'[24]

Although I respond to such suggestions with a large dose of scepticism, I must acknowledge that such questions are placed on the table as soon as one recognizes the existence of emergent levels in the natural world. Classical philosophers asked analogous questions when they wondered whether there could also be, beyond the level of mind, a level of spirit. Can emergence help to make sense of the predicates of spirit or even deity? Some have held, for example, that the divine grows and expands along with the expansion of the cosmos, life, and culture. The Lutheran theologian Wolfhart Pannenberg toyed with this idea early in his career: 'Thus it is necessary to say that, in a restricted but important sense, God does not yet exist.'[25] Or consider the more radical view of the Romantic philosopher Friedrich W. J. Schelling, who argued in his famous *Essay on Freedom* (*Freiheitsschrift*) that God was at one time merely potential and only gradually becomes actual over the course of history. Arguably, metaphysics in the tradition of Whitehead should also be emergentist, since it is a philosophy of pervasive becoming, even including the thesis that at least one 'pole' of the divine, the so-called consequent nature of God, emerges through the history of its interactions with finite occasions of experience.[26]

It is one thing, however, to use the term 'emergence' for whatever one thinks transcends or comes after mind, and quite another to work under the types of constraints that have guided the treatment of emergent levels since the opening of the present study. Take, for example, the notion of the emergence of spirit. If spirit (or Spirit) is introduced as a new type of *entity*, it diverges significantly from the way we were compelled to introduce mental causation, namely, as an emergent property of a complicated biological system. Is it possible to think a level beyond mind? Can one do so using similar methods to the ones we used in examining previous emergent levels? If applied directly—that is, in analogy with cases of emergence in the natural world—our inquiry to this point would suggest that 'spirit' or 'divinity' would have to be an emergent level or property within (or of) the natural world. Let us call this postulation *the emergence of deity*: the view that there is no substance or thing that is God but that 'deity' is a quality that *the universe* comes increasingly to possess over time. This emerging quality of deity (spiritedness?) could be imagined to feed back onto the world, in a way analogous to how mental phenomena affect physical states in the world. No God exists as a separate object, but there may be an increasing 'deification' of the universe over time.

As we saw in Chapter 1, Samuel Alexander's *Space, Time, and Deity* defends an emergentist theory of deity of precisely this sort: 'God is the whole world as possessing the quality of deity. Of such a being the whole world is the "body" and deity is the "mind".'[27] Alexander's metaphysic endorses a God who is in the process of coming to be: at one time there was no God, and now—to put it strangely—there is only partly God. No spiritual force set up the process in advance; instead, deity is radically dependent on the world.[28] This 'finite God', he writes, 'represent[s] or gather[s] up into its divine part its whole body' (ibid.). Alexander accepts, one might say, a verbal notion of God: the deity 'deisms' (his verb); and these 'deisings' or 'enjoyments of the God' are things that the world does. The *world* is the subject of these actions; *it* does them; but what the world *does* is to deify itself. God is verb only—as in the famous book by Rabbi David Cooper, *God is a Verb: Kabbalah and the Practice of Mystical Judaism*.[29] God does not create the world; the world 'deises' itself. One cannot be too squeamish if one is a radical theist of this sort. Pierre Bayle, the late seventeenth-century author of the *Dictionnaire historique et critique*, attacked the pantheism of Spinoza by ridiculing a God so tightly bound to world as to be indistinguishable from it: 'for one good thought the infinite Being will have a thousand foolish, extravagant, filthy, and abominable. It will produce in itself all the follies, idle fancies, lewd and unjust practices of mankind. . .; it will be united to them by the most intimate union that can be conceived'.[30] Alexander does not shy away from the pantheist conclusion: 'the body of God is the whole universe and there is no body outside his'.[31] To the extent that any features of deity are instantiated, they become true only of this world or of its inhabitants; humans may manifest 'godlike attributes' or 'divine love' without there existing a being or ground that is anything more than the natural world taken as a whole.

Indeed, one can find examples of philosophers who are yet more radical than Alexander in advocating the emergent property of deity without the separate existence of a God. Consider the work of Henry Wieman. Wieman writes famously that 'the only creative God we recognize is the creative event itself'.[32] We recognize creative good in the world, and yet we recognize it as 'supra-human', as 'different in kind' from ourselves (pp. 76–7). Wieman's response involves acknowledging the emergence of a property in the world— namely, 'there is production of unexpected good'[33]—while deriving from it the most minimal metaphysical entailments he possibly can. In one sense, Wieman admits, the creative event 'is not identical at all' with God; yet 'in whatsoever sense any concept of God can be identified with the reality of God, this concept can be' (Wieman, pp. 305–6).

Positions like those of Alexander and Wieman are not without their difficulties. Two aspects of Alexander's position in particular should give one pause: the divinization of humanity, and the finitization of God. It is, on reflection, perhaps an all-too-noble place to which his emergentism assigns humans: 'We are infinite because we are in relation to all Space-Time and to all things in it. Our minds are infinite in so far as from our point of view, our place or date, we mirror the whole universe; we are compresent with everything in that universe'.[34] Such a deification or divinization of humankind may have been attractive to Feuerbach, to Victorian England, or to German thinkers early in the twentieth century, infused as they were with the fiery certainty of cultural superiority. But the twentieth was, by any account, a bad century for the so-called infinite goodness of Man. There are also difficulties with the denial of all transcendence in deity. It is difficult to conceive what it means to ascribe godhood to the natural world. Mentality, yes, and perhaps even some deeper spiritual dimension. But if one is not inclined to affirm an object or dimension beyond the natural world, wouldn't it be more, well, natural to say that the predicate of deity is not instantiated—there is no x such that x is divine?

Nonetheless, the success of the sciences of emergence does provide some impetus in the direction of the emergence of deity. Such reflection has an ambiguous epistemic status: in one sense it is purely naturalist, since it does not assert the existence of any supernatural entities; in another sense it goes beyond naturalism by introducing predicates such as 'spirit' or 'deity' as aspects of the world.

This raises an interesting question: is the emergence of deity the only plausible metaphysical response to the new sciences of emergence? Or are there other conceptual positions that are consistent with these results? Finally, is *any* form of non-naturalist metaphysics still a live option in response to an emergent world?[35] To formulate this last question is to raise the contentious issue of whether there are any inherent limits to the domain of applicability of science.

THE LIMITS TO POSSIBLE SCIENTIFIC ENQUIRY

I ended the previous chapter with a defence of the human sciences as playing an irreducible role in the explanation of human behaviours. As obvious as it may seem that an adequate account has to preserve a role for what human beings do as persons, rather than just as biological or physical entities, that conclusion sometimes causes scientists to reject the emergence thesis. The underlying reason for the opposition has to do, perhaps, with tensions between standard scientific practice and the acknowledgement of novelty and irreducibility. When presented with the appearance of something new, the scientist's job is to show that, however novel it may look at first sight, the occurrence can eventually be explained in terms of underlying laws and structures.

Here is where the feud begins. Mind-body dualists—and in fact all those who maintain that the naturalistic approach needs to be supplemented—suggest that there is something inherently wrong with this approach. Because certain things that happen in the natural world are fundamentally different from what came before, they claim, science is misguided in its efforts to make them scientifically explicable. I have suggested that the resistance-in-principle to the scientific project, with its drive towards bottom-up explanations, is wrong-headed. Nonetheless, if humans are to gain the most accurate possible knowledge of the world around us, two things are necessary. We must make the most rigorous efforts possible to explain phenomena in terms of underlying causal mechanisms that may have produced them. Second, where explanations in terms of underlying mechanisms do not adequately account for the known or experienced data, we should acknowledge that shortcoming and seek to provide the most reasonable account of these limitations that we can find.

Although the latter requirement looks uncontroversial, it tends to bring the other side off the bench and into the feud. To deal with the shortcomings of scientific explanation in this manner, comes the retort, would be to acknowledge the possibility of some ultimate limits to scientific inquiry. But it is inadvisable to limit scientific inquiry in any manner. Moreover, it is dangerous, since it opens the door to superstition and dogmatism. Soon religious groups will start using their political power to impose artificial limits to scientific inquiry. Where scientists acknowledge gaps in bottom-up explanation, the superstitious will fill them in with gods, spirits, miracles, and magic.

Such thinking on both sides presupposes an irresolvable warfare of interests, with the one side championing the universality of bottom-up explanations and the other undercutting the value of such explanations. This warfare takes many forms. One smells the smoke of battle in debates between biological and more traditional psychological accounts of human action, or in no-holds-barred contests between scientific and metaphysical explanations of the world. The feud takes its archetypical form, however, in the warfare between science and religion. In the minds of some of the combatants, science must not *ever* acknowledge inherent dissimilarities across the natural world, lest religion declare a victory over science;

religion (replies the other side) must capitalize on every difficulty and set-back that arises in the pursuit of scientific knowledge. Among the regrettable results of this antagonism has been the stalemate between dogmatic physicalism and dogmatic dualism that has dominated scientific and philosophical writing over the last several centuries.

Obviously the stalemate has been unproductive; emergence theorists suggest it has also been unnecessary. In this chapter, and indeed in the book as a whole, I suggest a different model. Put in briefest form it is this: the line between what is explainable from the bottom-up and what is not is fluid; no one can specify in advance which phenomena can be reductively explained. The ideal response on the part of those with interests in metaphysical or meta-scientific or religious issues is to await the arrival of further scientific successes with enthusiasm and encouragement. God knows there will always be enough questions and enough unknowns that the door will never be permanently closed on the human responses of awe, wonder, and reverence. Scientific progress in one arena inevitably opens up new areas of mystery, as even a quick glance at the history of cosmology over the last fifty years will show. Or consider quantum physics: one of the most successful equations in history, the Schrödinger wave function, has led to the discovery of the mysteries of indeterminacy, the so-called collapse of the wave function, and the phenomena of quantum entanglement. It is unnecessary for religious thinkers to wrestle with scientists in the very domains where the latter have achieved their clearest successes. Conversely, scientists do not need to be dismissive of religious or metaphysical responses to the not-yet-known (and perhaps-never-scientifically-knowable), even when such responses are accompanied by the formation of corresponding religious or metaphysical beliefs.

As we saw in Chapter 2, emergence is a thesis about both what we know and what we do not know scientifically. Advocating strong emergence involves recognizing multiple levels of patterns and causes in the natural world, each of which allows for level-specific scientific study. But the flip side of this programme is an acknowledgement that human knowers are not in a position to reduce all these levels to manifestations of physics. Physics constrains the higher sciences, but it does not replace them. There is every reason to think that even the scientifically sophisticated humans of the future will require a place for the types of causation peculiar to life forms as they struggle to survive and reproduce and as they play and explore, as well as for the causes that we associate with the mental life.

Accordingly, in what follows I turn to some of the non-naturalist options that are raised by the emergence of mind or, more generally, by the apparent existence of multiple irreducible levels in the natural world. Emergence by itself does not compel one to take this step; it remains possible that strong emergence in biology and psychology is nothing more than an interesting feature of natural history. Nonetheless, the reasons I have explored—both the limitations of the naturalist standpoint and the potential explanatory strengths of the alternatives—provide sufficient motivation to take a very close look at the alternatives. It may just be that the phenomenon of mind is better explained in the context of transcendent mind than in the context of the denial of transcendence.

WHAT NATURALISTIC EXPLANATIONS LEAVE UNEXPLAINED

How universal is the presumption of naturalism? Is it ever defeasible? Are there certain contexts in which it would be rational not to accept it? Under what conditions might one override the presumption, and what sorts of reasons might one give for doing so? And what would replace it?

There are a variety of arguments against naturalism. The oldest stems from the perennial philosophical question, why is there anything at all? As even Kant had to admit (in his discussion of the antinomies of pure reason), there is something unsatisfying about explaining parts of the natural order only in terms of the other natural causes that help to produce them; one also wants to know what produced that natural order as a whole. This striving for a deeper reason, a deeper explanation, led Leibniz to formulate the requirement known as the principle of sufficient reason ('for anything that exists, there must be a reason why it exists rather than not existing'). The same motivation also underlies a number of the formulations of the traditional cosmological proof for the existence of God.

It is also questionable whether one can make sense of ethical obligation or moral striving given a purely naturalistic ontology. To derive an 'ought' from an 'is' is known as the Genetic Fallacy. If all that exists are the objective states of affairs described by the sciences, then all sense of obligation is ultimately an illusion. Humans may *feel* obligations, and there may be good biological, psychological, or sociological explanations for why they would feel this way. But no obligation qua obligation can be derived from such naturalistic explanations.[36]

Many claim to have had direct experiences that prove the falseness of naturalism. Obviously, those who indeed have self-authenticating religious experiences of a supernatural being or power have sufficient reason to reject the naturalist thesis (if the experiences are really self-authenticating). Those who have not had such experiences are in an epistemically more ambiguous situation, since the evidence at their immediate disposal can be no stronger than the general presumption in favour of testimony; and however strongly one interprets the presumption in favour of testimony, it certainly cannot match the weight of a self-authenticating experience. Still, there does appear to be a sort of cumulative case to be made from the history of religious traditions, which are repositories of human experience over multiple centuries. Moreover, despite differences in particular beliefs, the world's religious traditions do seem to be bound together by experiences that challenge the boundaries of naturalism. By the nature of the case, the argument from religious experience will never be decisive; but it is also not without some evidential weight.[37]

A related argument, also based on experience, may have broader appeal and validity. As humans we find ourselves confronted with the question of meaning and the need to find an account of our existence in the universe, and in our particular social context, that confers meaningfulness on it. In the absence of such an account many experience *anomie* (Durkheim) or 'nausea' (Sartre) or a sense of the absurd (Camus).[38] The argument then takes one of two forms. Some argue that naturalism is false because humans in fact possess accounts of the universe that make it meaningful. Thus Augustine writes from the certainty, 'For Thou hast made us for Thyself and restless is our heart until it comes to rest in Thee.'[39] But perhaps the stronger argument is not from the existence of an answer but from the existence of the question. Does not our preoccupation with the question of meaning suggest that there is something in our nature which is not and cannot be accounted for by any naturalistic explanation one could offer? What is true of the question of meaning might also be true of related phenomena: our longing for immortality, or at least survival of death;[40] our hope for an end of the universe, or for a state after that end, that would make the existence of intelligent life within the universe something other than futile; our preoccupation with the question of God. All of these questions serve, in Peter Berger's famous words, as 'intimations of transcendence'.[41]

Finally, the history of metaphysical reflection offers a series of sophisticated arguments against naturalism and systematic presentations of the views of reality that follow from these arguments.[42] In the absence of a deductively valid proof of the existence of God, it may be that metaphysical arguments will not compel assent from naturalists. But they certainly refute the claim that there are no coherent, nuanced accounts of reality other than naturalism.

There are other ways one could argue for the explanatory advantage of moving beyond the limits of naturalist explanations; each supplies reasons for considering theories that extend beyond the natural order as science comprehends it. In what follows I explore one example of such an argument. It should serve as a sort of roadmap for the remainder of the chapter, relating the steps of the argument and the varying conclusions to which it leads us.

The argument comes in four stages, two of which we have already encountered; looking back over the first two is the quickest way to motivate the third. In the first stage we found that the philosophy of physicalism is incompatible with the phenomenon of strong emergence, since it rules out those forms of natural causality that are more than merely a sum of physical forces. For example, the emergence account holds that humans are rational, moral animals who sometimes form true beliefs about themselves as psychophysical agents in the world based on the exercise of conscious rationality. By contrast, physicalism must reduce many of our beliefs about ourselves and our motives to their biological functions, which, ultimately, amount to changes in physical systems based on physical law. Since thought as such either does not exist in or cannot influence physical systems, a physicalist should not claim that he holds his position based on the force of the better argument. It may happen that his beliefs (which of course do not exist as such) correspond to the way things are. But his beliefs are not really responses to his (or anyone else's) arguments. Correctly described, they are states of a complicated physical system that we call the brain, or dispositions of another physical system, the body, to respond to external stimuli in a certain manner.

The second stage, as presented in the preceding chapter, goes beyond the conclusions that a purely naturalist study can support, but it in no way goes beyond the world of our experience. The argument was that the coherence of our mental states, and the causal influence that they clearly exercise in the world, is best understood as the product of a self-conscious mental agent. There was nothing non-naturalistic about this argument; instead, the claim was that such emergent phenomena are central to the naturalistic study of evolutionary history. The existence and nature of such an agent is nonetheless not something that scientific study could ever reconstruct; a mental agent as such could never play a direct role in a natural scientific theory. By contrast, no social scientific theory can avoid speaking in terms of personal agents. It would thus be misguided to treat the notion of a self-conscious agent as a 'merely regulative principle' in Kant's sense, namely as a 'pure fiction' of reason: pure fictions are not causal agents in the world, but you and I clearly are. We are thus theoretically justified in developing theories of human behaviour in terms that postulate mental agents or persons, although our theoretical justification does not come directly through any theory of natural science.

Stage one of the argument recognizes that mental states exercise causal force and that the resources of physicalism are inadequate to explain this causal force. No serious epistemic issues are raised by this move, since one remains within the domain of naturalism and scientific study. Hence, I have argued, one need not hesitate to expand one's ontology to include the variety of causes that one actually finds in the world. Stage two concludes that mental causes are best understood as the activities of agents, while acknowledging that the resources of scientific naturalism are inadequate to conceptualize agents. To the extent that the clear epistemic standards of naturalism will be hard to apply to language about agents, one feels some queasiness in including agents within one's inventory of the furniture of the universe. Somehow, it seems, one has to signal the more tenuous epistemic status of this particular concept as compared to, say, the idea that cells or organisms exist as entities and not just as aggregates of microphysical particles. I'll flag the difference by speaking of *the postulation of persons as self-conscious agents*. Again, 'postulation' does not mean 'fiction'; it means 'something known in a different manner than we know the existence of cells and organisms'. (This raises important questions about the hypothetical, 'constitutive' use of regulative postulates, which I have explored elsewhere.[43])

Stage one involved mental properties and stage two concerned agents; stage three is motivated by the question of the content of agents' beliefs. To believe something is to maintain that it is true. But naturalism, even enhanced by the postulation of personal agents, does not have the necessary conceptual resources to explain what it means for a belief to be true; nor can it say, in purely naturalistic terms, how a belief could be true. As reasoning agents we presuppose a fit, in many cases at least, between our beliefs and the external world. What must we postulate if we are to make sense of this core presupposition of human reason?

Thomas Nagel argues that, if we are to make sense of ourselves as reasoners, we must presume that there is some sort of ultimate fit between our epistemic dispositions and the world outside ourselves. 'What seems permanently puzzling about the phenomenon of reason, and what makes it so difficult to arrive at a satisfactory attitude toward it,' he writes, 'is the relation it establishes between the particular and the universal. If there is such a thing as reason, it is a local activity of finite creatures that somehow enables them to make contact with universal truths, often of infinite range.' Or, in a more pithy formulation, he argues that my reasoning is inevitably 'an attempt to turn myself into a local representative of the truth, and in action of the right'.[44] (The last words allude to Nagel's earlier, analogous argument that the rational commitment to justice involves a 'view from nowhere' in which the agent transcends her own interests and sees things from a perspective in which all agents have equal moral weight.[45])

To postulate that the world is inherently rational—that it is in its very nature such that it can be known by the exercise of human reason—is clearly an ontological step beyond the assumption of human agents.[46] But the postulation of a rational structure to the universe is necessary, Nagel argues, since the activity of reasoning cannot be explained without it. Indeed, it is sensible to require that our conception of the world should include an explanation of 'how beings like us can arrive at such a conception'.[47] We may not know *why* the universe should be such that this principle would hold, but we cannot imagine otherwise without falling into a scepticism that is contradicted by our own practices. Nagel concludes, 'We seem to be left with a question that has no imaginable answer: How is it possible for finite beings like us to think infinite thoughts?'[48]

Nagel's argument for the move to stage three is specifically directed at the insufficiency of evolutionary naturalism. Within its domain, naturalism offers the strongest explanations of which we are capable. The cell, the eye, and the brain are adequately explained as by-products of a random evolutionary process, but reason remains unexplained when treated in the same way. Reason makes sense only if there is an objective order consisting of 'logical relations among propositions'[49]; if there are only natural causes, no such order exists. For this reason Nagel declares himself a rationalist.

The stage three argument against naturalism stops at this point, which we might call *agnostic rationalism*. Nagel can acknowledge that there is something religious, or at least quasi-religious, about this world-picture, and he can express his hope that the religious picture is false.[50] But in the end, he thinks, reason does not enable one to give an explanation for the 'natural sympathy between the deepest truths of nature and the deepest layers of the human mind'.[51] Explaining the existence of knowledge—of reasonable, true beliefs—requires us to make the rationalist move, for we must assume that 'the capacity of the universe to generate organisms with minds capable of understanding the universe is itself somehow a fundamental feature of the universe'.[52] But that's as far as knowledge takes us. The trajectory of the argument points towards the mist-covered domain of a theistic world-picture. But reason, the agnostic rationalist holds, is not up to the task of ascending to such heights.

Nagel's arguments for the move to stage three are compelling. Still, one cannot help but sense an inconsistency in his unwillingness to follow his own argument through to its natural telos.[53] Nagel desists from applying the structure of his argument to his own conclusion. A world in which the conclusions of reason can be true must be one in which there is, as he puts it, 'a natural sympathy between the deepest truths of nature and the deepest layers of the human mind'; otherwise the fit of thought with the physical world, and hence the truth of our statements about it, remain unexplained. By the same logic, doesn't the fact of this sympathy between reason and the truths of nature *itself* require an explanation? Clearly no state of affairs internal to the natural world could provide the explanation, since the question is a second-order one: we want to know the reason for the 'natural sympathy' itself. Either the fact that the world is rational is a brute given, or it in turn has a reason. But the only reason that could function at this level is that the world was *made* to be reasonable, that is, that it was designed to be that way by an intentional agent.[54] The fourth stage of the argument, then, is one that goes one step deeper: the rationalism that Nagel has rightly been compelled to accept itself requires an explanation, which only an intentional creation would be able to provide.

A version of this argument has been widely discussed over the last decade or so under the heading of the 'evolutionary argument against naturalism', most often associated with the name of Alvin Plantinga.[55] The object of Plantinga's attack is metaphysical naturalism as supported by the standard evolutionary account of life in general and of human reasoners in particular. He argues that there is no reason to think that evolution (on the standard account) would ever have produced reliable belief-forming mechanisms. (Actually, Plantinga goes a step further and argues that the belief that one's own cognitive faculties are reliable, given the conjunction of metaphysical naturalism and standard evolutionary theory, is actually highly improbable.) As a result, the evolutionary naturalist has no reason to believe that any of the products of his cognitive faculties are true, including his belief in evolutionary naturalism. His position itself is self-defeating, since it brings with it a 'defeater' for every belief the naturalist's reason might lead him to form.

Part of the logic of Plantinga's argument maps nicely onto the case that Nagel makes for agnostic rationalism. But Plantinga's broader philosophical project involves an additional claim: we do not finally have reason to trust the deliverances of our reason unless we postulate a self-conscious, rational creator who is benevolently disposed towards humanity, that is, one who intends for humans to form true beliefs and who creates them and the world such that, at least in most cases, this goal will be fulfilled. It is not enough that we postulate that we are epistemically 'at home in the universe', as Nagel writes,[56] we must actually *be* at home in the universe. And this will only be the case if the rational fit between mind and world was intentionally created. Thus, according to Plantinga, only the theist, who believes that evolution is 'guided and orchestrated by God', is in the position to be able to explain the truth of her own beliefs, because only she offers a justification for the assumption of rationalism. She thus holds a conception of the world that actually meets Nagel's criterion that it include an explanation of 'how beings like us can arrive at such a conception'.[57]

Plantinga's argument is correct in underscoring the explanatory advantage of theism. What it does not acknowledge, however, is the cost of the move to theism, the cost that motivated Nagel's resistance to this final move. The benefits of theistic explanations may not outweigh the epistemic presumption in favour of naturalism that we encountered earlier. A full cost–benefit analysis reveals a much more nuanced decision than the 'winner takes all' rhetoric normally used by both sides in this debate. The naturalist is left with questions that cannot be answered, which is indeed a disadvantage; but she does have stronger empirical means at her disposal for resolving those questions that she does countenance. The theist has broader explanatory resources at his disposal, so that what were once brute givens come to have a place within an explanatory narrative; yet the reasoning that supports the position must venture beyond the well-known constraints and decision mechanisms provided by the natural world. If you think the cost of transcendence is too great, you have to pay the cost of unanswered questions. Of the two options, I have argued that the explanatory gain of transcendent mind is greater than what is lost by moving beyond the parameters of purely naturalistic explanations.

GOING BEYOND EMERGENCE

Having made the postulation of transcendent mind, one immediately faces a decision between two interpretations. On the one hand, one can interpret divine subjectivity on analogy with human subjectivity. In the human case mental phenomena are emergent from the complex physical system which is the central nervous system, while remaining dependent upon it. Extrapolate upwards, and one gets some form of emergentist theism, according to which deity emerges in the process of natural history. Deity, Alexander argued, is yet another emergent property of the universe, gradually appearing as it reaches certain stages of complexity. On the other hand, one can link emergence in the natural world with a nature-transcending ground or base. For example, one could hold that the divine was present as a being, force, or ground from the very beginning, even if some aspects of the divine agency only gradually became manifest as the universe proceeded to develop life, consciousness, and religious or spiritual experience. To the extent that divine mind is held to be transcendent or to precede the existence of the cosmos, the framework of emergence has been left behind. It can be reintroduced as a distinguishing feature of one's theistic conception, for example if one stresses the emerging, responsive nature of the divine experience in the way that process theologians do.[58] But if any element of mind precedes the cosmos as a whole or is not dependent on it, the resulting conception is not strictly an emergentist theory of mind.

There is a sense in which the first of these two options—Alexander's project of trying to account for the emergence of deity while working within the inventory of scientifically permissible things—is a logical extension of emergentist conclusions about the natural world. As such, it enjoys a kind of scientific support not available to advocates of transcendent mind. But is an immanence-based theory the *only* type of metaphysic that should be acknowledged? That claim is less convincing. With the last two sections behind us, it is easier to put into words what was strange about Samuel Alexander's 'emergence of deity'. Projects of this sort attempt to respond to the broader explanatory questions of the sort we have just explored, and even to find a place for qualities traditionally associated with God. Yet they make this effort while working only with the furniture of science, the list of physically existing things that a naturalistic study of the universe can provide. But if the framework of naturalism is inadequate for answering the explanatory questions raised by human existence, as the preceding argument suggests, then it is not clear why one should agree to work under the constraints of its ontology, limiting oneself to natural objects. If answering the broader questions forces us to employ concepts such as truth, necessity, rationality, or the good, the domain over which we predicate will have to be expanded as well.

Once the Nagel-like need for an expanded account is acknowledged, then, it is no longer clear that the broader questions are best answered merely by extending emergence one more step to include predicates such as deity. Perhaps this result is not so surprising. What we have encountered is a new field of questions that is constrained by the 'lower' levels but not determined by them. Thought cannot *break* physical laws; nonetheless there is sufficient room for the mental life even given the constraints set by physics and biology. Analogously, metaphysical proposals are constrained by the results of the sciences (a metaphysic cannot entail something that we know is scientifically false) and yet, within this limitation, a large number of possible metaphysical answers can be given.

When we raise the broader explanatory questions we are therefore forced to move beyond what empirical emergence can establish one way or the other. One can look for certain constraining factors: are the resulting theories compatible with the framework of emergence? Are they in a broad sense suggested by it? Do they begin with what humans have learnt about the higher levels of emergence in the natural world and then move beyond it in a manner that is motivated by the questions that science finds itself unable to address? In the end, however, it makes sense to defer to science only in the domain of its particular epistemic authority. When one is dealing with a field in which empirical inputs can usually decide between competing explanations, it is most rational to endorse that explanation that is best attested by the evidence. From physics to (at least the early stages of) the emergence of culture, appropriate evidence relationships can be established, resulting in discipline-based scientific study. But as one wanders deeper into the humanities, such controls are notably lacking. Of course, this raises no difficulties where the primary concerns are aesthetic, as in attempts to produce art or literature that is beautiful, meaningful, socially valuable, or politically empowering but that does not address explanatory questions. E. O. Wilson's famous proposal of a 'consilience' between science and the humanities, to name one oft-cited example, requires a purely aesthetic interpretation of the humanities, leaving all matters of true explanation to the sciences.[59] The humanities are not only about aesthetics, however; one also encounters ideas that claim not only to be true but also to be justified by reasons. If we are to avoid a draconian reduction of all questions in the humanities, and indeed all questions of human existence, to the epistemic authority of sciences, we will have to allow for another kind of explanation that is not based on scientific superiority alone.

Not surprisingly, some of the explanations put forward by humans in contexts other than the sciences extend beyond the natural world and its objects. Theists, for example, put forward explanations that involve a being or power which (if it exists) preceded the universe and created its laws and initial conditions. Claims with similar status but different content permeate the classical metaphysical systems and the world's religious traditions. Given their content, such claims require a different model of evaluation: experience gives rise to competing metaphysical explanations, but these explanatory candidates are not amenable to direct empirical testing. Faced with competing options and with reasons that incline one towards some and away from others, agents have no choice but to pursue the evaluation of the available options in the most sophisticated manner possible.

Convergence on a single answer, although a regulative goal for the endeavour, may not be likely, at least not in the sense in which one expects increasing agreement among scientists regarding which theories are the most empirically fruitful. But explanatory pluralism does not entail arbitrariness or irrationality. One has no idea how strong the arguments are or how much convergence may be achieved until one begins to marshal the case for and against the competing explanations. There is something suspect, bordering on self-contradictory, about attempts to use non-empirical arguments to show that only empirical arguments can be genuinely rational. After all, the relationship between science and philosophy or metaphysics is not constant and timeless; it varies as the theories and criteria for knowledge in the two domains change over time. For example, the science–metaphysics relationship in the 1780s, at the time of Kant's *Critique of Pure Reason*, does not correctly describe their relationship today: Newton's laws, we now know, are not universally valid; non-Euclidean geometries better describe the world of massive gravitational objects than Euclid's postulates did; cosmology is now an empirical science, not an idea of pure reason; and philosophy can rarely (if at all) achieve apodeictic certainty for its conclusions by means of syllogistic reasoning.

Once one has granted the viability of this sort of rational endeavour, one is no longer compelled to work within the restraints of a 'bottom–up' ontology. It *may* turn out that the broader questions are in the end best answered by metaphysical naturalism. Perhaps 'deity' is best understood, as Alexander believed, on analogy with properties such as 'reproduction', 'life', or 'thought', which we ascribe to cells, organisms, and minds respectively. But I have argued that more plausible accounts are achieved when one drops the stipulation of an empirical-world-only ontology. From an explanatory perspective it is unlikely that the sorts of qualities generally associated with deity—eternality, omnipresence, perfection, justice—correctly characterize inner-worldly objects. If such qualities are instantiated at all, as Alexander and Wieman think, they will be instantiated by an object that is different in kind from such intra-mundane properties.

The suggestion, in short, is that one conceive suprapersonal mind (or spirit or deity) not merely as an emergent quality of the natural world, but also as a source of agency in its own right.[60] It is most plausible to conclude *either* that the attributes generally associated with deity are not instantiated—they are not true of any object or objects—*or* that they are true of an entity or dimension that is not identical with the universe or any of its parts. This entity or dimension, even if it encompasses or includes the universe in its being, transcends it as well.

To make this move is to postulate transcendent mind. Of all the difficult issues one has to resolve in order to make sense of transcendent mind, one in particular is connected with the territory covered in the previous chapter: the notion of conscious agency. Providing a robust account of what is entailed in being a conscious human agent is one small step, though perhaps not a wholly insignificant one, in the project of making sense of the postulation of transcendent agency. Once one has given an adequate account of human agency, the door is at least open for theists to specify the ways in which the trans-empirical agent whom they postulate is like human agents and the ways in which it is distinct from them. That is, certain analogies must hold in virtue of the shared quality of agency, even if the two types of agents are otherwise quite different; otherwise talk of God as an agent is sheer equivocation. Once the minimal analogies are established, the discussion can move in two directions: thinking upwards to the metaphysical level from what is known about mental agency in the natural world, and thinking downwards from the theistic hypothesis to see how it may influence our understanding of human mind.

What are the prospects for conceiving divine agency? Using the concept of 'the image of God' (*imago dei*), theists have traditionally claimed that there are analogies between human persons, and in particular human minds, on the one hand, and God, understood as divine mind or Spirit, on the other. How is that analogy affected by the move to an emergentist theory of mind: is it undercut or is it strengthened? In some respects the results of this study are supportive for theistic claims; in other respects, however, the conceptual difficulties will force concessions that have not yet been widely accepted among theists. How will the emergentist be inclined to reconceive divine mind? What different conceptions of divine action will be entailed?

Before turning to this final question, it is necessary to step back from the argument for a moment and consider what happens epistemically when one begins to entertain the hypothesis of transcendent mind. While this position affirms that all mental phenomena in the empirical world are dependent on a biological substrate, it postulates that transcendent mind is not downwardly dependent in this way. This fact accounts for the ineliminable element of dualism in the theistic hypothesis. As we saw, the attractiveness of theism stems from the difficulties of reducing divinity or spirituality to the role of an attribute of the finite universe. Theism offers a broader framework within which the cosmos can be 'located' and explained. God serves as the source and (it is hoped) the ultimate culmination of the universe, its Alpha and Omega, the force or presence that underlies and sustains it. Yet this move, however metaphysically desirable it may be in the end, forces the chain of explanation beyond the framework that one otherwise uses to explain mental properties, in so far as it imagines a mind that is distinct in its essence from the natural order taken as a whole. The theist whose conception of human mind is drawn from emergence theory, as mine is, has avoided a dualistic response to the mind–body problem. But he has done so at the cost of opening up a theological dualism elsewhere in his system, namely in his conception of the relationship of the divine nature to the nature of the finite world.

In summary, the first half of this chapter has argued that there is a plausible argument leading from the fact of evolutionary emergence to God. Emergence theory represents an explanatory ladder leading from the big bang and fundamental physical laws through the process of biological evolution and up as far as the emergence of culture. The theistic emergentist then argues that the thought and action of *homo sapiens* (among other phenomena) confront us with certain predicates, qualities, and beliefs that are anomalous from the standpoint of natural law. Explaining these qualities and assessing the truth of these beliefs sets in motion an explanatory chain that eventually leads outside of natural science, and thus beyond the theoretical resources of emergence theory. One response is to infer the emergence of deity, or at least deity-predicates (Alexander); another is to postulate the rational nature of the universe as a brute given (Nagel); another is some form of theism. The theistic account concludes to a conscious intentional being or force that preceded the evolutionary process and whose creative intentions led, however indirectly, to the emergence of intelligent life. Depending on how high one estimates the costs to be of introducing transcendent explanations, one may be inclined to break the explanatory chain and remain within the epistemic constraints of naturalism, as in Nagel's agnostic rationalism. I argued, however, that these costs are not so high that one should resist linking strong emergence with theism, in so far as conjoining

the two brings with it explanatory strengths not available to naturalistic theories alone.

But theism, if it is to be more than the postulation of a divine
ground or a deistic divine source that has since grown mute, entails
some sort of divine involvement with the world. Thus the theist's
task is not complete without some account of divine action. Is this
idea compatible with the science of strong emergence? Indeed, is
there any sense in which the resources of emergence theory provide
more of an opening for conceiving divine action than do other
models of the natural world?

TRADING MIND—BODY DUALISM FOR THEOLOGICAL DUALISM

Theism is doubly hard to conceive in the contemporary context.
First, in the face of science's strong push towards immanent
explanations one must make the case that language about a
transcendent being or dimension is meaningful. Although I have
argued that the rejection of transcendence is unnecessary, clearly
the move to transcendent mind is one that many resist. Once it is
made, a second challenge arises: the task of making some sense of
the idea of divine causal activity in the world.

The second step is more difficult than the first: it is easier to hold
that there is a ground of all things than to maintain that this ground
also actively influences the world in some way. For example, a
creation of all things 'before the foundation of the world' does not
interfere in any way with scientific explanation, whereas a God who
would be doing things within the cosmos subsequent to the big
bang would be encroaching on the territory for which the sciences
are responsible. The possibility of direct conflicts is very real. Moreover, making this claim is metaphysically more difficult or, as one
might say, more 'expensive'. A God who carries out actions has
to be conceived not just as a ground or force but also as an
agent, which means that the divine must be somehow analogous to
human agents. Modern philosophy, at least until the middle of
the nineteenth century, represents a sustained struggle with the
difficulties of this notion.[61]

Part of the problem is that we are no longer sure what to make
of the notions of mind or spirit. The metaphysical resources of
the Western tradition—the conceptual worlds of *ruach, pneuma,
spiritus, Geist*—are difficult to reconcile with the attitude and results

of contemporary science.[62] One can of course still assert that 'God is Spirit, infinite and eternal in his being and perfections', to para-phrase the Westminster Confession,[63] one can affirm that humans are made 'in the image of God' (*imago dei*); and one can conclude that each human therefore possesses a God-like spirit or soul, as the Pope recently reaffirmed in his statement on evolution.[64] But whereas this view once accorded nicely with the natural science (natural philosophy) of a previous era, it stands in deep tension with the approaches and the results of the science of our own.

That is where the emergence argument comes in. If successful, this argument represents a *tertium quid* between physicalist treat-ments of mind, which leave no place for talk of spirit, and dualist treatments, which simply assume (in my view, too easily) the con-tinuing validity and usefulness of such language. Having followed the argument for strong emergence through the opening four chapters, and having traced the theory of mind that it supports, one now wants to know: how does it realign traditional views of the God–world relationship? If there is divine agency, how should it be reconceived in light of our new understanding of human agency?

Though the fact has not always been admitted, the relationship between understanding human agents and understanding the divine agent has always been a two-way street. Not infrequently, theories of the divine agent (theologies) have strongly influenced how human persons were conceived (the *imago dei* argument). But just as clearly, ideas about what humankind is—variously influ-enced by art, religion, philosophy, societal and political structures, and cultural practices—have provided models for how God is to be conceived. In an age of absolute monarchy and male dominance, God was naturally conceived as the King of Kings; in an age of deterministic physics, God was known as the Divine Watchmaker, the Ground of order and lawfulness; and in an age of dualism, God became pure spirit, pure mind (*nous noetikos*), independent of all things physical. In an age of emergence, how should the divine agent be conceived? In this context, what sense can be made of the idea of divine influence on the world? Or is that an idea that is simply no longer credible?

The dilemma that faces the theist is not difficult to state. The theist can construe human and divine agency as similar by seeing human mental activity as involving the introduction of a new, non-physical energy into the universe, in which case one ends up with a strongly dualistic picture of the mind–body relation; or one can preserve the continuity between mind and body, say by seeing the energy of mind as a sort of 'transduction' of biochemical energy (Christian de Duve),[65] in which case one ends up with a more dualistic picture of the God–world relation. In the latter case human agents are conceived as existing in much greater continuity with other natural processes and energies and hence as being ontologically more distant from the divine agent. As a result, however, it becomes more difficult to conceive the relation between the 'bottom–up' effects expressed as the operation of physical laws and the 'top–down' or focally intended divine actions through which God is imagined to communicate with human minds. I have advocated accepting the second horn of the dilemma, interpreting mind as in continuity with the natural world—in part because it preserves the possibility of neuroscience, and in part out of the conviction that, if one has to countenance some measure of dualism, the relation between an infinite God and a finite world is the right place to locate it. After all, as soon as one affirms the existence of a God who does not depend upon the existence of the physical world, has one not already advocated a position that is, at least in this respect, irreducibly dualistic?[66]

RETHINKING DIVINE ACTION

The various pieces are now in place for addressing the question of divine action. I have made the case for strong emergence in physics and biology; I have defended an understanding of mind that allows for mental causation without depending on a dualism that would obviate neuroscientific study; and I have explored a view of the God–world relation that radicalizes the immanence of God. What response to the problem of divine action is suggested by the resulting position?

It does not seem possible to defend physical miracles in a way that does not conflict with the approach, methods, and results of contemporary science. Now there may be one conceivable type of divine causal activity within the realm of physics that would circumvent the conflict, namely if one postulated that God affected the world at the quantum level (assuming that quantum events are indeed ontologically indeterminate), influencing this or that wave function collapse in one direction or another while still maintaining the overall probability distributions that are basic to quantum physics.

In this case no laws would be broken. The trouble, of course, is that we do not now and never could in the future possess any evidence that a God in fact influences the world at this level. Nor can we tell any convincing story of how God might amplify even billions and billions of such quantum-level interventions so as to convince (say) the hostage-taker not to kill the children who are under his control. The quantum approach encounters a further difficulty: if the level of the mental is anomalous (not governed by laws), then God could not, even in principle, determine the outcome of someone's thought through this mechanism, though in principle God could make one thought or another more probable. It remains important, for any assertion of actual divine influence on the world, that the physical world be an indeterminate system, since otherwise the physics would not leave room for the spontaneity of animal behaviour or the effects of downwards mental causation; and with these gone, the idea of divine influence on outcomes would become vacuous. Still, it is, I suggest, impossible to solve the problem of divine action at the quantum level alone.

Except for the quantum possibility, nothing in our exploration of science up to this point provides a way to make conceivable the idea of miracles in the physical world. Of course miracles in the strong sense—suspensions of natural law by God, who directly brings about some outcome without the mediation of finite causes—remain metaphysically possible: an infinitely powerful being (if one exists) could do anything it wanted in and with the world it created. Making this blanket assertion does not count as a solution to the problem of divine action, however. Because our knowledge of physics represents the most rigorous, most lawlike knowledge humans have of the world, there is never justification for assuming the falseness of physics except in so far as one is arguing for a new and better physics. Again, it can never be *ruled out* that there should be exceptions to physical law and that God should be the cause of one or more of these exceptions. And a given individual may be deeply convinced in some particular case that an exception has occurred and God was the cause of what happened. But when the alleged exception falls in the area of pure physical systems—those unaffected by human (and perhaps animal) agency—then her belief can never rise to the level of knowledge, understood as the process and results of intersubjective inquiry.

But matters are not the same when it comes to human action. (In principle, and *mutatis mutandis*, these arguments would apply to animals as well, though I do not explore that possibility here.) In the case of human thought and the actions that stem from it, no laws determine the decision-making process. Of course, given the structure of a brain, a given life history, and a specific set of environmental inputs, one result may be much more likely than others. But no natural laws are broken if, on the basis of a process of reflection, you do something different from what it was probable that you would do. I have argued that strong emergence is consistent both with the constraining effects of the relevant physical and biological systems and with the data on human behaviour, including introspective phenomena, whereas its competitors are not. Weak emergence does not do justice to the reality of mental causal agency. Dualism postulates the addition of qualitatively different energies by a qualitatively different kind of cause, reflecting the agency of an altogether different kind of substance. In addition to being unnecessary, the dualist response makes a mockery of the neurosciences, understood as the scientific study of the correlations between states of the central nervous system and the experienced phenomena of consciousness. If brain states are the result of inputs from a purely mental kind of energy that is unrelated to the electrochemical causal powers in the brain, then no knowledge of the interaction is possible; one would face a lawlike system that on a regular basis acts in a completely un-lawlike manner. By contrast, if conscious causes are emergent properties of the neurological systems that compose the brain, then some understanding of their operation is possible, even if they are not in the end controlled by overarching covering laws.

What then of divine influence on mental processes? Certainly it is not ruled out by the present conception. On this view, although thought is a natural phenomenon it is not determined by physical laws and is upwardly open to higher types of causality. It is permissible to construe divine causality as one of these higher levels of causality. Since human actions are already unpredictable on the basis of prior brain states and environmental factors, no determining conditions are broken when (if) a divine influence leads to a different outcome.

But how similar are these putative divine causes to mental causes understood as emergent? Here the theist faces a dilemma. The resources of emergence theory can help her introduce and defend divine action, but only if she construes the divine as the next emergent level in the cosmic evolutionary process. Earlier we considered theorists such as Samuel Alexander who were willing to make this move. For Alexander God was not a pre-existing being but a new type of property, 'deity', that comes to characterize the world at a certain point in its complexification. Obviously, this sort of theory, although it may offer a naturalized framework for speaking of the influence of deity, will not yield divine action in anything like its traditional form. Most forms of theism are (rightly) highly reticent to construe God as merely an emergent feature of the world.

Assuming then that one resists a fully emergentist theology, the resources of emergence will be of only limited assistance in formulating a theory of divine influence on human thought. The energy of divine causality, whatever it is, is not adapted or modified from energies elsewhere in the universe, because divine causes are not the product of the same natural system. Hence the principles that have been so fruitful in explaining human thought will not be able to do the same for divine influences. Consequently, divine causes will not be knowable in the same fashion, for the standard ways we come to know the processes of emergent systems and their products will not be available in this case.

When one looks back over the history of attempts to give a philosophical account of how God might influence human minds, one finds two distinct strategies employed. Each of the two has to find a way to interrelate three (among the many) levels of causality: physical causes, mental causes, and divine causes. The first strategy construes the human person on the model of the divine person or persons, following the biblical model of the creation of humanity 'in the image of God'. Here causal interactions between humans and God are unproblematic, since they are presupposed to be of fundamentally the same nature. This ease of interaction is bought with a price, however: the human soul or spirit is now different in nature from the physical world, so that comprehending mind–body interactions becomes difficult if not impossible. The concept of divine–human intercourse is made more manageable, but only at the cost of turning every impact of the mind on the body into a little miracle of its own. Let us call this dualistic view *the anthropology of the supernatural soul*. The second strategy construes the human person as a naturally occurring phenomena within the world; call it *the naturalized view* of the human person. The resulting family of positions makes it much easier to solve the mind–body problem, as we saw in the previous chapter. But now the dualism crops up in a different place—namely, in the relationship between human causality and divine causality—bringing with it the epistemic and ontological problems that are associated with any dualism.

What does and does not follow from the theological dualism that we have been forced to acknowledge? Once one abandons the thesis that divine causality is an emergent product of minds, the critic might complain, there is no longer any reason to expect that divine causation will be operative solely at the mental level. Given theological dualism, why should a direct divine influence on physical systems present any greater difficulties than a divine influence on human thought? I suggest however that this response is mistaken. First, the sciences of emergence have led to the recognition that nature is open to top–down influences. Indeterminacy at the bottom allows for whole–part constraint and downward causation (weak and strong emergence), but there is no sign that purposive directedness works from the bottom–up (unless of course it is built into the laws and initial conditions of the universe *ab initio*). Second, the level at which information could be communicated and understood is the level of conscious mental processing. Hence if information about the divine were to be conveyed to conscious agents one would expect it to come in a top–down manner. Finally, claims about divine interventions at lower levels face the unknowability problem. If a series of divine interventions at some level (say, quantum physics) radically realigned the expected probabilities, one would then have to speak of an occurrence much closer to a traditional miracle. If however no results are observed that are statistically very highly improbable, one will not have any reason to believe that any bottom-up divine influence has been operative.

Of course, the fact that bottom–up divine action would be forever undetectable does not make it impossible. But I should think that one would want *some* reason for advancing the idea that God is causally active right at the heart of physics, lest the claim appear meaningless. (Think of John Wisdom's famous parable of the invisible, undetectable gardener.[67]) Here the fundamental difference between physics-level and thought-level divine action becomes apparent. The nature of the causal relations at any given level is crucial. In physics, where we have detected the most rigorously lawlike behaviour of all, nothing in the theoretical framework suggests or requires that causes be meaningful or purposive. In fact, everything in the way we do physics forbids treating physical causes in this manner. By contrast, I have argued, adequate explanations of human behaviour and thought require reference to goals, intentions, and reasons. Thus, however the disputes about evidence turn out, there is at least a type–type fit in the latter case. The human sciences may not envision including a divine agent among the causal influences, but they at least have a place for agential causes, whereas agential causes are just not among the types of causes countenanced by physics.

Indeed, there is even a sense in which reference to transcendent or divine influences is a natural next step in one hierarchy: the hierarchy of meaning. When basic physical, emotional, and social needs are met, humans invariably raise questions of the 'ultimate meaning of it all'. In the quest to understand what reality is ultimately, and what is our place in it, humans often turn to the language of transcendence. This fact serves as reason to preserve a type of discourse that allows broader theoretical proposals to be formulated and perhaps even tested. Questions of this sort are not amenable to empirical resolution, since by their very nature they go beyond what empirical theories could ever establish; they could thus never become subsets of scientific theorizing. But nor is it obvious that they are nothing more than an expression of wishful thinking, affective response, and artistic licence. Intense debates take place at this level that involve careful conceptual distinctions, that build on previous arguments and traditions, and that are modified on the basis of criticisms and counterexamples.

Specifying the exact features of 'ultimate meaning' discourse and the methods for testing its assertions is a complicated task that would require a monograph of its own.[68] It is all too easy to conflate it with scientific discourse on the one hand or to dismiss it as subjective, relativistic nonsense on the other. As we have seen, a theory of the strong emergence of conscious phenomenal properties is the most that a discussion grounded in the sciences can produce. If there is a something in human beings that survives death and enjoys a post-mortem existence—say, a soul or some metaphysical ground for the subjective qualities that we experience—the empirical sciences could never fathom its nature or offer an exhaustive understanding of it. Still, even if ascertaining the existence of such a ground or mental substance by scientific means is not possible, its existence remains a live option, for metaphysical possibilities are not refuted by the fact that the empirical tests for them are not and can never be complete.[69] How then could one know? The best one can do is to extrapolate from what one does know empirically: constructing metaphysical 'sketches' that state the various possibilities as clearly as possible; fleshing out the broader models of human being that would be consistent with or entailed by these sketches; and attempting where possible to test the resulting claims by means of their internal consistency, coherence, fit with empirical results, and the fruitfulness of their implications.

INTEGRATING PERSONHOOD AND DIVINE ACTION

What happens when one tries to work out the specifics of divine action? What sort of account can be defended? Remember that the guiding challenge is compatibility or plausibility, not proof. The goal is not to demonstrate that specific divine actions have occurred, but to find out whether divine action would necessarily contradict natural law. Of course, it is always possible for believers to jettison all laws and regularities or to imagine them superseded by dramatic divine interventions. Thus one can imagine that, through a very large number of small miraculous interventions, God could create precisely those differentiated waves in the air that, upon striking the ear, the believer would hear as distinct words 'spoken' by God.[70] For many, however, such bold physical miracles no longer offer a credible picture of divine agency in the world.

One treads a delicate line here. The more vague the allusions to divine influences on the world, and the more they are based on a pure appeal to mystery, the less convincing they become for those who are sceptical in principle about the reasonableness of claims for divine action. Conversely, the more compatible such claims turn out to be with acceptable natural accounts of human agency, the more credible they become. Yet if the resulting account is *identical* to the natural accounts in everything it predicts, there is no reason to interpret it as an instance of divine action.

The most adequate account must lie somewhere between these extremes. On the one hand, it will locate some area or areas within nature that could in principle be upwardly open to divine influence. Macro-world physics, the physics of Newton's laws, represents the least plausible realm of all: we have strong reason to think that these physical processes are deterministic, and the theoretical framework that comprehends them leaves no place for talk of persons, intentions, meanings, or purposes. On the other hand, the concepts one uses to identify and describe the area of potential divine influence must be such that whatever influences take place could plausibly influence other parts of the natural world. As we have seen, a soul would meet the first criterion but fail at the second; a brain, or perhaps even the neural correlate of a specific idea, would meet the second but fail at the first. Therein lies the difficulty of the problem.

Given the discussion of mental causation in Chapter 4, dominated as it was by the challenge of relating brain states and specific mental states, it is tempting to conceive top–down divine causation as purely idea-based. One might imagine a sort of Platonic hierarchy (or Neoplatonic ascent), in which the various 'lower' levels are stripped away one by one. First, all physical causes are left behind, then the realm of the emotional or affective, followed by all 'merely personal' concerns, until only the realm of pure thought is left. Only at the level of pure thought, the highest level of emergence, where ideas are connected only by the purest bonds of logic and rationality, is God's causal agency is possible. This truly would be the model of God as the Great Mathematician!

One trouble with this conception is that it stands very far from the religious life. (Perhaps it represents the religious life as philosophers would like to see it.) The phenomenology of religion presents a picture in which highly concrete wishes are expressed and thanks are given, in which the affective life plays a much greater role, and in which that elusive question of the meaningfulness of one's existence often stands at centre stage. A Platonized view of divine action is highly abstract and disembodied, a far cry from the concrete symbols and concerns that characterize the religious life. At the same time, if any dimension of human existence is holistic, it is the religious dimension, for it invariably involves a personal sense of the meaning of one's existence as a whole. To raise the religious question is to ask about the unity of a personal life. Could it be that this holistic dimension would serve as a better locus for theories of divine action?

It appears that the one-to-one linking of thoughts and brain states that dominates the philosophy of mind has wrongly led philosophers of religion to look for ways of comprehending how divine influence could be at work in producing individual thoughts—or worse, in producing particular brain states so that certain thoughts would occur. There is no given brain state that is the concept of harmony, nor does it relate only two specific ideas; it represents a particular relation between ideas, which could be realized by a number of different idea combinations and hence by a very large number of different brain states. For similar reasons one would not expect a neuroscientific account of the meaningfulness of an individual life. As harmony implies a balance between some set of divergent factors, so meaningfulness involves a sense of fit between many diverse elements of a person's life. Factors external to the individual will play a crucial role in the account: certain types of interpersonal connections, a broad range of affective phenomena, a certain relation with one's environment, a perception of one's relation to her moral commitments and aspirations, and (often) some reference to non-empirical beings or forces. None of these can be explained as a state of a particular brain. At minimum the explanation would have to refer to the interrelationships between a very large number of brains, each standing in particular relation to its environment, memories, and affective states. It does not take much reflection to recognize the mind-boggling complexity of this state of affairs if viewed merely as a physical system. If one brain has 10^{14} neural connections and the firing potential of each synapse is expressed by a complex probabilistic function, how many variables would the biochemical equation have to contain to express the brain states of, say, a hundred people who share a single core value? Indeed, a neurological account is inconceivable for another reason: this (from the standpoint of physics) hopelessly complex physical system is not capable even in principle of referring to the state of affairs that we call 'the value of a human life', since it lacks the ideas and concepts to pick out and refer to such a thing.

Given these factors, it is easy to see what was wrong with divine action understood as God producing or helping to produce a specific idea formed within the brain of a specific person at some time.[71] It appears that talk of producing thoughts in a bottom–up manner by manipulating brain states is not the right level of analysis for approaching the question of divine action. There is a way to conceive divine agency at the appropriate level of complexity and with the appropriate concepts, but only if one introduces the idea of the emergent level of 'the person as such' or 'the person as a whole'. We might define it as *that level that emerges when an integrated state is established between a person and her body, her environment, other persons, and her overall mental state, including her interpretation of her social, cultural, historical, and religious context.* States of the person as such might include happiness, contentment, conflict, or fulfilment. Thus the person in this sense might experience *anomie*, in Emile Durkheim's sense of the term, or she might experience that sense of meaningfulness which Peter Berger connects with the idea of a 'sacred canopy'.[72]

It is not necessary to commit oneself to a particular understanding of the ontological status of the person in order to speak of its causal role. In this regard, note the parallels between this topic and the discussion of agents in the previous chapter. There I noted that the presumption of naturalism makes it problematic to slip into the assumption that mental causation is the manifestation of a spiritual soul or substance. Nonetheless, it was possible to accept an irreducible causal role for mental causes in so far as one can not make sense of human behaviour without them. A similar epistemic caution is warranted in the present case. It is justified to postulate that the person as such plays a causal role in those various behaviours that we speak of as personal actions. As long as the integrated level presupposed in the idea of personal action plays this vital explanatory, causal role, we do not need to dismiss it as a mere fiction. But accepting the reality of personal action also, and in my view rightly, demands a more complex account of the relations between individual mental causes and the broader (explanatory and causal) concept of personal intentions. Mental causes are more tightly correlated with particular brain states, though they are not identical to them. Likewise, the intentions of a person as such are dependent on individual mental causes, though again without being identical to them. The layered nature of these relationships makes it more difficult to formulate explanations that jump over multiple levels. It is hard to draw direct correlations, for example, between person-level intentions and specific brain states. Such intentions invariably involve not just the relation between a particular idea and a particular brain state but reference outwards to many different ideas, to other persons, to culture and history, and perhaps to the divine.

Among certain critics there will be a strong temptation to reduce talk of 'the person as such' to a merely affective state of an individual body and brain. After all, have Damasio, LeDoux, and others not shown that thought is a higher-order expression of 'the emotional brain', giving causal-explanatory priority to the affective centres?[73] But for those of us who accept the causal agency of thought, as argued in the previous chapter, it is natural to distinguish between two levels of the human affective life. Hormonal changes such as the release of oestrogen or testosterone correlate with specific, relatively undifferentiated affective responses such as fear and aggression, and increased levels of beta endorphins may reduce the intensity of pain or produce a general sense of euphoria.

But humans also experience higher-order affective responses of much greater complexity, such as the sense of harmoniousness or well-being or dissonance. Once one has accepted mental causality, it becomes gratuitous to equate all such higher-order affective responses with releases of hormones and neurotransmitters. Ironically, it is this reductionism of the emotional realm which undergirds a seemingly very different response, the Platonic ascent to disembodied thought discussed above. Emotions, seen as primitive and undifferentiated, must be left behind if the highest levels of human cognition are to appear in their pure form. In contrast to both views, human existence in the world suggests that the conscious life—experiencing our most complex interrelationships, solving the most complex sorts of problems, synthesizing diverse dimensions into an integrated response or attitude—is accompanied by a higher-order affective state that is just as differentiated, as general, and as efficacious as the corresponding mental processes.

This integrative state of the person thus has affective as well as intellectual and social dimensions. Clearly, it can have an ethical dimension as well. The treatment of ethics within, for example, evolutionary psychology has a tendency to reduce higher-order ethical aspirations and contents to the underlying biological values. Thus a biology-dominant assessment of the altruistic actions of an individual will tend to explain her motivations in terms of kin selection or the hope for reciprocal treatment in the future. By contrast, according to the non-reductive standpoint taken here it is plausible that individuals are sometimes motivated by genuine (i.e. not reductively explicable) concerns for the well-being of others.[74] As a result, the desire to be ethical can be understood as itself a kind of causal force or motivation that does not need to be explained in terms of social gains or selection pressures.

All the various factors just outlined play some role in constituting that sense of integrated selfhood that in turn motivates a myriad of specific actions. One can grant this conclusion without needing to posit a separate soul as the ground for this sense. Personhood may be an emergent quality of the natural world without being conceived as some specific mental 'thing'. In fact, the penchant to locate all such higher-order mental properties within a specific soul-substance is itself a kind of reductive move: the world can only contain mental properties if they are located within specific mental things such as souls. For a monist position like the present one, it is sufficient to note that the one 'stuff' of the world takes a wide variety of forms and manifests some amazing features; one cannot conclude from this fact that all of these states are direct manifestations of a specific kind of stuff. For the Cartesian dualist there must be two radically different substances (*res cogitans* and *res extensa*) because there are mental properties and physical properties. But for the emergentist monist there is, as Christian de Duve puts it, 'vital dust':[75] the one stuff of the world whose history we work to reconstruct, taking on the surprising forms of gravitational attraction, quantum entanglement, reproduction, spontaneous play, conscious awareness, moral striving, and the quest for meaning.

I have argued that the human person, understood as integrated self or psychophysical agent-in-community, offers the appropriate level on which to introduce the possibility of divine agency. Here, and perhaps here alone, a divine agency could be operative that could exercise downward causal influence without being reduced to a manipulator of physical particles or psychotropic neurotransmitters. Only an influence that worked at the level of the person as such could influence the kinds of dimensions that are religiously significant without falling to the level of magic: a person's sense of her relations with others, her higher-order affective states, her ethical striving, and her sense of the meaningfulness of her existence in relation to the world around her.

By the nature of the case, one cannot give a very precise account of how the agency of an integrated person might be related to neurophysiological processes; reconstructing this type of agency requires the tools of the human sciences (psychology, sociology, and anthropology, but also history, the arts, ethics, etc.). It cannot be a direct relationship between an idea and a brain state but must involve the broader social and cultural context as well—which gives us reason, once again, to conclude that the human sciences are unlikely ever to be reduced to neurophysiology. As persons, and as social scientists, we nevertheless have good reason to think that persons do in fact do things qua persons in the world.

The situation for theists is similar, albeit one step further removed. The theist will be unable to explain in human-scientific terms how it is that God affects the person as such. We do know—or at least it is a core postulation of science—that all natural influences on the affective or mental state of persons are mediated through some sort of physical inputs to the person: spoken words, gestures, texts, artistic creations. By the nature of the case, the divine influence posited by theists would not be mediated in this fashion. This makes divine influence disanalogous to all other influences on human persons, again reflecting the dualistic moment in any account of divine action. Nevertheless, we have found a way to construe that influence that does not require negating or setting aside what is known scientifically about mind and emergence. The model I have employed—an influence at the level of integrated persons, which in turn influences specific mental, affective, and physical processes—avoids the implausibilities of the competing models of divine action. For example, it avoids the impression that divine action could only take place through breaking physical laws or through a direct, idea-to-idea influence. The former conflicts with standard scientific assumptions about how human thought works, and the latter is based on an inaccurately Platonic picture of persons as thinking souls. The model of the human person, understood as an integrated system of influences, may make the causal questions more obscure, but it does correspond to our best overall account of human personhood. If one is to defend a notion of divine influence on human persons, is this not the level at which one should formulate one's account?

CLOSING OBJECTIONS

I close with a consideration of the chief objections that will be raised from both sides. The physically oriented philosopher or scientist may wonder how one can ascribe any causal role to something as amorphous as an integrated self. At least in the case of a set of emergent mental properties that are correlated with states of some specific brain, one can identify the physical unit that the mental causes are supposed to operate on, and one can imagine how the mental causes might themselves have been produced by a particular brain. Is the same true of a self?

The answer lies in the dispositional element of mental causation first presented in the previous chapter. The present view does not ontologize the self into a substance in its own right. Operationally, the self is best understood as a disposition to act in certain ways or to have particular conscious thoughts or experiences in response to particular stimuli. Clearly, human dispositions *do* make a difference in the world. Mary's dispositions—her tendency to react angrily to confrontation, or her tendency to look for the best in others—will express themselves over a potentially immense variety of stimuli. Nor are such dispositions plausibly reduced to some state of Mary's brain. As we saw in Chapter 2, a system described using the tools of physics, or for that matter neurological descriptions, cannot even pick out states such as 'the tendency to look for the best in others', much less explain their causal efficacy. Behavioural tendencies and dispositions can only be defined in a conceptual and causal context that includes persons, moral predicates, linguistic conventions, and social institutions. A further advantage of this approach is that such dispositions may be broad enough to include many of the sorts of features traditionally associated with religious experience: meta-physical concepts, higher-order affects, the concern with ethical obligations, the quest for personal integration, and the search for meaning within the world.

A second objection poses a dilemma for theists concerning the extent of the divine influence on the world. If theism implies that God influences the physical evolution of the cosmos or guides evolution at the biochemical level in order (say) to produce human beings, then it is committed to the strong notion of physical miracles that I have otherwise eschewed. But if God does not begin influencing the world until organisms complex enough to manifest mental causality appear on the scene, then how can God be understood as causally responsible for the emergence of mental agents in the first place?

The objection rightly draws attention to the altered notions of divine creation and providence that are required for any theology that would seek to be consistent with the natural sciences. There is no such thing as a scientific account of the origin of the funda-mental laws, the physical constants, and the initial conditions that structure the physical universe as a whole; hence there is no obstacle to belief in an initial creative act by God. It is an empirical question whether, given the laws, constants, and initial conditions, the emergence of intelligent life was probable. To the extent that Simon Conway Morris and others are right in assigning a high probability to the evolution of intelligence, it becomes plausible that God could have initiated this natural process with the intention of bringing about intelligent life. How early in the evolutionary process God could begin to influence individual organisms will depend on one's understanding of emergence in evolution, and hence on further scientific study. To the extent that other primates manifest cog-nition, awareness, and even early forms of consciousness, the same openness to divine influence would be present that we have found in the case of humans. The studies of animal behaviour and cognition by Marc Bekoff and others reveal the extent of spontaneous behaviour in animals: highly complex, genetically and environmentally underdetermined actions, such as revealed in studies of animal play.[76] This opens the door in principle to divine influences at a much earlier point in biological evolution. Of course, if one is a panpsychist, as in Whitehead's panexperientialist philosophy, the divine lure could be at work from the first moment of creation. But the evidence for spontaneity in atoms is rather more spotty than it is in the case of animal behaviour studies.

From the opposite side come the objections from theologians. Assuming that God were able to make connection with human beings in the way described in these pages, would the connection be specific enough to allow for any sort of divine revelation or guidance? If it turns out that no content whatsoever can be communicated by these means, even in principle, then it is hard to see how the resulting position is of any help to theists. Perhaps a general divine tug towards 'the spiritual' or 'higher things' would be sufficient to preserve some sort of generic religiosity, but it would certainly fall far short of what, traditionally, theists have looked for in divine–human interaction.

Perhaps some re-evaluation of the mode and concreteness of divine communication, even in principle, will indeed be necessary. It has become difficult to conceive of the divine directly implanting sentences into the consciousness of human beings. That notion involves the somewhat spooky idea of a God something like a human listener, sitting in a corner of one's mind and eavesdropping on the flow of one's thoughts. Moreover, as we saw at the top of the previous section, it is impossible to conceive direct, verbal communication without relying on a series of physical miracles—God's either directly producing sound waves in the earth's atmosphere or directly changing the electrochemical balance in billions of synaptic junctures in the brain. Belief in the occurrence of literal divine speech also has a more disturbing aspect. If God has the capacity to introduce specific propositions into the minds of humans at will, then God becomes responsible for every occasion in history in which immense suffering or evil has arisen out of God's failure to act. Why would God not implant into the mind of the teacher the thought, 'Move your class of children away from the building' before the mud slide descended upon their school? Even 'Run,

run, run!' would probably be sufficient. A God who is capable in principle of communicating highly specific propositional information to humans, and who regularly does so, yet who often fails to communicate even a minimal warning when huge amounts of pointless suffering could be avoided as a result, would seem to be morally culpable for the results of this silence. This wilful inactivity would raise the problem of evil to unanswerable proportions.

What would be the nature of the communication on the present view? If the communication occurs at the level of the person as such, the content of communication cannot be understood primarily as a set of true assertions with specific propositional content. Divine revelation interpreted as a set of propositions would leave out the affective, ethical, and holistic dimensions that are an inherent part of the phenomenology of the religious life. Yet the divine input cannot be completely non-propositional either if some sort of communication is actually to take place. A completely non-propositional understanding of divine influence—say, a sense of undifferentiated love broadcast to all living beings at all times—also runs the risk of reducing the divine to an impersonal force. Such a view is untenable for theists, who maintain that, whatever the divine ultimately is, it is *not less than* personal. To be more-than-personal is to have the volitional, intellectual, and communicative abilities that humans have, and presumably infinitely more as well. What is communicated might well be more than propositional, but one cannot consistently hold that it would be less.

Without claiming to know the specific content of divine revelation (or even whether it has actually occurred), one can without difficulty conceive a rather differentiated lure of the divine on humans. After all, an individual person's sense of self represents a highly differentiated complex of factors, combined as it is with complex dispositions to respond in vastly different ways in different social, ethical, and moral contexts. Certainly God, understood as infinitely-more-than-personal-being, would have the capacity to form highly differentiated responses to each living person (and, for that matter, towards all living things). The problem lies not on the divine side but on the side of the persons who must comprehend the communication. Here it makes sense to imagine a great variation in the receptive abilities of individual persons. At this moment my inexpensive radio is barely able to capture the beautiful melodies of Brahm's first symphony, but the finely tuned equipment in the office next to mine is reproducing the details of the broadcast with unbelievable fidelity. Presumably the openness of an individual to differentiated divine communications might be enhanced by various meditative or spiritual practices, just as it might be blocked by the voice of his ego or the strength of his certainty that such communication is impossible. Available conceptual and cultural resources would also in principle affect the process. One could imagine a specific constellation of factors that reduced a person's receptivity to a minimum, and one can formulate factors that would presumably make one maximally responsive to divine leading. All of these factors taken together would have an impact on the degree of clarity with which the communication might take place.

It will continue to be a matter of dispute which putative divine revelations are indeed veridical and what their actual propositional content is. The argument sketched in these pages provides strong reason to suspect that the particular beliefs and dispositions of different cultural and religious groups greatly affect what they take to be divine communications. A prior belief in Yahweh or Allah or Brahman will strongly predispose the recipient to construe any actual divine influences in a highly specific way. Indeed, one would expect that the idiosyncratic influences are not limited to the cultural level: the symbols, metaphors, and culturally plausible ideas available to each individual presumably colour significantly how she interprets her own religious experiences.[77] In the end, it could be that a certain faith perspective—namely, belief in the plausibility of some form of transcendent mind or spirit[78]—will be necessary before individuals are willing even to entertain the question of which, if any, putative revelations might actually serve in some way as guides to the divine nature.

CONCLUSION

The overall argument of this book consists of two distinct parts. The first part defends (strong) emergence as the most accurate description of what occurs in the evolutionary process from quarks to cells to brains to thought. On the one hand, life appears different enough from non-living physical systems, and mental properties appear different enough from their neural substrate, that dualists have been inclined to view them as different kinds of substance altogether. But scientific work on the origins of life and on the neural correlates of consciousness has undercut arguments for the explanatory incommensurability between the two sides. Differences remain, but not dichotomies. On the other hand, the aspirations for a complete reduction to microphysics have not been realized. To the contrary, the natural world increasingly reveals distinct levels of organization, with each level characterized by its own irreducible types of causal influence and explanation. The conclusion is not that scientific study is futile or misguided; it is that scientific study reveals a vastly more complicated world, with vastly more complex interactions between different levels of organization, than the reductionist programme ever envisioned. Attempting to balance these various considerations led us to an emergentist understanding of the relations between the various levels, and hence between the sciences that study them.

The case in the first part of the book is independent of the case for transcendent mind explored in the present chapter. Nonetheless, the more speculative argument developed here grows naturally out of what came before. Suppose one grants that animals manifest distinct forms of awareness not found elsewhere in the natural world, and that humans evidence mental qualities unparalleled in the other animals. And suppose that one concludes that something like the theory of strong emergence provides the best account of these mental properties and their causal role in the world. It seems hard to deny that these two conclusions lead inevitably to confrontation with some of the 'big questions' of philosophy—questions about agency and freedom, about higher-order levels of mind, and about transcendent or divine mind. Debates about such topics are necessarily speculative; one will not be able to achieve the levels of certainty that one attains in more science-oriented topics. Nevertheless, discussions of dualism, reduction, and emergence are so clearly connected to certain of the enduring philosophical questions that only a loss of nerve would keep one from following the line of argument as far as it leads.

But something bigger is at issue in combining the first and second parts of the argument: the relationship between scientific and non-scientific factors as humans seek to understand their place in the universe. The exponential growth of scientific knowledge, perhaps more than any other single factor, has transformed our sense of who we are and what kind of a world we inhabit. Given science's astounding success, it is natural to assume that the growth of scientific knowledge will be limitless, that in the end nothing will lie outside its purview. Some embrace this prediction with melioristic exuberance; others recoil from what appear to be its dehumanizing effects, opposing the advance of science on all fronts.

Emergence as presented here steers a middle course between these two responses; it is both a response to science's successes and failures and a prediction of the long-term outcome. The question at issue is not whether nature manifests itself in distinct levels of phenomena but whether the natural sciences will eventually be able to comprehend *all* of the levels that are relevant for a causal explanation of phenomena in the universe. I have suggested that the evidence, and not a whiggish science-phobia, supports a negative answer. Some levels of reality are ideally suited for mathematical deterministic explanations (macro-physics), others for explanations that are mathematical but not deterministic (quantum physics), and others for explanations that focus on structure, function, and development (the biological sciences from genetics to neurophysiology). But at other levels laws play a more minimal role and idiosyncratic factors predominate; hence narratives tend to replace measurements and prediction becomes difficult at best. It appears that much of the interior life of humans, and whatever social interactions or creative expressions are based on this interiority, fall into this category. Social scientists can reach shared understandings of psychological and cultural phenomena and thus achieve a growth of knowledge over time. The natural sciences contribute to good social science—but not by making it a mere extension of themselves.

The ladder of levels of complexity does not end there, however. Persons ask questions about the meaningfulness of the natural and social worlds in which they live and move. Once again, a level of explanation becomes a part of a broader whole, and thinkers are invited to participate in the quest for knowledge at the next higher level. Without doubt the *questions* rise to a level beyond the social scientific. But does the possibility of discerning better and worse answers keep up with the questions, or do they now outstrip all human capacity for rational evaluation? To take an analogous example, cosmology poses questions that, it seems, a physical science could never answer: what is the source of the big bang? If there is a multiverse, why do certain laws hold across all of its diverse regions? In short: when one follows the line from emergent mind to transcendent mind, does the reach of the questions exceed the grasp of discussable answers?

The continuing explosion of scientific knowledge in the twenty-first century will tempt many to conclude that beyond the reach of natural science there is no knowledge, only opinion and affect. The emergence argument that I have traced in these pages is one way, though certainly not the only one, to show why the equation of knowledge and natural science is mistaken. As tenuous as our grasp may be on knowledge (that is, proposals that are open to inter-subjective criticism and assessment) when the questions extend beyond what is empirically decidable, critical discussion by no means has to come to an end when the boundaries of physics and biology are reached. Indeed, does not rational debate of the 'really big questions'—debates not dominated by appeals to tradition, force, or absolute authority—become increasingly important as the human mind continues to expand the limits of its knowledge, and the knowledge of its limits, in an age of science?

NOTES

1. There is fairly good evidence that the biblical traditions do not treat the mental substance as the essence of humanity in the way that Greek philosophy did, if only because of their stress on the resurrection of the body; hence in the biblical traditions, at least, there is strong reason to question this sharp separation of mind and body. This thesis represents a core premise of the essays in Warren S. Brown, Nancey Murphy, and H. Newton Malony (eds.), *Whatever Happened to the Soul? Scientific and Theological Portraits of Human Nature* (Minneapolis: Fortress Press, 1998).

2. Paul Churchland, *Matter and Consciousness* (Cambridge, Mass.: MIT Press, 1984), 21.

3. See Stephen J. Gould and R. C. Lewontin, 'The Spandrels of San Marco and the Panglossian Paradigm: A Critique of the Adaptationist Programme', in *Proceedings of the Royal Society of London*, Series B, *Biological Sciences* ('The Evolution of Adaptation by Natural Selection'), 205 (1979), 581–98.

4. This seems to be the view implied by Ursula Goodenough's notion of 'horizontal transcendence'. See Goodenough, *The Sacred Depths of Nature* (New York: Oxford University Press, 1998) and 'Causality and Subjectivity in the Religious Quest', *Zygon*, 35/4 (2000), 725–34. She cites Michael Kalton, 'Green Spirituality: Horizontal Transcendence', in M. E. Miller and P. Young-Eisendrath (eds.), *Paths of Integrity, Wisdom and Transcendence: Spiritual Development in the Mature Self* (New York: Routledge, 2000).

5. See Frank Tipler, *The Physics of Immortality: Modern Cosmology, God, and the Resurrection of the Dead* (New York: Doubleday, 1994). The most famous twentieth-century advocate of this position was Teilhard de Chardin.

6. Friedrich Nietzsche, 'Ueber Wahrheit und Lüge im aussermoralischen Sinne', *Nietzsche Werke*, ed. Giorgio Colli and Mazzino Montinari, ii/3 (Berlin: Walter de Gruyter, 1973), 369; translated in Daniel Brazeale (ed.), *Philosophy*

and Truth: Selections from Nietzsche's Notebooks of the Early 1870s (Atlantic Highlands, NJ: Humanities Press, 1979, 1993), 79.

7. See John Wheeler, *At Home in the Universe* (New York: Springer-Verlag, 1996); *Geons, Black Holes, and Quantum Foam: A Life in Physics* (New York: Norton, 1998); 'Information, Physics, Quantum: The Search for Links', in Anthony J. G. Hey (ed.), *Feynman and Computation: Exploring the Limits of Computers* (Cambridge, Mass.: Perseus Books, 1999).

8. See Paul Davies, *The Cosmic Blueprint: New Discoveries in Nature's Creative Ability to Order the Universe* (Philadelphia, Pa: Templeton Foundation Press, 2004) and *The Mind of God: The Scientific Basis for a Rational World* (New York: Simon & Schuster, 1992). The argument is a variant on the earlier 'anthropic principle', on which see esp. John D. Barrow and Frank Tipler, *The Anthropic Cosmological Principle* (New York: Oxford University Press, 1986).

9. Michael Denton, *Evolution: A Theory in Crisis* (Bethesda, Md: Adler & Adler, 1986) and *Nature's Destiny: How the Laws of Biology reveal Purpose in the Universe* (New York: Free Press, 1998).

10. Simon Conway Morris, *Life's Solution: Inevitable Humans in a Lonely Universe* (Cambridge: Cambridge University Press, 2003).

11. Christian de Duve, *Life Evolving: Molecules, Mind, and Meaning* (Oxford: Oxford University Press, 2002).

12. William Dembski, *The Design Inference: Eliminating Chance Through Small Probabilities* (New York: Cambridge University Press, 1998); *Intelligent Design: The Bridge between Science and Theology* (Downers Grove, Ill: InterVarsity Press, 1999); *No Free Lunch: Why Specified Complexity Cannot be Purchased without Intelligence* (Lanham, Md.: Rowan & Littlefield, 2002); and Dembski (ed.), *Signs of Intelligence: Understanding Intelligent Design* (Grand Rapids, Mich.: Brazos Press, 2001). The Intelligent Design argument is clearly summarized by Del Ratzsch, *Nature, Design and Science: The Status of Design in Natural Science* (Albany: NY: SUNY Press, 2001), and a (partisan) history is given in Thomas Woodward, *Doubts about Darwin: A History of Intelligent Design* (Grand Rapids, Mich.: Baker Books, 2003). For a related argument see Michael Behe, *Darwin's Black Box: The Biochemical Challenge to Evolution* (New York: Free Press, 1996).

13. Cited in H. Margenau, *Scientific Indeterminism and Human Freedom* (Latrobe, Pa: Archabbey Press, 1968).

14. See Arthur Peacocke, *Theology for a Scientific Age* (Minneapolis: Fortress Press, 1993) and *Paths from Science towards God: The End of All Our Exploring* (Oxford: OneWorld, 2001); see also Arthur Peacocke and Ann Pederson, *The Music of Creation, with CD* (Minneapolis: Fortress Press, 2006).

15. See Philip Hefner, *The Human Factor: Evolution, Culture, and Religion* (Minneapolis: Fortress Press, 1993).

16. See A. N. Whitehead, *Process and Reality*, corrected edn. (New York: Free Press, 1975); Lewis Ford, *The Lure of God: A Biblical Background for Process Theism* (Philadelphia, Pa: Fortress Press, 1978); David Ray Griffin, *Reenchant-*

ment without Supernaturalism: A Process Philosophy of Religion (Ithaca, NY: Cornell University Press, 2001).

17. See David Hume, *Dialogues Concerning Natural Religion*, ed. Norman Kemp Smith (Indianapolis Bobbs-Merrill (Library of Liberal Arts), 1979), and Hume, *Of Miracles* (La Salle, Ill: Open Court, 1985).

18. See David Chalmers, 'Facing up to the Problem of Consciousness', first published in a special issue of the *Journal of Consciousness Studies* in 1995, and now available in Hameroff, Kaszniak, and Scott, (eds.), *Toward a Science of Consciousness* (Cambridge, Mass.: MIT Press, 1996).

19. Albert-László Barabási, *Linked: The New Science of Networks* (Cambridge, Mass.: Perseus, 2002), 25–40.

20. James Lovelock, *Gaia: A New Look at Life on Earth* (Oxford: Oxford University Press, 1995); Lovelock, *Homage to Gaia: The Life of an Independent Scientist* (Oxford: Oxford University Press, 2001).

21. John E. Stewart, *Evolution's Arrow: The Direction of Evolution and the Future of Humanity* (Canberra, Australia: Chapman Press, 2000). For further references in defence of the idea of a 'global brain' or superorganism, see http://pespmc1.vub.ac.be/GBRAINREF.html (verified 30 Mar, 2004).

22. Robert Wright, *Non-Zero: The Logic of Human Destiny* (New York: Pantheon Books, 2000).

23. Marc Pesce, 'Virtually Sacred', in W. Mark Richardson and Gordy Slack (eds.), *Faith in Science: Scientists Search for Truth* (London and New York: Routledge, 2001), 109, 112.

24. Steven Johnson, *Emergence: The Connected Lives of Ants, Brains, Cities, and Software* (New York: Simon & Schuster Touchstone, 2001), 117.

25. Wolfhart Pannenberg, *Theology and the Kingdom of God* (Philadelphia,:Pa.: Westminster, 1969), 56.

26. See Whitehead, *Process and Reality*, 343–51. Thus Nancy Frankenberry argues that Whitehead's notion of the consequent nature of God 'is a suggestive application of certain theological resources ingredient in the use of the emergent paradigm' in 'The Emergent Paradigm and Divine Causation', *Process Studies*, 13 (1983), 202–17, p. 205. Despite Frankenberry's provocative suggestions, process thinkers have not interacted in any significant detail with contemporary emergence theory. One major process thinker who argues for the compatibility of process and emergence theory is Ian Barbour; see e.g. 'Neuroscience, Artificial Intelligence, and Human Nature: Theological and Philosophical Reflections', in Robert J. Russell, Nancey Murphy, Theo Meyering, and Michael Arbib (eds.), *Neuroscience and the Person: Scientific Perspectives on Divine Action* (Vatican City State: Vatican Observatory Publications, 1999), 249–80.

27. Samuel Alexander, *Space, Time, and Deity*, the Gifford lectures for 1916–18, 2 vols. (London: Macmillan, 1920), ii. 353.

28. 'A substance or piece of Space-Time which is mental is differentiated in a portion of its mental body so as to be divine, and this deity is sustained by all the

Space-Time to which it belongs', quoted in Charles Hartshorne and William Reese, *Philosophers Speak of God* (Chicago: University of Chicago Press, 1953), 367.

29. David Cooper, *God is a Verb: Kabbalah and the Practice of Mystical Judaism* (New York: Riverhead Books, 1997).

30. Pierre Bayle, 'Spinoza', *Dictionnaire historique et critique de Pierre Bayle*, new edn. (Paris: Desoer Libraire, 1820), xiii. 416–68. See *Mr Bayle's Historical and Critical Dictionary: The Second Edition* (London, 1738), v, 'Spinoza'.

31. Alexander, *Space, Time, and Deity*, ii. 357. He then draws an interesting, apparently panentheistic inference from this immanentist theology: 'All we are the hunger and thirst, the heart-beats and sweat of God'. Alexander's position is both similar to and different from the Eastern Orthodox concept of *theosis*, according to which God gradually brings it about that the world is permeated by God's presence and becomes deised, conforming increasingly to God's nature.

32. Henry N. Wieman, *The Source of Human Good* (Chicago: University of Chicago Press, 1946), 7, also quoted in Hartshorne and Reese, *Philosophers Speak of God*, p. 396.

33. The phrase is used by Hartshorne and Reese, ibid. 404.

34. Alexander, *Space, Time, Deity*, ii. 358.

35. One could of course simply respond, 'But I don't believe in an emergent God; I believe in an eternal God above history.' The route of appeals to faith or to private religious experience is of course still open to the believer. But the present study makes a different methodological commitment. My goal is to see what parts of the classical metaphysical and religious responses might still be plausible given the results of the previous chapters.

36. See John Hare, 'Is there an Evolutionary Foundation for Human Morality?', in Philip Clayton and Jeffrey Schloss (eds.), *Evolution and Ethics: Human Morality in Biological and Religious Perspective* (Grand Rapids Mich.: Eerdmans, 2004). Hare's argument would be undercut if the Kantian attempt to derive ethical obligations from pure practical reason alone is justified.

37. Although many have argued in this fashion, Peter Berger has given a particularly nuanced form of the argument. See the works cited in the following notes 38 and 41.

38. See Peter L. Berger, *The Sacred Canopy: Elements of a Sociological Theory of Religion* (New York: Anchor Books, 1967).

39. St Augustine, *The Confessions*, I. 1, quoted from *The Confessions of Saint Augustine*, tr. Edward B. Pusey (New York: Collier Books, 1972), 11.

40. Cf. Thaddeus Metz, 'The Immortality Requirement for Life's Meaning', *Ratio*, 16/2 (2003), 161–77.

41. See Phillip H. Wiebe, *God and Other Spirits: Intimations of Transcendence in Christian Experience* (Oxford: Oxford University Press, 2004); cf. George F. R. Ellis, 'Intimations of Transcendence: Relations of the Mind to God', in Robert J. Russell et al. (eds.), *Neuroscience and the Person*. Among the works by Peter L. Berger see *A Rumor of Angels: Modern Society and the Rediscovery of the Supernatural* (Garden City, NY: Doubleday, 1969); *The Heretical Imperative: Contem-*

porary Possibilities of Religious Affirmation (Garden City, NY: Anchor Books, 1980); and his most recent work, *Questions of Faith: A Skeptical Affirmation of Christianity* (Malden, Mass.: Blackwell, 2004); cf. Linda Woodhead with Paul Heelas and David Martin (eds.), *Peter Berger and the Study of Religion* (London: Routledge, 2001).

42. I have covered these in some detail in *The Problem of God in Modern Thought* (Grand Rapids, Mich.: Eerdmans, 2000).

43. See the presentation and critique of Kant's theory of regulative principles in Clayton, *The Problem of God in Modern Thought*, chs 1 and 5.

44. Thomas Nagel, *The Last Word* (New York: Oxford University Press, 1997), 118.

45. Thomas Nagel, *The View from Nowhere* (New York: Oxford University Press, 1986). He later argues that, in moral reasoning, 'I find within myself the universal standards that enable me to get outside of myself' (*The Last Word*, 117). I do not here reconstruct Nagel's arguments concerning justice, freedom, and the first-person perspective, but clearly if they are valid they further support the position being defended in the text.

46. Cf. Tadeusz Szubka, 'The Last Refutation of Subjectivism?', *International Journal of Philosophical Studies*, 8 (2000), 231–7.

47. T. Nagel, *View from Nowhere*, 74.

48. T. Nagel, *The Last Word*, 74.

49. See the closing chapter of *The Last Word*, 'Evolutionary Naturalism and the Fear of Religion', 129.

50. In describing the 'fear' of religion, Nagel writes, 'I speak from experience. It isn't just that I don't believe in God and, naturally, hope that I'm right in my belief. It's that I hope there is no God! I don't want there to be a God; I don't want the universe to be like that' (*The Last Word*, 130).

51. Ibid.

52. Ibid 132.

53. For a treatment that pushes Nagel to acknowledge that his position is only consistent if he takes the religious step, see Gilbert Meilaender, 'The (Very) Last Word', *First Things*, 94 (1999), 45–50.

54. I suppose one could say that the universe just had to be reasonable, but that rejoinder merely repeats the 'brute given' response. Perhaps one could say that if the universe were not reasonable we would not know it, though it is not clear to me why this should be the case.

55. For the *locus classicus* of this argument, see Alvin Plantinga, *Warrant and Proper Function* (New York: Oxford University Press, 1993), ch. 12, and the final book of his trilogy, *Warranted Christian Belief* (New York: Oxford University Press, 2000). Background articles by the same author include 'When Faith and Reason Clash: Evolution and the Bible', *Christian Scholar's Review*, 21 (1991), 8–33; 'Evolution, Neutrality, and Antecedent Probability: A Reply to Van Till and McMullen', *Christian Scholar's Review*, 21 (1991), 80–109; 'On Rejecting The Theory of Common Ancestry: A Reply to Hasker', *Perspectives on Science*

and Christian Faith, 44 (1992), 258–63; 'Darwin, Mind and Meaning', *Books and Culture* (May/June 1996). The argument is not original with Plantinga; probably the closest source for his formulation of the argument is C. S. Lewis, *Miracles: A Preliminary Study* (New York: HarperCollins , 2001), ch 3, 'The Cardinal Difficulty of Naturalism'. A good cross-section of the critical debate appears in James K. Beilby (ed.) *Naturalism Defeated?: Essays on Plantinga's Evolutionary Argument against Naturalism* (Ithaca, NY: Cornell University Press, 2002). For important criticisms see the two chapters on the topic in Robert Pennock, *Intelligent Design Creationism and its Critics: Philosophical, Theological, and Scientific Perspectives* (Cambridge, Mass.: MIT Press, 2001); Evan Fales, 'Plantinga's Case against Naturalistic Epistemology', *Philosophy of Science*, 63 (1996), 432—51; and Branden Fitelson and Elliott Sober, 'Plantinga's Probability Arguments against Evolutionary Naturalism', *Pacific Philosophical Quarterly*, 79 (1998), 115–29, the last of which is available online at http://philosophy.wisc.edu/fitelson/PLANT/PLANT.html (verified 24 Feb 2004).

56. See T. Nagel, *The Last Word*, concluding chapter, p. 130.

57. T. Nagel, *View from Nowhere*, 74.

58. Yet even this claim needs nuancing. On the one hand, there is something very un-emergentist about Whiteheadian theologies, since they hold awareness or experience to be fully present from the very first moment of the universe's history, albeit it in rather primitive form. On the other hand, there are resources already in the Patristic theologians, and certainly in theologies influenced by Neoplatonism, which have a strongly emergentist flavour to them.

59. See E. O. Wilson, *Consilience: The Unity of Knowledge* (New York: Knopf, 1998).

60. Note that the logic of emergence allows for this move, though it does not require it. Emergentists in biology e.g. construe cells and organisms as agents in their own right.

61. For an overview of the difficulties and the major responses see Clayton, *Problem of God*.

62. For a perplexing account of the perplexities see Jacques Derrida's *De l'espirit*, tr. Geoffrey Bennington and Rachel Bowlby as *On Spirit* (Chicago: University of Chicago Press, 1989).

63. 'There is but one only, living, and true God, who is infinite in being and perfection, a most pure spirit, invisible, without body, parts, or passions; immutable, immense, eternal, incomprehensible, almighty, most wise, most holy, most free, most absolute', *Westminster Confession of Faith*, chapter 2, 'Of God and of the Holy Trinity', part 1 (available e.g. at http://www.pcanet.org/general/cof_chapi-v.htm, verified 28 Feb 2004)

64. The (conditional) endorsement of evolution was made by Pope John Paul II in an address to the Pontifical Academy of Sciences on 22 Oct 1996; see http://www.newadvent.org/docs/jpo2tc.htm, verified 28 Feb., 2004.

65. See de Duve, *Life Evolving*, 208–26, esp. 223–4. De Duve's solution allows for mental causation in a manner that clearly is not dualist, and yet it preserves a fully bidirectional interaction between body and mind.

66. I have been influenced here by some formulations of Steven Knapp (pers. correspondence).

67. Recall the famous closing words from Anthony Flew's challenge, which refer to John Wisdom's metaphor of the elusive gardener: 'At last the Sceptic despairs, "But what remains of your original assertion? Just how does what you call an invisible, intangible, eternally elusive gardener differ from an imaginary gardener or even from no gardener at all?"' See Anthony Flew, 'Theology and Falsification', repr. in Baruch Brody (ed.), *Readings in the Philosophy of Religion: An Analytic Approach* (Englewood Cliffs, NJ: Prentice-Hall, 1974), 308.

68. I have given a detailed defence of this sort of discourse in *Problem of God*, esp ch 1.

69. Ibid., ch 5. I argue that Kant is wrong to rule out in advance any knowledge whatsoever of claims of this type.

70. Something like this position seems to be implied in some of the examples given by Nicholas Wolterstorff in *Divine Discourse: Philosophical Reflections on the Claim that God Speaks* (Cambridge: Cambridge University Press, 1995).

71. There are resources in mainstream philosophy of mind that are potentially more useful to philosophers of religion, such as treatments of dispositional states or the framework of multiple realizability that I discussed in ch 4.

72. See Berger, *Sacred Canopy*.

73. See Antonio Damasio, *The Feeling of What Happens: Body and Emotion in the Making of Consciousness* (New York: Harcourt Brace, 1999); Damasio, *Looking for Spinoza: Joy, Sorrow, and the Feeling Brain* (Orlando, Fla.: Harcourt, 2003); Joseph LeDoux, *The Emotional Brain: The Mysterious Underpinnings of Emotional Life* (New York: Simon & Schuster, 1996).

74. See Philip Clayton and Jeffrey Schloss (eds.), *Evolution and Ethics: Human Morality and Religious Perspective* (Grand Rapids, Mich.: Eerdmans; 2004).

75. See Christian de Duve, *Vital Dust: Life as a Cosmic Imperative* (New York: Basic Books, 1995).

76. See Marc Bekoff and John A. Byers (eds.), *Animal Play: Evolutionary, Comparative, and Ecological Perspectives* (Cambridge: Cambridge University Press, 1998); Marc Bekoff, Colin Allen, and Gordon M. Burghardt (eds.), *The Cognitive Animal: Empirical and Theoretical Perspectives on Animal Cognition* (Cambridge, Mass.: MIT Press, 2002); Colin Allen and Marc Bekoff, *Species of Mind: The Philosophy and Biology of Cognitive Ethology* (Cambridge, Mass.: MIT Press, 1997); cf. Gordon M. Burghardt and Marc Bekoff (eds.), *The Development of Behavior: Comparative and Evolutionary Aspects* (New York: Garland STPM Press, 1978).

77. See Wayne Proudfoot, *Religious Experience* (Berkeley, Calif.: University of California Press, 1985); John Hick, *An Interpretation of Religion* (New Haven: Yale University Press, 1989).

78. See Clayton, 'The Emergence of Spirit', *CTNS Bulletin*, 20/4 (Fall 2000), 3–20, and, in a condensed and more popular form, 'The Emergence of Spirit', *The Christian Century*, 121/1 (13 Jan. 2004), 26–30; cf. Clayton, *God and Contemporary Science* (Grand Rapids, Mich.: Eerdmans, 1997); Michael Welker,

Gottes Geist: Theologie des Heiligen Geistes, tr. John Hoffmeyer as *God the Spirit* (Minneapolis: Fortress Press, 1994); Peter Hodgson, *Winds of the Spirit: A Constructive Christian Theology* (Louisville, Ky.: Westminster John Knox Press, 1994); and Bradford Hinze and D. Lyle Dabney (eds.), *Advents of the Spirit: An Introduction to the Current Study of Pneumatology* (Milwaukee, Wis.: Marquette University Press, 2001).

Bibliography

Abel, Theodore F., *The Foundation of Sociological Theory* (New York: Random House, 1970).

Agazzi, Evandro (ed.), *The Problem of Reductionism in Science*, Episteme, 18 (Dordrecht: Kluwer Academic Publishers, 1991).

—— and Luisa Montecucco (eds.), *Complexity and Emergence* (River Edge, NJ: World Scientific, 2002).

Alexander, Samuel, *Space Time, and Deity*, the Gifford lectures for 1916–18, 2 vols. (London: Macmillan, 1920).

Allen, Colin and Marc Bekoff, *Species of Mind: The Philosophy and Biology of Cognitive Ethology* (Cambridge, Mass.: MIT Press, 1997).

—— and George Lauder (eds.), *Nature's Purposes: Analyses of Function and Design in Biology* (Cambridge, Mass.: MIT Press, 1998).

Allen, T. F. H. and T. W. Hoekstra, *Toward a Unified Ecology* (New York: Columbia University Press, 1992).

Anderson, Phil W., 'More is Different: Broken Symmetry and the Nature of the Hierarchical Structure of Science', *Science*, 177 (4 Aug. 1972), 393–6.

Arbib, Michael, 'Schema Theory', in S. Shapiro (ed.), *The Encyclopedia of Artificial Intelligence* (New York: Wiley, 1992), 1427–43.

—— and Mary B. Hesse, *The Construction of Reality* (Cambridge: Cambridge University Press, 1986).

——, E. Jeffrey Conklin, and Jane C. Hill, *From Schema Theory to Language* (New York: Oxford University Press, 1987).

Archinov, Vladimir and Christian Fuchs (eds.), *Causality, Emergence, Self-Organisation*, a publication of the international working group on 'Human Strategies in Complexity: Philosophical Foundations for a Theory of Evolutionary Systems' (Moscow: NIA-Priroda, 2003).

Audi, Robert, 'Mental Causation: Sustaining and Dynamic', in John Heil and Alfred Mele (eds.), *Mental Causation* (Oxford: Oxford University Press, 1993).

Baars, Bernard, *In the Theater of Consciousness: The Workspace of the Mind* (New York: Oxford University Press, 1997).

Baddeley, Roland, Peter Hancock, and Peter Földiák (eds.), *Information Theory and the Brain* (Cambridge: Cambridge University Press, 2000).

Barabási, Albert-László, *Linked: The New Science of Networks* (Cambridge, Mass.: Perseus Books, 2002).

——and Reka Albert, 'Emergence of Scaling in Random Networks', *Science*, 286 (15 October 1999), 509–12.

Barbour, Ian, 'Neuroscience, Artificial Intelligence, and Human Nature: Theological and Philosophical Reflections', in Robert J. Russell, Nancey Murphy, Theo Meyering, and Michael Arbib (eds.), *Neuroscience and the Person: Scientific Perspectives on Divine Action* (Vatican City State: Vatican Observatory Publications, 1999).

Barrow, John D. and Frank Tipler, *The Anthropic Cosmological Principle* (New York: Oxford University Press, 1986).

Batchelor, G. K., *An Introduction to Fluid Dynamics* (Cambridge: Cambridge University Press, 2000).

Bayle, Pierre, 'Spinoza', *Dictionnaire historique et critique de Pierre Bayle*, new edn. (Paris: Desoer Libraire, 1820), xiii. 416–68.

Beckermann, Ansgar, Hans Flohr, and Jaegwon Kim (eds.), *Emergence or Reduction: Essays on the Prospects of Nonreductive Physicalism* (New York: W. de Gruyter, 1992).

Bedau, Mark, 'Weak Emergence', *Philosophical Perspectives*, 11: *Mind, Causation, and World* (Atascadero, Calif.: Ridgeview, 1997).

Behe, Michael, *Darwin's Black Box: The Biochemical Challenge to Evolution* (New York: Free Press, 1996).

Beilby, James K. (ed.), *Naturalism Defeated? Essays on Plantinga's Evolutionary Argument against Naturalism* (Ithaca, NY: Cornell University Press, 2002).

Bekoff, Marc, Colin Allen, and Gordon M. Burghardt (eds.), *The Cognitive Animal: Empirical and Theoretical Perspectives on Animal Cognition* (Cambridge, Mass.: MIT Press, 2002).

——and John A. Byers (eds.), *Animal Play: Evolutionary, Comparative, and Ecological Perspectives* (Cambridge: Cambridge University Press, 1998).

Berger, Peter L., *The Sacred Canopy: Elements of a Sociological Theory of Religion* (New York: Anchor Books, 1967).

——*A Rumor of Angels: Modern Society and the Rediscovery of the Supernatural* (Garden City, NY: Doubleday, 1969).

——*The Heretical Imperative: Contemporary Possibilities of Religious Affirmation* (Garden City, NY: Anchor Books, 1980).

——*Questions of Faith: A Skeptical Affirmation of Christianity* (Malden, Mass.: Blackwell, 2004).

Bishop, John, 'Agent-Causation', *Mind*, NS 92 (1983), 61–79.

Blitz, David, *Emergent Evolution: Qualitative Novelty and the Levels of Reality*, Episteme, 19 (Dordrecht: Kluwer, 1992).

Brandon, Robert N., 'Reductionism versus Wholism versus Mechanism', in R. N. Brandon (ed.), *Concepts and Methods in Evolutionary Biology* (Cambridge: Cambridge University Press, 1996), 179–204.

Broad, C. D., *The Mind and its Place in Nature* (London: Routledge & Kegan Paul, 1925).

Brown, Terrance and Leslie Smith (eds.), *Reductionism and the Development of Knowledge* (Mahwah, NJ: L. Erlbaum, 2003).

Brown, Warren S., Nancey Murphy, and H. Newton Malony (eds.), *Whatever Happened to the Soul? Scientific and Theological Portraits of Human Nature* (Minneapolis: Fortress Press, 1998).

Buchanan, Bob, Wilhelm Gruissem, and Russell Jones, *Biochemistry and Molecular Biology of Plants* (Somerset, NJ: John Wiley and Sons, 2000).

Buller, David J. (ed.), *Function, Selection, and Design* (Albany, NY: SUNY Press, 1999).

Burghardt, Gordon M. and Marc Bekoff (eds.), *The Development of Behavior: Comparative and Evolutionary Aspects* (New York: Garland STPM Press, 1978).

Butterfield, Jeremy and Constantine Pagonis (eds.), *From Physics to Philosophy* (Cambridge: Cambridge University Press, 1999).

——, Mark Hogarth, and Gordon Belot (eds.), *Spacetime* (Brookfield, Vt.: Dartmouth Publishing Co., 1996).

Byrne, Richard W., *The Thinking Ape* (Oxford: Oxford University Press, 1995).

Callicot, J. Baird, 'From the Balance of Nature to the Flux of Nature', in Richard L. Knight and Suzanne Riedel (eds.), *Aldo Leopold and the Ecological Conscience* (Oxford: Oxford University Press, 2002), 90–105.

Campbell, Donald, '"Downward Causation" in Hierarchically Organised Biological Systems', in F. J. Ayala and T. H. Dobzhansky (eds.), *Studies in the Philosophy of Biology* (Berkeley: University of California Press, 1974), 179–86.

—— 'Levels of Organisation, Downward Causation, and the Selection-Theory Approach to Evolutionary Epistemology', in G. Greenberg and E. Tobach (eds.), *Theories of the Evolution of Knowing* (Hillsdale, NJ: Lawrence Erlbaum, 1990), 1–17.

Campbell, Neil, *Biology* (Redwood City, Calif: Benjamin Cummings, 1991).

Cartwright, John, *Evolution and Human Behaviour: Darwinian Perspectives on Human Nature* (Cambridge, Mass.: MIT Press, 2000).

Chalmers, David, *The Conscious Mind: In Search of a Fundamental Theory* (New York: Oxford Univ. Press, 1996).

—— 'Facing up to the Problem of Consciousness', repr. in Jonathan Shear (ed.), *Explaining Consciousness: The 'Hard Problem'* (Cambridge, Mass.: MIT Press, 1997).

Chisholm, Roderick M., 'The Agent as Cause', in Myles Brand and Douglas Walton (eds.), *Action Theory* (Dordrecht: D. Reidel, 1976).

—— *Person and Object* (La Salle, Ill.: Open Court, 1976).

Churchland, Paul, *Matter and Consciousness* (Cambridge, Mass.: MIT Press, 1984).

Clancey, W. J., 'The Biology of Consciousness: Comparative Review of Israel Rosenfield, *The Strange, Familiar, and Forgotten: An Anatomy of Consciousness* and Gerald M. Edelman, *Bright Air, Brilliant Fire: On the Matter of the Mind in Artificial Intelligence*, 60 (1991), 313–56.

Clark, Austen, *Psychological Models and Neural Mechanisms: An Examination of Reductionism in Psychology* (Oxford: Clarendon Press, 1980).

Clarke, Randolph, 'Toward a Credible Agent-Causal Account of Free Will', *Nous*, 27 (1993), 191–203.

Clayton, Philip, *Explanation from Physics to Theology* (New Haven: Yale University Press, 1989).

—— *God and Contemporary Science* (Grand Rapids, Mich.: Eerdmans, 1997).

—— 'The Emergence of Spirit', *CTNS Bulletin*, 20/4 (2000), 3–20.

—— 'Neuroscience, the Person and God: An Emergentist Account', *Zygon*, 35 (2000), 613–52.

—— *The Problem of God in Modern Thought* (Grand Rapids, Mich.: Eerdmans, 2000).

—— 'Emergence: Us for It', in John D. Barrow, Paul C. W. Davies, and Charles L. Harper, Jr. (eds.), *Science and Ultimate Reality: Quantum Theory, Cosmology and Complexity* (Cambridge: Cambridge University Press, 2004), 577–606.

—— *From Hegel to Whitehead: Systematic Responses to the Modern Problem of God* (in preparation).

—— and Paul Davies (eds.), *The Re-emergence of Emergence* (Oxford: Oxford University Press, 2006).

—— and Jeffrey Schloss (eds.), *Evolution and Ethics: Human Morality in Biological and Religious Perspective* (Grand Rapids, Mich.: Eerdmans, 2004).

Cockburn, Andrew, *An Introduction to Evolutionary Ecology* (Oxford: Blackwell Scientific Publications, 1991).

Comte, Auguste, *Cours de philosophie positive*, trans. as *Introduction to Positive Philosophy*, ed Frederick Ferré (Indianapolis: Hackett Pub. Co., 1988).

Cooper, David, *God is a Verb: Kabbalah and the Practice of Mystical Judaism* (New York: Riverhead Books, 1997).

Cotterill, Rodney M. J., 'Did Consciousness evolve from Self-Paced Probing of the Environment, and not from Reflexes?', *Brain and Mind*, 1 (2000), 283–98.

—— 'Evolution, Cognition and Consciousness', *Journal of Consciousness Studies*, 8 (2001), 3–17.

Coulson, C. A., *Christianity in an Age of Science* (London: Oxford University Press, 1953).

—— *Science and the Idea of God* (Cambridge: Cambridge University Press, 1958).

—— *Science, Technology, and the Christian* (New York: Abingdon Press, 1960).

Cowen, George *et al.*, *Complexity: Metaphors, Models, and Reality* (Boulder, Co.: Perseus Book Group, 1999).

Crane, Tim, 'The Significance of Emergence', in Carl Gillett and Barry Loewer (eds.), *Physicalism and its Discontents* (Cambridge: Cambridge University Press, 2001).

Crick, Francis, *The Astonishing Hypothesis* (New York: Charles Scribner's Sons, 1994).

—— and Christof Koch, 'The Unconscious Homunculus', in Thomas Metzinger (ed.), *Neural Correlates of Consciousness: Empirical and Conceptual Questions* (Cambridge, Mass.: MIT Press, 2000).

Crysdale, Cynthia S. W., 'Revisioning Natural Law: From the Classicist Paradigm in Emergent Probability', *Theological Studies*, 56 (1995), 464–84.

Csete, Marie E. and John C. Doyle, 'Reverse Engineering of Biological Complexity', *Science*, 295 (1 March 2002), 1664–9.

Damasio, Antonio, *The Feeling of What Happens: Body and Emotion in the Making of Consciousness* (New York: Harcourt Brace, 1999).

—— *Looking for Spinoza: Joy, Sorrow, and the Feeling Brain* (Orlando, Fla.: Harcourt, 2003).

Davidson, Donald, 'Thinking Causes', in John Heil and Alfred Mele (eds.), *Mental Causation* (Oxford: Oxford University Press, 1995).

Davidson, Eric H. *et al.*, 'A Genomic Regulatory Network for Development', *Science*, 295 (1 March 2002), 1669–78.

Davidson, Julian M. and Richard J. Davidson (eds.), *The Psychobiology of Consciousness* (New York: Plenum Press, 1980).

Davidson, Richard J. and Anne Harrington (eds.), *Visions of Compassion: Western Scientists and Tibetan Buddhists examine Human Nature* (Oxford: Oxford University Press, 2002).

Davies, Paul, *The Mind of God: The Scientific Basis for a Rational World* (New York: Simon & Schuster, 1992).

—— *The Cosmic Blueprint: New Discoveries in Nature's Creative Ability to order the Universe* (Philadelphia, Pa.: Templeton Foundation Press, 2004).

Dawkins, Richard, *The Blind Watchmaker: Why the Evidence of Evolution Reveals a Universe without Design* (New York: Norton, 1987).

—— *A Devil's Chaplain: Reflections on Hope, Lies, Science, and Love* (Boston: Houghton Mifflin Company, 2003).

Deacon, Terrence, *The Symbolic Species: The Co-Evolution of Language and the Brain* (New York: W. W. Norton, 1997).

—— 'The Hierarchic Logic of Emergence: Untangling the Interdependence of Evolution and Self-Organization', in Bruce H. Weber and David J. Depew (eds.), *Evolution and Learning: The Baldwin Effect Reconsidered* (Cambridge, Mass.: MIT Press, 2003).

Deamer, David W. and Gail R. Fleischaker, *Origins of Life: The Central Concepts* (Boston: Jones and Bartlett, 1994).

de Duve, Christian, *Vital Dust: Life as a Cosmic Imperative* (New York: Basic Books, 1995).

—— *Life Evolving: Molecules, Mind, and Meaning* (Oxford: Oxford University Press, 2002).

Dembski, William, *The Design Inference: Eliminating Chance through Small Probabilities* (New York: Cambridge University Press, 1998).

—— *Intelligent Design: The Bridge between Science and Theology* (Downers Grove, Ill.: InterVarsity Press, 1999).

—— *No Free Lunch: Why Specified Complexity cannot be Purchased without Intelligence* (Lanham: Rowan and Littlefield, 2002).

—— (ed.), *Signs of Intelligence: Understanding Intelligent Design* (Grand Rapids, Mich.: Brazos Press, 2001).

Dennett, Daniel, *Consciousness Explained* (Boston: Little, Brown, and Co., 1991).

Denton, Michael, *Evolution: A Theory in Crisis* (Bethesda, Md.: Adler & Adler, 1986).

—— *Nature's Destiny: How the Laws of Biology reveal Purpose in the Universe* (New York: Free Press, 1998).

Derrida, Jacques, *Of Spirit: Heidegger and the Question*, trans. Geoffrey Bennington and Rachel Bowlby (Chicago: University of Chicago Press, 1989).

d'Espagnat, Bernard, *Veiled Reality: An Analysis of Present-day Quantum Mechanical Concepts* (Reading, Mass.: Addison-Wesley, 1995).

Diaz, Jose Luis, 'Mind–Body Unity, Dual Aspect, and the Emergence of Consciousness', *Philosophical Psychology*, 13 (Spring 2000), 393–403.

Dilthey, Wilhelm, *Introduction to the Human Sciences*, ed. Rudolf Makkreel and Frithjof Rodi (Princeton: Princeton University Press, 1989).

—— *Hermeneutics and the Study of History*, ed. Rudolf Makkreel and Frithjof Rodi (Princeton: Princeton University Press, 1996).

Dupré, John, *The Disorder of Things: Metaphysical Foundations of the Disunity of Science* (Cambridge, Mass.: Harvard University Press, 1993).

Durham, William, *Coevolution: Genes, Culture, and Human Diversity* (Stanford, Calif.: Stanford University Press, 1991).

Dyson, Freeman, *Infinite in All Directions*, Gifford Lectures 1985 (New York: Harper & Row, 1988).

Edelman, Gerald M., 'Bright Air, Brilliant Fire: On the Matter of the Mind', *Artificial Intelligence*, 60 (1991), 313–56.

—— *Bright Air, Brilliant Fire: On the Matter of the Mind* (New York: Basic Books, 1992).

—— and Giulio Tononi, 'Reentry and the Dynamic Core: Neural Correlates of Conscious Experience', in Thomas Metzinger (ed.), *Neural Correlates of Consciousness: Empirical and Conceptual Questions* (Cambridge, Mass.: MIT Press, 2000).

—— *A Universe of Consciousness: How Matter becomes Imagination* (New York: Basic Books, 2001).

Ekman, Paul and Richard J. Davidson (eds.), *The Nature of Emotion: Fundamental Questions* (New York: Oxford University Press, 1994).

Eldridge, Niles and Stephen J. Gould, 'Punctuated Equilibria: An Alternative to Phyletic Gradualism', in Thomas J. M. Schopf (ed.), *Models in Paleobiology* (San Francisco, Calif: W. H. Freeman, Cooper, 1972).

el-Hani, Charbel Nino and Antonio Marcos Pereira, 'Higher-Level Descriptions: Why should We Preserve Them?' in Peter Bøgh Andersen, Claus Emmeche, Niels Ole Finnemann, and Peder Voetmann Christiansen (eds.), *Downward Causation: Minds, Bodies and Matter* (Aarhus: Aarhus University Press, 2000).

Ellis, George F. R., 'Intimations of Transcendence: Relations of the Mind to God', in Robert J. Russell *et al.* (eds.), *Neuroscience and the Person* (Vatican City: Vatican Observatory Press, 1999).

—— 'True Complexity and its Associated Ontology', in John Barrow, Paul Davies, and Charles Harper, Jr. (eds.), *Science and Ultimate Reality: Quantum*

Theory, Cosmology, and Complexity (Cambridge: Cambridge University Press, 2004).

Emmeche, Claus, Simo Køppe, and Frederik Stjernfelt, 'Levels, Emergence, and Three Versions of Downward Causation', in Peter Bøgh Andersen, Claus Emmeche, Niels Ole Finnemann, and Peder Voetmann Christiansen (eds.), *Downward Causation: Minds, Bodies and Matter* (Aarhus: Aarhus University Press, 2000), 13–34.

Fales, Evan, 'Plantinga's Case against Naturalistic Epistemology', *Philosophy of Science*, 63 (1996), 432–51.

Fitelson, Branden and Elliott Sober, 'Plantinga's Probability Arguments against Evolutionary Naturalism', *Pacific Philosophical Quarterly*, 79 (1998) 115–29.

Flew, Anthony, 'Theology and Falsification', repr. in Baruch Brody (ed.), *Readings in the Philosophy of Religion: An Analytic Approach* (Englewood Cliffs, NJ: Prentice-Hall, 1974).

Fodor, Jerry, 'Special Sciences, or the Disunity of Science as a Working Hypothesis', in Ned Block (ed.), *Readings in Philosophy of Psychology*, 2 vols. (Cambridge, Mass.: Harvard University Press, 1980).

Ford, Lewis, *The Lure of God: A Biblical Background for Process Theism* (Philadelphia, Pa: Fortress Press, 1978).

Frankenberry, Nancy, 'The Emergent Paradigm and Divine Causation', *Process Studies*, 13 (1983), 202–17.

Gadamer, Hans-Georg, *Truth and Method*, ed. Garrett Barden and John Cumming (New York: Seabury Press, 1975).

Gell-Mann, Murray, *The Quark and the Jaguar: Adventures in the Simple and the Complex* (New York: W. H. Freeman and Co., 1994).

Giddens, Anthony, *New Rules of Sociological Method: A Positive Critique of Interpretive Sociologies* (London: Hutchinson, 1976).

Gillett, Carl, 'Non-Reductive Realization and Non-Reductive Identity: What Physicalism does not Entail', in Sven Walter and Heinz-Dieter Heckmann (eds.), *Physicalism and Mental Causation* (Charlottesville, Va.: Imprint Academic, 2003).

—— 'Physicalism and Panentheism: Good News and Bad News', *Faith and Philosophy*, 20/1 (2003), 1–21.

—— 'Strong Emergence as a Defense of Non-Reductive Physicalism: A Physicalist Metaphysics for "Downward" Determination', *Principia*, 6 (2003), 83–114.

—— and Barry Loewer (eds.), *Physicalism and its Discontents* (New York: Cambridge University Press, 2001).

Goodenough, Ursula, *The Sacred Depths of Nature* (New York: Oxford University Press, 1998).

—— 'Causality and Subjectivity in the Religious Quest', *Zygon*, 35/4 (2000), 725–34.

Goodwin, Brian, *How the Leopard changed its Spots: The Evolution of Complexity* (Princeton: Princeton University Press, 2001).

Gordon, Deborah M., *Ants at Work: How an Insect Society is organized* (New York: W. W. Norton, 2000).

Gould, Stephen J. and R. C. Lewontin, 'The Spandrels of San Marco and the Panglossian Paradigm: A Critique of the Adaptationist Programme', *Proceedings of the Royal Society of London*, Series B, Biological Sciences ('The Evolution of Adaptation by Natural Selection'), 205 (1979), 581–98.

Gregersen, Niels Henrik, 'The Idea of Creation and the Theory of Autopoietic Processes', *Zygon*, 33 (1998), 333–68.

——'Autopoiesis: Less than Self-Constitution, More than Self-Oganization: Reply to Gilkey, McClelland and Deltete, and Brun', *Zygon*, 34 (1999), 117–38.

—— (ed.), *Complexity to Life: On the Emergence of Life and Meaning* (Oxford: Oxford University Press, 2003).

Griffin, David Ray, *Unsnarling the World-Knot: Consciousness, Freedom, and the Mind–Body Problem* (Berkeley: University of California Press, 1998).

—— *Reenchantment without Supernaturalism: A Process Philosophy of Religion* (Ithaca, NY: Cornell University Press, 2001).

Gulick, Walter, 'Response to Clayton: Taxonomy of the Types and Orders of Emergence', *Tradition and Discovery: The Polanyi Society Periodical* 29/3 (2002–3), 32–47.

Hardcastle, Valerie Gray, *The Myth of Pain* (Cambridge, Mass.: MIT Press, 1999).

Hare, John, 'Is There an Evolutionary Foundation for Human Morality?', in Philip Clayton and Jeffrey Schloss (eds.), *Evolution and Ethics: Human Morality in Biological and Religious Perspective* (Grand Rapids, Mich.: Eerdmans, 2004).

Harré, Rom and E. H. Madden, *Causal Powers: A Theory of Natural Necessity* (Oxford: Blackwell, 1975).

Hartshorne, Charles and William Reese (eds.), *Philosophers speak of God* (Chicago: University of Chicago Press, 1953).

Hasker, William, *The Emergent Self* (Ithaca, NY: Cornell University Press, 1999).

Hefner, Philip, *The Human Factor: Evolution, Culture, and Religion* (Minneapolis: Fortress Press, 1993).

Heil, John, 'Multiply Realized Properties', in Sven Walter and Heinz-Dieter Heckmann (eds.), *Physicalism and Mental Causation: The Metaphysics of Mind and Action* (Exeter: Imprint Academic, 2003).

Hempel, Carl, *Aspects of Scientific Explanation and Other Essays in the Philosophy of Science* (New York: Free Press, 1965).

——and Paul Oppenheim, 'Studies in the Logic of Explanation', *Philosophy of Science*, 15 (1948), 135–75.

Hick, John, *An Interpretation of Religion* (New Haven: Yale University Press, 1989).

Hinze, Bradford and D. Lyle Dabney (eds.), *Advents of the Spirit: An Introduction to the Current Study of Pneumatology* (Milwaukee, Wis.: Marquette University Press, 2001).

Hodgson, Peter, *Winds of the Spirit: A Constructive Christian Theology* (Louisville, Ky.: Westminster John Knox Press, 1994).

Holcombe, Mike and Ray Paton (eds.), *Information Processing in Cells and Tissues* (New York: Plenum Press, 1998).

Holland, John, *Emergence: From Chaos to Order* (Cambridge, Mass.: Perseus Books, 1998).

Hume, David, *Dialogues Concerning Natural Religion*, ed. Norman Kemp Smith (Indianapolis, Ind.: Bobbs-Merrill (Library of Liberal Arts), 1979).

—— *Of Miracles* (La Salle, Ill.: Open Court, 1985).

Jasper, Herbert H., L. Descarries, V. Castelluci, and S. Rossignol (eds.), *Consciousness: At the Frontiers of Neuroscience* (Philadelphia: Lippencott-Raven, 1998).

Johnson, Steven, *Emergence: The Connected Lives of Ants, Brains, Cities, and Software* (New York: Simon & Schuster Touchstone, 2001).

Kalton, Michael, 'Green Spirituality: Horizontal Transcendence', in M. E. Miller and P. Young-Eisendrath (eds.), *Paths of Integrity, Wisdom and Transcendence: Spiritual Development in the Mature Self* (New York: Routledge, 2000).

Kass, Leon, *The Hungry Soul: Eating and the Perfecting of Our Nature* (Chicago: University of Chicago Press, 1999).

Kauffman, Stuart, 'Whispers from Carnot: The Origins of Order and Principles of Adaptation in Complex Nonequilibrium Systems', in George Cowen, David Pines, and David Meltzer (eds.), *Complexity: Metaphors, Models, and Reality*, Sante Fe Institute Studies in the Sciences of Complexity, Proceedings, 19 (Reading, Mass.: Addison-Wesley, 1990).

—— *At Home in the Universe: The Search for Laws of Self-Organization and Complexity* (New York: Oxford University Press, 1996).

—— *Investigations* (New York: Oxford University Press, 2000).

Kim, Jaegwon, 'The Non-Reductivist's Troubles with Mental Causation', in John Heil and Alfred Mele (eds.), *Mental Causation* (New York: Oxford University Press, 1993).

—— *Supervenience and Mind: Selected Philosophical Essays* (Cambridge: Cambridge University Press, 1993).

—— 'Making Sense of Emergence', *Philosophical Studies*, 95 (1999), 3–36.

—— *Mind in a Physical World: An Essay on the Mind–Body Problem and Mental Causation* (Cambridge, Mass.: MIT Press, 1998).

—— 'Mental Causation and Consciousness: The Two Mind-Body Problems for the Physicalist', in Carl Gillett and Barry Loewer (eds.), *Physicalism and its Discontents* (Cambridge: Cambridge University Press, 2001).

—— (ed.), *Supervenience* (Aldershot, England: Ashgate, 2002).

Kitano, Hiroaki, *Foundations of Systems Biology* (Cambridge, Mass.: MIT Press, 2001).

—— 'Systems Biology: A Brief Overview', *Science*, 295 (1 March 2002), 1662–4.

Kosslyn, Stephen and Oliver Koenig, *Wet Mind: The New Cognitive Neuroscience* (New York: Free Press, 1992).

Laland, Kevin N., 'The New Interactionism', *Science*, 300 (20 June 2003), 1879–80.

Landis, Wayne G. and Ming-Ho Yu, *Introduction to Environmental Toxicology*, 3rd edn. (New York: Lewis Publishers, 2004).

Laughlin, Robert B., 'Nobel Lecture: Fractional Quantization', *Reviews of Modern Physics*, 71 (1999), 863–74.

LeDoux, Joseph, *The Emotional Brain: The Mysterious Underpinnings of Emotional Life* (New York: Simon & Schuster, 1996).

Lewes, G. H., *Problems of Life and Mind*, 2 vols. (London: Kegan Paul, Trench, Turbner, and Co., 1875).

Lewin, Roger, *Complexity: Life at the Edge of Chaos*, 2nd edn. (Chicago: University of Chicago Press, 1999).

Lewis, C. S., *Miracles: A Preliminary Study* (New York: HarperCollins, 2001).

Loewenstein, Werner, *The Touchstone of Life: Molecular Information, Cell Communication, and the Foundations of Life* (New York: Oxford University Press, 1999).

Lovelock, James, *Gaia: A New Look at Life on Earth* (Oxford: Oxford University Press, 1995).

—— *Homage to Gaia: The Life of an Independent Scientist* (Oxford: Oxford University Press, 2001).

Lowe, E. J., 'The Causal Autonomy of the Mental', *Mind* 102, No. 408 (1993), 629–44.

McGinn, Colin, *The Character of Mind: An Introduction to the Philosophy of Mind* (Oxford: Oxford University Press, 1997).

—— *The Mysterious Flame: Conscious Minds in a Material World* (New York: Basic Books, 1999).

—— *The Making of a Philosopher: My Journey through Twentieth-Century Philosophy* (New York: Harper Collins, 2002).

MacKay, Donald, *The Clockwork Image* (London: InterVarsity Press, 1974).

—— *Science, Chance and Providence* (Oxford: Oxford University Press, 1978).

—— *Human Science and Human Dignity* (Downers Grove, Ill.: InterVarsity Press, 1979).

—— *Science and the Quest for Meaning* (Grand Rapids, Mich.: Eerdmans, 1982).

—— *Behind the Eye*, 1986 Gifford Lectures, ed. Valery MacKay, (Oxford: Basil Blackwell, 1991).

Margenau, H., *Scientific Indeterminism and Human Freedom* (Latrobe, Pa: Archabbey Press, 1968).

Markosian, Sed Ned, 'A Compatibilist Version of the Theory of Agent Causation', *Pacific Philosophical Quarterly*, 80 (1999), 257–77.

Marvin, Walter, *A First Book in Metaphysics* (New York: Macmillan, 1912).

Maturana, Humberto, *Autopoiesis and Cognition: The Realization of the Living* (Dordrecht: D. Reidel, 1980).

—— and Francisco Varela, *The Tree of Knowledge: The Biological Roots of Human Understanding*, trans. Robert Paolucci (New York: Random House, 1998).

Meilaender, Gilbert, 'The (Very) Last Word', *First Things*, 94 (1999), 45–50,

Metz, Rudolf, *A Hundred Years of British Philosophy*, ed. J. H. Muirhead (London: G. Allen & Unwin, 1938).

Metz, Thaddeus, 'The Immortality Requirement for Life's Meaning', *Ratio*, 16/2 (2003), 161–77.

Metzinger, Thomas (ed.), *Neural Correlates of Consciousness: Empirical and Conceptual Questions* (Cambridge, Mass.: MIT Press, 2000).

Michal, Gerhard (ed.), *Biochemical Pathways: An Atlas of Biochemistry and Molecular Biology* (New York: John Wiley & Sons, 1999).

Milo, R. *et al.*, 'Network Motifs: Simple Building Blocks of Complex Networks', *Science*, 298 (2002), 824–7.

Mingers, John, *Self-Producing Systems: Implications and Applications of Autopoiesis* (New York: Plenum Press, 1995).

Morowitz, Harold, *The Emergence of Everything: How the World became Complex* (New York: Oxford University Press, 2002).

Morris, Simon Conway, *Life's Solution: Inevitable Humans in a Lonely Universe* (Cambridge: Cambridge University Press, 2003).

Murphy, Nancey, 'Divine Action in the Natural Order: Buridan's Ass and Schrödinger's Cat', in Robert J. Russell, Nancey Murphy, and Arthur Peacocke (eds.), *Chaos and Complexity: Scientific Perspectives on Divine Action* (Vatican City: Vatican Observatory Publications, 1995), 325–59.

Nagel, Ernst, *The Structure of Science: Problems in the Logic of Scientific Explanation* (London: Routledge and Kegan Paul, 1961).

Nagel, Thomas, 'What is it like to be a Bat?', in Ned Block (ed.), *Readings in Philosophy of Psychology*, 2 vols. (Cambridge, Mass.: Harvard University Press, 1980). i. 159–68.

—— *The View from Nowhere* (New York: Oxford University Press, 1986).

—— *The Last Word* (New York: Oxford University Press, 1997).

Nietzsche, Friedrich, 'Ueber Wahrheit und Lüge im aussermoralischen Sinne', *Nietzsche Werke*, ed. Giorgio Colli and Mazzino Montinari, ii/3 (Berlin: Walter de Gruyter, 1973).

O'Connor, Timothy, 'Emergent Properties', *American Philosophical Quarterly*, 31 (1994), 97–8.

—— (ed.), *Agents, Causes, and Events: Essays on Indeterminism and Free Will* (New York: Oxford University Press, 1995).

Olson, Everett C. and Jane Robinson, *Concepts of Evolution* (Columbus, Ohio: Charles E. Merrill, 1975).

Oltvai, Zoltán and Albert-László Barabási, 'Life's Complexity Pyramid', *Science*, 298 (2002), 763–4.

Ornstein, Jack H., *The Mind and the Brain: A Multi-Aspect Interpretation* (The Hague: Nijhoff, 1972).

O'Shaughnessy, Brian, *The Will: A Dual Aspect Theory* (New York: Cambridge University Press, 1980).

Oyama, Susan, *The Ontogeny of Information: Developmental Systems and Evolution*, 2nd edn. (Durham, NC: Duke University Press, 2000).

Pannenberg, Wolfhart, *Theology and the Kingdom of God* (Philadelphia: Westminster, 1969).

Pap, Arthur, 'The Concept of Absolute Emergence', *British Journal for the Philosophy of Science*, 2 (1952), 302–11.

Pattee, Howard H. (ed.), *Hierarchy Theory: The Challenge of Complex Systems* (New York: George Braziller, 1973).

Peacocke, Arthur, *An Introduction to the Physical Chemistry of Biological Oganization* (Oxford: Clarendon Press, 1983, 1989).

—— *Theology for a Scientific Age: Being and Becoming—Natural, Divine, and Human*, enlarged edn. (Minneapolis: Fortress Press, 1993).

—— *God and the New Biology* (Gloucester, Mass.: Peter Smith, 1994).

—— 'The Sound of Sheer Silence', in Robert J. Russell *et al.* (eds.), *Neuroscience and the Person* (Vatican City: Vatican Observatory Publications, 1999).

—— *Paths from Science towards God: The End of All Our Exploring* (Oxford: OneWorld, 2001).

Pennock, Robert, *Intelligent Design Creationism and its Critics: Philosophical, Theological, and Scientific Perspectives* (Cambridge, Mass.: MIT Press, 2001).

Pepper, Stephen, 'Emergence', *Journal of Philosophy*, 23 (1926), 241–5.

Pesce, Marc, 'Virtually Sacred', in W. Mark Richardson and Gordy Slack (eds.), *Faith in Science: Scientists Search for Truth* (London and New York: Routledge, 2001).

Placek, Tomasz and Jeremy Butterfield (eds.), *Non-Locality and Modality* (Dordrecht: Kluwer Academic, 2002).

Plantinga, Alvin, 'When Faith and Reason Clash: Evolution and the Bible', *Christian Scholar's Review*, 21 (1991), 8–33.

—— 'Evolution, Neutrality, and Antecedent Probability: A Reply to Van Till and McMullen', *Christian Scholar's Review*, 21 (1991), 80–109.

—— 'On Rejecting the Theory of Common Ancestry: A Reply to Hasker', *Perspectives on Science and Christian Faith*, 44 (1992), 258–63.

—— *Warrant and Proper Function* (New York: Oxford University Press, 1993).

—— 'Darwin, Mind and Meaning', *Books and Culture* (May/June 1996).

—— *Warranted Christian Belief* (New York: Oxford University Press, 2000).

Polanyi, Michael, *The Tacit Dimension* (Garden City, NY: Doubleday Anchor Books, 1967).

—— *Knowing and Being: Essays*, ed. Marjorie Grene (London: Routledge and Kegan Paul, 1969).

—— and Harry Prosch, *Meaning* (Chicago: University of Chicago Press, 1975).

Prigogine, Ilya, *Order out of Chaos: Man's New Dialogue with Nature* (New York: Bantam Books, 1984).

Primas, Hans, *Chemistry, Quantum Mechanics and Reductionism: Perspectives in Theoretical Chemistry*, 2nd corr. edn. (Berlin: Springer-Verlag, 1983).

Proudfoot, Wayne, *Religious Experience* (Berkeley: University of California Press, 1985).

Pylyshyn, Z. E., 'What the Mind's Eye tells the Mind's Brain: A Critique of Mental Imagery', *Psychological Bulletin*, 80 (1973), 1–24.

Ramachandran, V. S. and Sandra Blakeslee, *Phantoms in the Brain: Probing the Mysteries of the Human Mind* (New York: William Morrow, 1998).

Ratzsch, Del, *Nature, Design and Science: The Status of Design in Natural Science* (Albany, NY: SUNY Press, 2001).

Ridley, Matt, *Nature via Nurture: Genes, Experience, and What makes us Human* (New York: HarperCollins, 2003).

Robert, Jason Scott, *Embryology, Epigenesis, and Evolution: Taking Development Seriously* (Cambridge: Cambridge University Press, 2004).

Rollo, David, C., *Phenotypes: Their Epigenetics, Ecology, and Evolution* (London: Chapman and Hall, 1995).

Rosenfeld, Israel, *The Strange, Familiar, and Forgotten: An Anatomy of Consciousness* (New York: Alfred A. Knopf, 1992).

Rottschaefer, William W., *The Biology and Psychology of Moral Agency* (Cambridge: Cambridge University Press, 1998).

Rowe, William L., *Thomas Reid on Freedom and Morality* (Ithaca, NY: Cornell University Press, 1991).

—— 'The Metaphysics of Freedom: Reid's Theory of Agent Causation', *American Catholic Philosophical Quarterly*, 74 (2000), 425–46.

Ruse, Michael, *Darwin and Design: Does Evolution have Purpose?* (Cambridge, Mass.: Harvard University Press, 2003).

Russell, Robert J., Nancy Murphy, and Arthur Peacocke (eds.), *Chaos and Complexity: Scientific Perspectives on Divine Action* (Vatican City: Vatican Observatory Publications, 1995).

—— Theo Meyering, and Michael Arbib (eds.) *Neuroscience and the Person* (Vatican City State: Vatican Observatory Publications, 1999).

Schulze, Ernst-Detlef and Harold A. Mooney (eds.), *Biodiversity and Ecosystem Function* (Berlin: Springer-Verlag, 1994).

Schuster, Peter, 'How do RNA Molecules and Viruses Explore Their Worlds', in George Cowen, David Pines, and David Meltzer (eds.), *Complexity: Metaphors, Models, and Reality*, Sante Fe Institute Studies in the Sciences of Complexity Proceedings, 19 (Reading, Mass.: Addison-Wesley, 1990), 383–414.

Searle, John, 'Minds, Brains, and Programs', *Behavioral and Brain Sciences*, 3 (1980), 417–24.

—— *The Rediscovery of the Mind* (Cambridge, Mass.: MIT Press, 1992).

Seife, C., 'Cold Numbers unmake the Quantum Mind', *Science*, 287 (4 Feb. 2000).

Sellars, Wilfrid, *Science, Perception and Reality* (New York: Humanities Press, 1971).

Senchuk, Dennis M., 'Consciousness Naturalized: Supervenience without Physical Determinism', *American Philosophical Quarterly*, 28 (1991), 37–47.

Sheets-Johnstone, Maxine, 'Consciousness: A Natural History', *Journal of Consciousness Studies*, 5 (1998), 260–94.

Sheldrake, Rupert, *A New Science of Life: The Hypothesis of Morphic Resonance* (Rochester, Vt.: Park Street Press, 1981, 1995).

Silberstein, Michael, 'Emergence and the Mind–Body Problem', *Journal of Consciousness Studies*, 5 (1998), 464–82.

—— 'Converging on Emergence: Consciousness, Causation and Explanation', *Journal of Consciousness Studies*, 8 (2001), 61–98.

—— and John McGreever, 'The Search for Ontological Emergence', *Philosophical Quarterly*, 49 (1999), 182–200.

Singer, Wolf, 'Consciousness from a Neurobiological Perspective', in Thomas Metzinger (ed.), *Neural Correlates of Consciousness* (Cambridge, Mass.: MIT Press, 2000).

Smith, Brian Cantwell, *On the Origin of Objects* (Cambridge, Mass.: MIT Press, 1996).

Snow, C. P., *The Two Cultures*, 2nd edn. (Cambridge: Cambridge University Press, 1964).

Sober, Elliott, 'The Multiple Realizability Argument against Reductionism', *Philosophy of Science*, 66 (1999), 542–64.

Spaulding, E. G., *The New Rationalism* (New York: Henry Holt and Co., 1918).

Sperry, Roger, 'A Modified Concept of Consciousness', *Psychological Review*, 76 (1969), 532–6.

—— 'Mental Phenomena as Causal Determinants in Brain Function', in G. G. Globus, G. Maxwell, and I. Savodnik (eds.), *Consciousness and the Brain* (New York: Plenum, 1976).

—— 'Mind–Brain Interaction: Mentalism, Yes; Dualism, No', *Neuroscience*, 5 (1980), 195–206.

—— 'Consciousness and Causality', in R. L. Gregory (ed.), *The Oxford Companion to the Mind* (Oxford: Oxford University Press, 1987).

—— 'In Defense of Mentalism and Emergent Interaction', *Journal of Mind and Behaviour*, 12 (1991), 221–46.

St Augustine, *The Confessions*, trans. Edward B. Pusey (New York: Collier Books, 1972).

Stapp, Henry P., *Mind, Matter, and Quantum Mechanics* (Berlin and New York: Springer-Verlag, 1993).

Stewart, John E., *Evolution's Arrow: The Direction of Evolution and the Future of Humanity* (Canberra, Australia: Chapman Press, 2000).

Szubka, Tadeusz, 'The Last Refutation of Subjectivism?', *International Journal of Philosophical Studies*, 8 (2000), 231–7.

Taylor, Richard, *Action and Purpose* (Atlantic Highlands, NJ: Humanities Press, 1973).

Tegmark, Max, 'The Quantum Brain', *Physical Review E* (2000), 1–14.

Thompson, Evan (ed.), *Between Ourselves: Second-Person Issues in the Study of Consciousness* (Thorverton, UK: Imprint Academic, 2001).

Tipler, Frank, *The Physics of Immortality: Modern Cosmology, God, and the Resurrection of the Dead* (New York: Doubleday, 1994).

Tononi, Giulio and Gerald M. Edelman, 'Consciousness and Complexity', *Science*, 282 (1998), 1846–51.

Tracy, Thomas F., 'Particular Providence and the God of the Gaps', in Robert J. Russell, Nancey Murphy and Arthur Peacocke (eds.), *Chaos and Complexity* (Vatican City: Vatican Observatory Press, 1995).

Van Gulick, Robert, 'Reduction, Emergence and Other Recent Options on the Mind–Body Problem: A Philosophic Overview', *Journal of Consciousness Studies*, 8 (2001), 1–34.

Varela, Francisco, with Natalie Depraz and Pierre Vermersch, *On Becoming Aware: A Pragmatics of Experiencing* (Amsterdam: J. Benjamins, 2003).

—— and Jonathan Shear (eds.), *The View from Within: First-Person Approaches to the Study of Consciousness* (Bowling Green, Ohio: Imprint Academic, 1999).

——, Evan Thompson and Eleanor Rosch, *The Embodied Mind: Cognitive Science and Human Experience* (Cambridge, Mass.: MIT Press, 1991).

Velmans, Max, *Understanding Consciousness* (London: Routledge, 2000).

—— 'How could Conscious Experiences affect Brains?', *Journal of Consciousness Studies*, 9 (2002), 3–29.

—— 'Making Sense of Causal Interactions between Consciousness and Brain', *Journal of Consciousness Studies*, 9 (2002), 69–95.

von Wright, Georg Henrik, *Explanation and Understanding* (Ithaca NY: Cornell University Press, 1971).

Walter, Sven and Heinz-Dieter Heckmann (eds.), *Physicalism and Mental Causation: The Metaphysics of Mind and Action* (Exeter: Imprint Academic, 2003).

Watson, James D. *et al.* (eds.), *Molecular Biology of the Gene*, 4th edn. (Menlo Park, Calif.: Benjamin/Cummings, 1987).

Weber, Bruce and Terrence Deacon, 'Thermodynamic Cycles, Developmental Systems, and Emergence', *Cybernetics and Human Knowing*, 7 (2000), 21–43.

Weber, Bruce H. and David J. Depew, *Evolution and Learning: The Baldwin Effect Reconsidered* (Cambridge, Mass.: Mit Press, 2003).

Welker, Michael, *Gottes Geist: Theologie des Heiligen Geistes*, trans. John Hoffmeyer as *God the Spirit* (Minneapolis: Fortress Press, 1994).

Wheeler, John, *At Home in the Universe* (New York: Springer-Verlag, 1996).

—— *Geons, Black Holes, and Quantum Foam: A Life in Physics* (New York: Norton, 1998).

—— 'Information, Physics, Quantum: The Search for Links', in Anthony J. G. Hey (ed.), *Feynman and Computation: Exploring the Limits of Computers* (Cambridge, Mass.: Perseus Books, 1999).

Whitehead, A. N., *Process and Reality*, corrected edn., ed. David Ray Griffin and Donald Sherburne (New York: Free Press, 1975).

Wiebe, Phillip H., *God and Other Spirits: Intimations of Transcendence in Christian Experience* (Oxford: Oxford University Press, 2004).

Wieman, Henry N., *The Source of Human Good* (Chicago, Ill.: University of Chicago Press, 1946).

Wilson, E. O., *Sociobiology: The New Synthesis* (Cambridge, Mass.: Harvard University Press, 1975).

—— *Consilience: The Unity of Knowledge* (New York: Knopf, 1998).

Wimsatt, William C., 'The Ontology of Complex Systems: Levels of Organization, Perspectives, and Causal Thickets', *Canadian Journal of Philosophy*, Suppl. vol. 20 (1994) 207–74.

Windelband, Wilhelm, 'History and Natural Science' tr. Guy Oakes, *History and Theory*, 19/2 (1980), 165–85.

Wolfram, Stephen, *A New Kind of Science* (Champaign, Ill.: Wolfram Media, 2002).

Wolterstorff, Nicholas, *Divine Discourse: Philosophical Reflections on the Claim that God Speaks* (Cambridge: Cambridge University Press, 1995).

Woodhead, Linda with Paul Heelas and David Martin (eds.), *Peter Berger and the Study of Religion* (London: Routledge, 2001).

Woodward, Thomas, *Doubts about Darwin: A History of Intelligent Design* (Grand Rapids, Mich.: Baker Books, 2003).

Wright, Robert, *Non-Zero: The Logic of Human Destiny* (New York: Pantheon Books, 2000).

Yockey, Hubert, *Information Theory and Molecular Biology* (Cambridge: Cambridge University Press, 1992).

Zeleny, Milan (ed.), *Autopoiesis: Dissipative Structures, and Spontaneous Social Orders* (Boulder, Colo.: Westview Press, 1980).

Zurek, Wojciech, 'Decoherence and the Transition from Quantum to Classical', *Physics Today*, 44/10 (1991) 36–44.

—— 'Decoherence and the Transition from Quantum to Classical—Revisited', *Los Alamos Science*, 27 (2002), 14.

Index

LaVergne, TN USA
13 September 2009
157701LV00002B/4/P